The Gospel and the Land of Promise

The Gospel and the Land of Promise
Christian Approaches to the Land of the Bible

Edited by
PHILIP CHURCH
PETER WALKER
TIM BULKELEY
TIM MEADOWCROFT

☙PICKWICK *Publications* · Eugene, Oregon

THE GOSPEL AND THE LAND OF PROMISE
Christian Approaches to the Land of the Bible

Copyright © 2011 Wipf and Stock Publishers. All rights reserved. Except for brief quotations in critical publications or reviews, no part of this book may be reproduced in any manner without prior written permission from the publisher. Write: Permissions, Wipf and Stock Publishers, 199 W. 8th Ave., Suite 3, Eugene, OR 97401.

An earlier version of chapter 4 was previously published as Church, Philip. "The Promised Land in the New Testament and in Particular in Hebrews," in *Israel: 5 Views on People, Land, and State*. Auckland, Vision Network of New Zealand: 15–25. All rights reserved.

Pickwick Publications
An Imprint of Wipf and Stock Publishers
199 W. 8th Ave., Suite 3
Eugene, OR 97401

www.wipfandstock.com

ISBN 13: 978-1-60899-545-5

Cataloging-in-Publication data:

The gospel and the land of promise : christian approaches to the land of the Bible / edited by Philip Church, Peter Walker, Tim Bulkeley, and Tim Meadowcroft.

xiv + 188 p. ; 23 cm. Including bibliographical references and index.

ISBN 13: 978-1-60899-545-5

1. Land. 2. Bible—Theology. 3. Palestine in the Bible. I. Title. II. Church, Philip. III. Walker, Peter. IV. Bulkeley, Tim. V. Meadowcroft, Tim.

BS1199 P26 G55 2011

Manufactured in the U.S.A.

Contents

Contributors / vii

Acknowledgments / viii

Preface / ix

Abbreviations / xiii

1. Introduction—*Peter Walker* / 1
2. From Promised Land to Reconciled Cosmos: Paul's Translation of "Worldview," "Worldstory," and "Worldperson" —*Mark Strom* / 14
3. Paul's Answer to the Threats of Jerusalem and Rome (Phil 3) —*Mark Keown* / 28
4. "Here We Have No Lasting City" (Heb 13:14): The Promised Land in the Letter to the Hebrews—*Philip Church* / 45
5. The Kingdom of God and the Land: The New Testament Fulfillment of an Old Testament Theme —*Alistair Donaldson* / 58
6. "Exile away from His Land": Is Landlessness the Ultimate Punishment in Amos?—*Tim Bulkeley* / 75
7. A "Fifth Gospel" Less Torn and More Legible? On Recent Attempts to Retrieve Herodian Galilee—*Bob Robinson* / 86
8. The Old Testament: Friend or Foe of Palestinian Christians? Exploring the Insights of Palestinian Theologian Naim Ateek—*Gordon Stewart* / 103

9   Evangelical Social Conscience and the Challenge of Christian Zionism—*Stephen Tollestrup* / 121

10 When Land Is Layered: Jacob in Conversation with Colonizer (James Cook) and Colonized (Te Horeta Te Taniwha) —*Steve Taylor* / 133

11 "God Has by No Means Rejected His People" (Rom 11:1): A Response to the Accusation of "Replacement Theology" —*Philip Church* / 147

12 The Gospel and the Land of Promise: A Response —*Tim Meadowcroft* / 158

Bibliography / 167

Index of Ancient Sources / 179

Contributors

Tim Bulkeley, Lecturer, Old Testament, Carey Baptist College, Auckland, NZ

Philip Church, Senior Lecturer, School of Theology, Mission and Ministry, Laidlaw College, Auckland and Christchurch, NZ

Alistair Donaldson, Lecturer, School of Theology, Mission and Ministry, Laidlaw College, Christchurch, NZ

Mark Keown, Senior Lecturer, School of Theology, Mission and Ministry, Laidlaw College, Auckland and Christchurch, NZ

Tim Meadowcroft, Head of School of Theology, Mission and Ministry and Senior Lecturer in Biblical Studies, Laidlaw College, Auckland, NZ

Bob Robinson, Senior Lecturer, School of Theology, Mission and Ministry, Laidlaw College, Auckland and Christchurch, NZ

Gordon Stewart, Senior Lecturer, School of Theology, Mission and Ministry, Laidlaw College, Auckland and Christchurch, NZ

Mark Strom, Former National Principal, Laidlaw College, Auckland, NZ

Stephen Tollestrup, Executive Director, TEAR Fund, NZ

Steve Taylor, Senior Lecturer, Flinders University, and Director of Missiology and Postgraduate Coordinator, Uniting College of Leadership and Theology, Adelaide, Australia

Peter Walker, Associate Vice-Principal & Director of Development, Wycliffe Hall, University of Oxford, United Kingdom

Acknowledgments

As indicated, Scripture quotations from:

Holy Bible, New International Version®, NIV®. Copyright © 1973, 1978, 1984 by Biblica, Inc.™ Used by permission of Zondervan. All rights reserved worldwide. www.zondervan.com.

Holy Bible, Today's New International Version®. TNIV®. Copyright © 2001, 2005 by Biblica, Inc.™ Used by permission of Zondervan. All rights reserved worldwide. www.zondervan.com.

New Revised Standard Version Bible, copyright © 1989 Division of Christian Education of the National Council of the Churches of Christ in the United States of America. Used by permission. All rights reserved.

Good News Bible, copyright © 1994 published by Bible Societies/HarperCollins Publishers Ltd UK. Good News Bible, copyright © American Bible Society 1966, 1971, 1976, 1992. Used with permission.

Preface

Most of the essays in this volume had their origin in a one-day colloquium entitled "The Gospel and the Land," held at the Laidlaw-Carey Graduate School in Auckland, New Zealand, on July 9, 2009. The Laidlaw-Carey Graduate School is a joint venture between Laidlaw College and Carey Baptist College, and offers advanced degrees in theology. This colloquium was part of a master of theology course entitled "Biblical Theology: Land, City, Temple and People of God," taught by Peter Walker, who contributes the first chapter of the book. This chapter introduces the subject with a brief discussion of six questions, or "sticking points": questions concerning the theology of the land that are answered differently by Palestinian and Jewish Christians.

After the introduction, the next four essays examine the theme of land in different parts of the New Testament. Mark Strom considers Paul as a "worldperson," an expression he coins to show how Paul was the first translator of a worldview out of its original cultural soil. He argues that Paul's silence about the land is a "loud silence" that needs to be noticed, for it evidences a complete disinterest in the question of land. Paul's vision of what Christ had accomplished by his death and resurrection was global and cosmic: it left no room for national or geographic containment.

Mark Keown's essay is an exegetical study of Phil 3, in which he argues that Paul is countering two distinct issues faced by the Philippian church: that of Judaizers (Jerusalem) and that of unbelievers with a Greco-Roman mindset (Rome) seeking to compromise the gospel in the interests of empire. To the Judaizers Paul claims that he, a Hebrew of the Hebrews, had put aside all the religious trappings of Judaism outside of Jesus, including Jewish territorial theology; and to the Greco-Roman unbelievers he presents the hope of the return of Christ, accompanied by bodily transformation and a cosmic victory that transcends any geographical location, whether Rome or Jerusalem.

Philip Church considers theme of land in the book of Hebrews, the only book in either the Old or the New Testament to use the expression "the promised land" (Heb 11:9). He argues that while there is almost complete silence about the promised land elsewhere in the New Testament, the author of Hebrews mentions Jerusalem and the land, only to negate it in favor of the heavenly Jerusalem, the city to come, whose architect and builder is God.

Alistair Donaldson notes that while land is a constant theme in the Old Testament, it is almost entirely absent in the New. On the other hand, the expression "the kingdom of God" appears suddenly in the New Testament, while it is completely absent from the Old. It appears frequently on the lips of Jesus, and over one hundred times in the Synoptic Gospels alone. He argues that the notion of God's rule over the entire cosmos has replaced the idea of God's rule over Israel.

In the next essay Tim Bulkeley turns to the Old Testament and examines the theme of the loss of land in Amos, concluding that this is not the ultimate punishment for the unfaithfulness of God's people; the ultimate punishment is the loss of Yahweh's favor because his people have ignored his requirement to act appropriately as the chosen and gifted people. Those who claim that Yahweh has given them their land are obligated to live as Yahweh requires in that land, or they will lose both Yahweh's favor and his land.

The essays having a biblical studies theme end with chapter 7 where the focus changes a little. Here Bob Robinson looks back to the era of Second Temple Judaism and considers what one specific part of the land of promise—the region of Galilee—had come to look like in the early Roman period.

Gordon Stewart's essay signals a partial shift away from biblical studies, as he looks at the use of the Old Testament in the writings of Palestinian theologian Rev. Dr. Naim Ateek, founder and head of the Sabeel Ecumenical Liberation Theology Center in Jerusalem. Traditionally Zionist Christians have used such Old Testament texts as Gen 12:1–3 to exclude the Palestinian people from their land. This essay examines texts that have been used in this way, and then looks at the way Ateek responds to these readings, seeking to read them with an authentic christological focus.

Stephen Tollestrup has had many years involvement in peace activism and social concern. His essay grows out of a passionate desire to see the Palestinian people liberated from oppression, and argues that an important contribution to that liberation could come from western evangelical churches as they are freed from Zionist readings of the Bible. He concludes his chapter with a set of proposals that could contribute to this.

Steve Taylor gives a postcolonial reading of Gen 28:10–18, where Jacob "came to a certain place and stayed there for the night" (v. 10). He reads this text in the light of James Cook's diary record of his arrival in New Zealand to take possession of it for the British Empire in November 1769; and also in the light of the way a twelve-year-old Maori remembered and recorded the same event later in life. "Our tribe was living there at the time," he wrote. Cook came to take possession of New Zealand on behalf of the Queen to be sure, but when he did this the land was already occupied. Parallels with the formation of the state of Israel in 1948 are clear.

Frequently those who critique Zionism are faced with the charge of "replacement theology," the notion that the church has replaced Israel in the purposes of God. The penultimate essay in the volume critiques this charge, taking as its text the claim of Rom 11:1 that God has not rejected the people of Israel. Philip Church argues in this chapter, however, that God's faithfulness to his promises to Israel are seen not in the latter-day existence of the state of Israel, but in the ways in which Jewish people become followers of Jesus, and are grafted into the one people of God, the true descendants of Abraham.

Tim Meadowcroft completes the volume with a response to each chapter, examining them in the light of four themes: the land and pilgrimage, the land and politics, the land and her people, and the land and its scriptures. In so doing he offers a valuable critique of the book as a whole, in particular introducing the significant counterpoint that, in their efforts to downplay the significance of the Land of Promise in the New Testament, the authors leave themselves open to the danger of downplaying the importance of landed space for all people, and in particular, the Israeli and Palestinian peoples.

Today the land of promise is a spark in the tinder-dry atmosphere of Middle Eastern affairs. Events there continue to wield influence amongst peoples and in places well beyond the region itself. This raises for Christians the acute theological problem of how to relate to the land of promise today and in light of the land of the Bible. Our hope is that this volume of essays will contribute to a more informed and theologically coherent response to issues surrounding the land of promise. We have prepared it in the name of peace for all peoples in that place and amongst those who continue to look to her as a place of promise.

Philip Church
for the editorial team

Abbreviations

ABR	*Australian Biblical Review*
AGJU	Arbeiten zur Geschichte des antiken Judentums und des Urchristentums
ANF	*The Ante-Nicene Fathers*, edited by Alexander Roberts and James Donaldson (Bellingham: Logos Research Systems, 2001)
BDAG	*A Greek-English Lexicon of the New Testament and Other Early Christian Literature.* 3rd edition, edited by F. W. Danker (Chicago, IL/London: University of Chicago Press, 2000)
BECNT	Baker Exegetical Commentary on the New Testament
Bib	*Biblica*
BNTC	Black's New Testament Commentaries
BSac	*Bibliotheca sacra*
BST	The Bible Speaks Today
BTB	*Biblical Theology Bulletin*
BZ	*Biblische Zeitschrift*
CBQ	*Catholic Biblical Quarterly*
CMES	*Critical Middle Eastern Studies*
CSR	*Christian Scholar's Review*
DJG	*Dictionary of Jesus and the Gospels*, edited by J. B. Green and S. McKnight (Downers Grove: InterVarsity, 1992)
EB	Earth Bible
FM	*Faith and Mission*
HALOT	*The Hebrew and Aramaic Lexicon of the Old Testament.* 1st English edition, edited by Ludwig Koehler and Walter Baumgartner (Leiden: E. J. Brill, 1993-2000).
ICC	International Critical Commentary
KB	*Lexicon in Veteris Testamenti Libros*, edited by Ludwig Koehler and Walter Baumgartner (Leiden: E. J. Brill, 1985)

JSJ	*Journal for the Study of Judaism*
JSJSup	Journal for the Study of Judaism Supplement Series
JSOTSup	Journal for the Study of the Old Testament Supplement Series
JTSA	*Journal of Theology for Southern Africa*
MES	*Middle Eastern Studies*
NAC	New American Commentary
NCB	New Century Bible
NICNT	New International Commentary on the New Testament
NIDB	*New International Dictionary of the Bible*
NIGTC	New International Greek Testament Commentary
NIVAC	NIV Application Commentary
NSBT	New Studies in Biblical Theology
NTS	*New Testament Studies*
NovT	*Novum Testamentum*
OBT	Overtures to Biblical Theology
PBM	Paternoster Biblical Monographs
PNTC	Pillar New Testament Commentary
PTMS	Princeton Theological Monograph Series
SBLDS	Society of Biblical Literature Dissertation Series
SBLMS	Society of Biblical Literature Monograph Series
SEHT	Studies in Evangelical History and Thought
SFSHJ	*South Florida Studies in the History of Judaism*
SNTSMS	Society for New Testament Studies Monograph Series
ST	*Studia Theologica*
TDNT	*Theological Dictionary of the New Testament*
THNT	Theologischer Handkommentar zum Neuen Testament
THNTC	Two Horizons New Testament Commentary
TS	*Theological Studies*
TynBul	*Tyndale Bulletin*
VT	*Vetus Testamentum*
WBC	Word Biblical Commentary
WTJ	*Westminster Theological Journal*
WUNT	Wissenschaftliche Untersuchungen zum Neuen Testament
ZAW	*Zeitschrift für die alttestamentliche Wissenschaft*

1

Introduction

Peter Walker

The dispute still rages over the promised land: how today are biblically-rooted Christians to view this unique land—the focus of God's promises in the Old Testament? What is its present significance and role within God's purposes? Does it belong by "rights" to any particular people? And what are God's expectations, indeed requirements, of those who live there?

These key questions, which percolate throughout this present volume and which were the basis for lively discussions in New Zealand when I visited to teach a course in biblical theology (focused on the issues of temple, city, land, and people), are naturally matters of even more vital concern for those Christian believers who actually live in the "land" themselves. Far from being abstract or merely "academic," they are vitally urgent, coloring every aspect of life—religious, political, and practical.

This became abundantly clear for me, personally, when invited to participate in a series of four annual consultations that brought together Jewish and Palestinian Christians to discuss the "Theology of the Land." In this chapter I highlight some of the major sticking points that we encountered in the midst of those lively debates. To keep this brief, the points of dispute will be listed under the original six headings.[1]

1. These consultations took place in Cyprus and then at Bethlehem Bible College between 1996 and 2000. For the sake of simplicity, I highlight the differences between the "messianic" and "Palestinian" viewpoints, but this terminology necessarily hides the fact that these are generalizations; that the nuanced position of any individual normally associated with that label is not truly represented here; and also, of course, that there were "Westerners" present in the consultations who might well have adopted a mixture of these positions without themselves being, strictly, either "messianic believers" or

INHERITANCE

This key biblical word is sometimes used in the Old Testament of Israel (with the nation being seen as God's inheritance) but is also used of the physical land that Israel inherited.[2] Used in this way it reminded the Israelites that they were strictly "tenants" (with God himself as the prime owner of the land) but equally that they had received an undeserved gift of grace.[3] But how does the New Testament use this word "inheritance" and who can claim to be its true inheritors?

The Palestinian viewpoint would note how the New Testament now applies this language of "inheritance" not to a land but to that which all believers graciously receive through Christ (1 Pet 1:3–4). They would also highlight Paul's insistence that *all* believers, both Jew and Gentile, are now equally "heirs" of God's promises in Christ (Rom 8:16–17). Paul is adamant on this point in Gal 3:26–29, where he builds his argument on the idea that Christ himself is ultimately the true "seed" (singular), the inheritor and guarantor of the divine promises.[4] Thus, on this view, the notion of an "inherited land" has been transformed in the New Testament era. Moreover, if there *were* any continuing sense in which the "seed of Abraham" still inherited the physical land, then arguably the implication of Galatians is that the true inheritors of this land promise are not those physically descended from Abraham, but rather those who by faith have been incorporated into Israel's Messiah.

A messianic viewpoint, however, would see the promise of this land inheritance in the Old Testament as not being overthrown by the New, but rather as continuing (in parallel to the "spiritual inheritance" now enjoyed by Gentile Christians): the promise still stands and those of Jewish descent are the rightful "heirs." They would also highlight that, even within the Old Testament, there are several instances (principally during the exile) when the Israelites were not strictly in active

---

"Palestinian Christians." Some of the papers were later published by Bethlehem Bible College in Loden, Wood, and Walker (eds.), *The Bible and the Land*. A version of this present chapter will also appear shortly in a revised and updated version of that book.

2. For the land as Israel's "inheritance," see Num 26:53; 36:2; Deut 4:21, 38; 15:4 etc.; Josh 11:23; Pss 105:11; 135:12; 136:21; Isa 58:14; Jer 3:19; Ezek 45:1; 48:29.

3. See Lev 25:23 ("the land is mine"). It also undergirded the prophetic concern that no Israelite should be sold into slavery and thereby disinherited or removed from his ancestral connection to the promised land: see, e.g., 1 Kgs 21:1–16, Ahab's attack on Naboth's "inheritance."

4. For other relevant NT texts, see Eph 2:11–23; 1 Pet 2:9–10.

"possession" of the land, but nevertheless were still (by divine promise) its rightful "owners." This distinction between "possession" and underlying "ownership" then explains how the promise of their inheritance has not been broken through nearly two thousand years of not "possessing" the land of Israel. Jewish descendants of Abraham have always been its rightful owners, even though "dispossessed," and this applies to the present day—even if some parts of the land are currently "occupied" or administered by others.

COVENANTS

The Bible is a book based on God's covenant promises. There are several episodes in biblical history where God makes such covenant promises (e.g., Noah, Abraham, Moses, David), and the promises of a "new covenant" (Jer 31:31–34) give rise to the second half of the Bible being described *in toto* as the "New Testament" (or "New Covenant"). Yet this then gives rise to much dispute as to whether these apparently successive covenants are all aspects of but *one* overarching divine covenant-promise, or whether there are several covenants (which then relate to each other in various ways, perhaps by contrast or perhaps with a later covenant superseding an earlier covenant). In particular, were the important covenants (to Abraham and again to David) strictly unconditional or were they conditional in some way? Could the recipients of the promise eventually lose out on that which was promised? Indeed could the promise effectively be terminated (and thus totally removed from divine consideration) or is there something about them that is "eternal" and lasts "forever" (come what may)?

A messianic viewpoint would focus on the eternal and unconditional nature of these covenants. In particular, the divine promise of the land (an integral part of the covenant with Abraham) was explicitly stated to be "forever" (Gen 17:7–8). This cannot be revoked—neither by the passage of time, nor by the dawning of a "new covenant," nor by the disobedience of the descendants of Abraham. The Israelites would eventually go into exile (the curse of the covenant for such disobedience), but they were "restored" to the land—precisely because the gift of the land was itself unconditional.

A Palestinian response would highlight that there are other divine promises that, though explicitly stated as being "forever," do not appear to have been fulfilled;[5] so perhaps the Hebrew word forever (*le'olam*) does not mean literally "to the end of the eternity" but only "for a very long time." Alternatively, if David was promised that there would always be a descendant on his throne (and that his dynasty would last "forever": 2 Sam 7:13, 16), then there is a manifest problem in Old Testament history when the kings of Judah are taken into exile, never to return. This dashing of the divine promise evidently causes much heart searching for subsequent biblical writers (e.g., Pss 74 and 79). The solution to this dilemma, however, is given in the New Testament when the angel announces at Jesus' birth that he "will sit on the throne of his father David and his kingdom will have no end" (Luke 1:32–33); this then is underscored when the apostles proclaim Jesus as Israel's Messiah, the true Davidic King (Acts 2–3 etc.). So here is an instance of an "eternal" promise continuing over into the New Testament era (and indeed into eternity)—but, crucially, in a form or mode that is not literal or "political" in the same way as the original promise sounded.

This then suggests, by parallel reasoning, that the divine promise of the land also might continue into the present but *in a different mode*. Hence there are New Testament references to the "ends of the earth" now coming within God's kingdom rule under Christ (Acts 1:8) and to Abraham's "inheriting the world" (Rom 4:13)—indications that the apostles saw the land promise as now fulfilled in a maximalist and global fashion; hence too the references in Hebrews to the enduring "Sabbath rest" for God's people as the ultimate fulfillment of the promised land as established under Joshua (Heb 3–4). Thus, Hebrews' portrait of the temple, Jerusalem, and the land as all being viewed differently in the light of the coming of Jesus needs to be heeded today—not least by messianic believers (the contemporary equivalent of the first-century "Hebrew" believers). In the days of the "new covenant" (Heb 8:7–13), believers are to focus elsewhere, not on the original physical form of the promise, but on what the promise eternally signified; and they must not be tempted back into merely Jewish ways of seeing matters, ignoring the divinely intended fulfillment of those realities as now revealed in Jesus.

---

5. A small but interesting example is that of the Rechabites, whose tribe, according to Jer 35:18–19, will last "forever."

THE ROLE OF JESUS IN FULFILLING THE COVENANT

Within this framework of covenant fulfillment, there is then much dispute concerning the role of Jesus himself. As Israel's Messiah he presumably came to fulfill the Abrahamic and Davidic covenants in some way, but how did he do so? So the questions we have just raised can also be phrased like this: Does the fulfillment that he accomplished cause the covenants to continue after him in much the same way as before, only deeper (as might be argued from a messianic position)? Or instead does his fulfilling them somehow bring their original shape to an end, with them now being supplanted by something slightly different, which yet reflects God's original and eternal intention (as might be argued from a Palestinian position)? Thus a messianic believer might argue that, even if Jesus is the true Davidic king in a non-political sense, the original promise suggests that we might still expect a king over Israel in a more obviously literal sense. Or again, Jesus may have come as a fulfillment of God's promise to Abraham, thus bringing God's blessing to "all nations," but surely that does not annul the promise within that Abrahamic covenant concerning his descendants' ownership of the land?

This same point might be construed diagrammatically as follows. For the messianic position, the covenant promises in the Old Testament are like a straight line, which then is *supplemented* by extra aspects of fulfillment brought about by the coming of Jesus. For the Palestinian position, however, those covenant promises are *funneled down* onto Jesus and then re-emerge in the New Testament in a "new" form. In the former scheme there is an emphasis on continuity, but with additions; in the latter, there is a greater note of *dis*continuity, pointing instead to what might be termed "intentional transformation." The latter scheme seems to work well for a biblical theme like the temple: for the New Testament clearly teaches that we no longer need a physical temple, because Jesus himself is the true temple and because he has offered the ultimate sacrifice for sin.[6] However, the former scheme seems to work better for a biblical theme like the land: for at first sight there does not seem to be any substantial New Testament teaching that overturns the Old Testament's perspective on this key topic. The Palestinian position (indebted to Hebrews) might therefore more frequently talk in terms of typology—where the reality revealed in the New Testament is God's

---

6. See John 1:14; 2:21; Heb 10:10–22; for Christian believers constituting a new temple in Christ, see also 1 Cor 3:16–17; 6:19; Eph 2:21–22; 1 Pet 2:4–8.

intended pattern or "type," which has been preceded or foreshadowed by an Old Testament "anti-type" that might (outwardly) appear quite different. The messianic position would use this category more sparingly, fearing that such typological fulfillment might effectively undermine the Old Testament promises or seemingly render them null and void.

These differences, located at the level of how we construct our overall biblical framework, are then matched by differences at the more detailed level—namely when we look at Jesus' public ministry and try to assess his attitude to the Abrahamic promises concerning the land. The messianic position would highlight that Jesus' teaching seems to pass over this topic in silence (thus presumably leaving the promise unchanged in the New Testament era). The Palestinian position would argue that in his one explicit reference to the "land issue" (in Matt 5:5) Jesus is universalizing its scope (from the promised land to the whole "earth"). Moreover, he was clearly opposed to the nationalistic desires of his fellow Jews (and the "Zealots") for political independence, warning instead that fighting Rome would only bring down God's judgment upon Jerusalem;[7] if so, then he must have disagreed with the Zealots' interpretation of the Old Testament land promises that inspired them to hope for Israel's independent kingdom. Jesus did not see those promises being fulfilled in that way and, arguably, through his own ministry was revealing a quite different way in which they were being fulfilled. To this the messianic position might reply: "Yes, Jesus in his own day was not working for a 'political' or physical fulfillment, but that may simply be for *reasons of timing*: now, two thousand years later, it *is* God's time for those land-promises to come back into play." In other words, the land promises were not transformed (still less, annulled) by Jesus in the first century; they were simply left untouched. If, then, we were to extend our imaginary diagram into the present era, we would need to depict how God's Old Testament promises about the land were "put on hold" for many centuries (perhaps with a dotted line) but have recently come back into operation.

A key text at this point in the discussion is Acts 1. The risen Jesus answers the disciples' insistent question about the "restoration of the kingdom to Israel" with: "it is not for you to know the seasons . . . but you will be witnesses . . . to the ends of the earth." A messianic reading of this text would hear Jesus saying that this political restoration has

---

7. See, e.g., Luke 13:35; 19:41–44; 21:20–24; 23:28–31.

simply been delayed: it will come about in the future but only after the disciples have first gone out to the world in evangelism. A Palestinian response, by contrast, might say that Jesus' own teaching (in v. 3) had expressly had a different emphasis (being focused on the "kingdom of God," not of Israel) and thus his reply offers a redefinition of their misguided restoration hope: the kingdom will come and Israel will truly be restored *by the very means* of their going out to the world with the news of Jesus as Israel's true King and Messiah; when the "ends of the earth" come under the rule of Jesus as Lord, *that* will be the true fulfillment of God's promises to restore his people.

These two quite different interpretations of Jesus' understanding of Israel's restoration come to the surface in other places within the Gospels and Acts. In each case the essential dispute looks like this: was Jesus leaving the restoration-hopes of Israel to one side and focusing on fulfilling other aspects of Old Testament prophecy? Or was he claiming that his ministry was the surprising fulfillment of those hopes and that he was indeed restoring Israel but at a deeper level—inaugurating her true return from exile, redeeming her from sin, and regathering her around himself as the true centre of God's people? The former (messianic) view then opens the door to see the establishment of the modern state of Israel as a fulfillment of those Old Testament hopes of restoration; but the latter view questions whether we can apply these "restoration" categories to this modern event because (on this view) Jesus and the New Testament writers have given a definitive re-interpretation of this restoration theme— a reinterpretation that is authoritative and thus disallows us from seeking fulfillment of these promises in ways that seem to undermine the reality of the fulfillment offered by Jesus.

OTHER NEW TESTAMENT QUESTIONS

The shape of the debate is gradually becoming clear. Within this framework we can now list (more briefly) some other points of dispute in interpreting the New Testament:

- What is the significance of the New Testament's teaching about the redundancy of the Jerusalem temple? Can that rightly be used to set up a paradigm of "fulfillment by transformation" that can then be applied (as above) to other Old Testament realities (the city of Jerusalem, the land of Israel, the people of Israel)? And within this, how do we interpret those more positive references to the temple in Acts (with the apostles still using it for worship and teaching)?[8] Was this merely an interim necessity or should we receive this as somehow potentially "normative" (such that a rebuilt temple today would still be compatible with Hebrews' teaching about its redundancy)?[9]

- What are the implications of the widespread teaching in the New Testament that Jesus is a New Moses who has performed a new "exodus" for God's people?[10] Does this imply that there is effectively a corresponding new "promised land" towards which this new Moses figure is leading us?

- When Paul uses his frequent tag "in Christ," is he using this in a *locative* sense—seeing it as the New Covenant equivalent of being "in the land" (as the sphere of God's blessing)? Why are there so few references to the land in his writings? Does this reflect his disinterest in this non-issue? Or was he an ardent Jewish nationalist before his conversion (even a "proto-Zealot"?) who had now consciously abandoned this "political" interpretation in the light of Christ?[11]

- If the New Testament writers all assert that Gentiles are now included within God's people as Gentiles, does this necessarily mean that all Jewish distinctives have to be abolished? Would Paul have discouraged Jewish believers in Jesus from circumcising their sons? Can Jewish practices (e.g., in regard to Sabbath and dietary regulations) be observed without countermanding Paul's desire that such things not erect a barrier between Jew and Gentile, or encourage a two-tier element within God's one people in Christ (as encouraged in Eph 2:14)?[12] If they can, then presumably the Jewish privilege of being

---

8. Acts 3:1; 21:26.

9. This raises a key historical question about the book of Hebrews: was it written before the destruction of the temple (such that its teaching proactively dismisses the temple's significance in the light of Christ)? Or was it written in the aftermath of 70 CE, thus being merely a reflective interpretation of how to live in a post-temple world (which could thus be ignored if a new temple were built)? The majority viewpoint is for a date in the 60s CE: see commentaries by Bruce, Guthrie and Lane; for a post-70 reflection, see, e.g., Isaacs, *Sacred Space*. See further my *Jesus and the Holy City*, 227–32.

10. See, e.g., Luke 9:29–30; Matt 2–5; John 6–8; 1 Cor 10:1–4; Heb 3:1–6; Rev 15:3.

11. Paul twice uses the word "zeal" to describe his pre-Christian stance (Gal 1:14; Phil 3:6).

12. See also Rom 3:29–30; Phil 3:2–9; 1 Pet 2:9–10.

"owners" of the land can continue in the New Covenant era without disposing Gentile believers? But, if they cannot, then the converse may be true.

- In particular, how are we to understand Jesus' teaching about Jerusalem being "trampled upon until the *times of the Gentiles* are fulfilled" (Luke 21:24)? Is this a long-term future prophecy, suggesting a nearly two-thousand-year period of Gentile rule over Jerusalem (until 1967?), which matches in some way Paul's references to the "fullness of the Gentiles" (Rom 11:25)? Or is it simply the Lukan parallel to the verses found in Matthew and Mark that speak about God's mercifully limiting (or "cutting short") the length of those days "for the sake of the elect" (Matt 24:22; Mark 13:20)? In other words, the force of the phrase is that the "times of the Gentiles" (when they besiege the city and then gloat over its defeat) will actually be kept short; the severe trauma will not last more than a few years (perhaps matching 67–72 CE?).

- This raises the multiple questions relating to Rom 11—a text that can often dominate the entire proceedings! In sum, is Paul predicting a distinctive end-times scenario when God will "save Israel" (either through Christ or in some other distinctive and "mysterious" way)? Or is he advocating that Israel will be saved (in some smaller, less spectacular way) through the normal process of Jewish people responding to the Good News of their Messiah Jesus? If there is such a distinctive end-times period, then special rules might apply to that season in God's purposes (e.g., God fulfilling literally prophecies that previously had been fulfilled in Christ in a different way). If there is not, however, then we must be careful not to be led astray from the norms laid down by the apostles.

THE RETURN TO THE LAND

This last point leads on to dispute about how to evaluate the return of Jewish people to the land of Israel in our own day:

- Is this a straightforward fulfillment of Old Testament prophecies (e.g., Ezek 36–39), showing the enduring nature of the promise in Gen 12? Or is it an event that, whilst under the providence of the God of the Bible, is not strictly a fulfillment of those passages (with them having been fulfilled either in sixth and fifth centuries BCE, or through the "restoration" accomplished in Messiah Jesus)? If the latter, what might these deeper providential purposes of God be (for example, might it be a means of God showing the descendants of Abraham that their ultimate salvation and *shalom* is precisely *not* to be found in the land, but only in their Messiah as revealed in Jesus)?

- Yet, even if it *were* granted that this return is indeed a fulfillment of Old Testament prophecy, there would then be a subsequent series of disputed points:

- If Israel has been returning to the land, why are we not seeing the parallel movement of a "returning" to the *Lord* (which is what Ezekiel's prophecies were primarily about)? What is the relationship of these two returnings? Why was nineteenth-century Zionism principally espoused by secular Jews? And what are we to make of this secular atheism continuing to be the majority position within contemporary Israeli society? If there has thus been only a minimal "returning to the Lord," does that begin to throw back questions as to whether this is indeed a fulfillment of Ezekiel?

- And in this period of supposed prophetic fulfillment, how much is strictly the work of God alone and how much is the responsibility of human beings to bring about? Should we be actively encouraging "*aliyah*" (enabling the "returning" to the land) and be proactive in evangelism (enabling the "returning" to the Lord) or should believers adopt a more passive stance? In particular, since witnessing to Messiah Jesus amongst Jewish people is historically so complex, should believers simply adopt an acquiescent (and often uncritical) role of "loving Israel"—in the hope that through this loving support God will do *his* work of bringing them to himself?

- Above all, even if we are in prophetic times, what are the biblical mandates for justice that still remain? Does the "prophetic" right to return to the land trump and render irrelevant the bracing demands for justice and righteousness—as expressed so forcefully by those same Old Testament prophets? Do Israel's *prophetic rights to the land* somehow excuse them from *moral and social righteousness in the land*? Just because something has been prophesied, this does not mean we are locked into a deterministic sequence of events, where we are absolved of our human responsibilities to "seek justice, love mercy and walk humbly with our God" (Mic 6:8).

- Following on from this: if Ezekiel himself acknowledged the political and social rights of those who had come to live in the land during the period since Israel's deportation into exile (Ezek 47:22–23), then equally God has a concern for the Palestinians who, in our own day, are resident in this promised land. If the models of conquest (as espoused uniquely in the days of Joshua) were consciously not invoked by Ezekiel, then presumably they should not be invoked today.[13] In theory, of course, it should be possible to adhere to a belief in the land as being rightfully "owned" by Israel, without then desiring to expel all non-Jewish residents from its borders; yet in practice this conviction about ownership can all too easily fuel an inhospitable exclusivism. The biblical mandates concerning the "alien in your midst" then become even more important.[14]

MISSION ISSUES FROM THE WIDER MIDDLE EAST

Finally, these disputes over detail reflect some wider differences of perspective with regard to mission. How does our theology of the land affect the wider Christian community in its promotion of the gospel in the Middle East, both amongst Jews and Muslims?

Relating to Judaism

With regard to Judaism, when Christians adopt a positive and "prophetic" interpretation of Israel's return to the land, this presumably is seen positively amongst many Israeli Jews. Even if they themselves do not read the Old Testament with an attitude of faith in the God of Israel, presumably they are grateful for this Christian support of Israel and this expression of solidarity after a long period when relations between church and synagogue have been historically sour. By contrast, were Christians

---

13. One fascinating possibility is that the writer of Acts intended his work to be the New Testament analogue of Joshua in the Old Testament. There are some intriguing parallels: between the fates of Achan and Ananias/Sapphira and the repeated refrains that punctuate each narrative ("rest from war" in Joshua; "growth of the word" in Acts). If so, *Joshua's* going into the promised land has now been outmoded through the going out of *Jesus'* disciples into the whole inhabited world.

14. See, e.g., Lev 23:22; 24:22; Num 15:15–16; Deut 10:18–19.

to take a more negative view (especially if they become pointedly critical of Israel's political and moral stances), this might well have the effect of undermining the promotion of the gospel—not least because criticism of Israel is so often perceived as an expression of anti-Semitism.

Yet, there remains the key point (alluded to above) that this stance of support for Israel can easily become in the minds of many Christians not a means to an end, but a sufficient end in itself; in other words, the goal of evangelistic mission is effectively forgotten in the bid to "comfort Israel"—seemingly at all costs. This then effectively begins to undermine and work *against* the gospel of Jesus—with Israelis gratefully taking the Christian support offered in the name of Jesus but "digging in their heels" in response to the Christian claims that this Jesus is their Messiah.

Relating to Islam

With regard to Islam, of course, the issues largely work in entirely the opposite direction. Missionaries working in the wider Middle East are constantly aware of the negative effect for mission and outreach amongst Muslims that results from Christian support for Israel. For this support can easily be seen by Muslims as effectively support for their enemies in the region—and indeed as a modern-day outworking of a Crusader mentality within Western Christendom. This is deeply resented. There is then a strong incentive for Christians in Arab countries to distance themselves from Christian Zionist groups, whose advocacy for Israel has such unfortunate effects within this local context.

There is also an urgent need for such Christians to offer an intelligent approach to the Old Testament; for in the eyes of the Muslims it is this portion of the Christian Bible that has encouraged this undesired support of Israel. Thus the divine promises to Abraham, the conquest narrative under Joshua, and the later prophecies about a "return" all need to be interpreted sensitively in this context. No wonder there can be a strong temptation for Christians in the wider Middle East to play down their commitment to the Old Testament. Certainly, they find they have an urgent task of interpreting the Old Testament "Christianly" (rather than in a merely "Jewish" fashion), developing a truly Jesus-centered biblical theology.

All this is driven by the missionary imperative and by the desire to promote the gospel of Jesus—demonstrating how the Christian faith offers a coherent and distinct middle ground between Judaism and

Islam—but there are real dangers of dismissing the Old Testament too much or of becoming overly critical of Israel. For, just as Christians who are seeking to witness amongst Jewish people can end up supporting Israel too easily, so Christians working amongst Muslims can end up being too uncritical of Islamic fundamentalism or some of the extreme positions found within Palestinian nationalism.

IN CONCLUSION

These six areas of dispute proved to be quite major sticking points in our debates. They revealed disagreement on matters both large and small—both "big framework" ideas as well as points of exegetical detail on particular words. Yet it was important to let all these issues come out "onto the table" (though this often required much godly patience with one another!). My hope is that those who now read these reflections will build on what we discovered and will now take the debate forward in further creative ways—ways that foster both biblical faithfulness and Christian charity.

2

From Promised Land to Reconciled Cosmos

Paul's Translation of "Worldview," "Worldstory," and "Worldperson"

Mark Strom

BACKGROUND TO THE ENQUIRY AND PROPOSAL

In various Pauline statements we can discern a nascent recasting of major intellectual traditions. I am thinking of such statements as these among others: "Where is the wise man, scholar, and philosopher?," "Has not God made foolish the wisdom of the world?," "God chose the foolish things of the world to shame the wise" (1 Cor 1:20, 27)[1]; "In Christ are hidden all the treasures of wisdom and knowledge" (Col 2:3); "We have the light of the knowledge of the glory of God in the face of Christ" (2 Cor 4:6); "We take every thought captive to Christ" (2 Cor 10:5); and, "Do not conform to the patterns of this world but be transformed by the renewing of your mind" (Rom 12:2).[2] To mix labels ancient and modern, in these and other Pauline statements, we may hear the apostle reorienting theology, anthropology, epistemology, ethics, and history around Christology. In short, the entire intellectual enterprise was shown a new axis.

---

1. Unless otherwise noted, all Bible quotations are from the NIV.

2. On this last text, note that classical philosophy and society overwhelmingly censured change. Paul's use of the language of "transformation" (*metamorpheō*) was a striking innovation. See Judge, "Cultural Conformity," 3–24.

Readers of Paul usually emphasize his value for Christians. But the legacy of his letters is also public. Paul's letters belong among the greats of classical literature for the seminal and lasting influence they have had on Western life and thought.[3] In this paper, the question of land and cosmos in Paul's letters will serve as a point of departure for a reading of Paul's broader intellectual legacy.

HYPOTHESIS IN A NUTSHELL

Paul was the first translator of a worldview out of its original cultural soil. Ever. Anywhere. A summary of the argument will help to clarify what I *am* claiming and what I am *not*:

Paul saw Israel's Messiah as the "worldmessiah," the king of a "worldkingdom," and the second truly representative human, the second Adam, the true "worldperson." My awkward neologisms seek to dramatize the Pauline categories of thought; in particular, that a Pharisee came to believe that the story carried by Israel could no longer be confined within Judaism or his ancestral home. The covenantal and prophetic promise of land had been recalibrated in the gospel declaration of the reconciliation of the whole earth. As Saul, he had devoted his life to the Jewish story, worldview, and place. As Paul, he devoted himself to proclaiming this story and its surprising resolution to peoples he formerly excluded from it. Paul did not invite Gentiles to join a Jewish story and way of life. Rather, he radically altered the categories and referents of the Jewish story and worldview. Paul sought to make the story intelligible to Athenians, Corinthians, and Ephesians on their own terms as their own story. Certainly Paul continued to teach Gentiles the Jewish origins of the story. This was a crucial strategy. But the story he now told excluded any claim by any group to nationalistic, geographic, imperial, cultural or intellectual priority. The story and worldview Paul proclaimed could be embraced by any group for it was the story of the cosmos and for the cosmos. Accordingly, it could be expressed in the linguistic, social, and intellectual patterns familiar to Gentiles (even if the story also critiqued those patterns). No prophet had ever done this (though perhaps Ezekiel and Daniel pointed in this direction). Neither had Jesus. Indeed, it may

---

3. This is a point acknowledged by Christian and non-Christian intellectuals alike. See for example Alain Gignac's discussion of the reading of Romans by neo-Marxist and postmodern philosophers Alain Badiou, Jacob Taubes, and Giorgio Agamben. See Gignac, "Reception." My thanks to Gavin Drew for this link.

be that no figure in antiquity had ever done this. If so, then arguably Paul was the first translator of a worldview out of its original cultural soil.

Paul's originality among Jewish forebears and contemporaries is not hard to demonstrate. But my larger hypothesis is of course impossible to prove. No one can hope to compare adequately the impact of every influential figure of antiquity. Nonetheless, the scale of impact I am claiming for Paul narrows the field of contenders. How many ancient leaders or writers triggered profound and lasting shifts that were *both* intellectual and social? Such a comparison is feasible within those traditions that have shaped the West up to and including the time of Paul: chiefly Greece, Rome, Egypt, and the ancient Near East. All I can do here is assume the hypothesis has something going for it, and then frame an argument around it. At the least I hope to arouse suspicion that, whether first or not, what Paul accomplished is possibly without equal in scope and enduring impact.

LOCATING THIS HYPOTHESIS WITHIN THE QUESTION OF THE LAND

Paul never used the vocabulary of "land." His references to Israel are to the people, not to the land. There is of course considerable debate about how Paul viewed the ultimate place of his people in the economy of his gospel. Whatever ways we read Rom 9–11 (and other texts), Paul never included Israel's homeland in the hope held out to his people, nor to the Gentiles. And while Zion appears within Old Testament quotations cited in his most extensive treatment of the place of Israel in the gospel (Rom 9–11; see 9:33; 11:26), Zion serves as the place *from* which Yahweh has acted, not as the *telos* of the story.[4] Jerusalem only appears in statements

---

4. Rom 9:33 refers to Yahweh doing something for Israel in Zion that causes them to stumble. Paul locates this action in Jesus. The reference does not indicate any ongoing significance of geographical Zion as the locus of promise. If anything, it suggests that, though what has been done took place where Israel would expect, it now only means shame for them. Rom 11:26 refers to Yahweh doing something for Israel from Zion that blesses Jacob (Israel). Note also the change in preposition in the quote. The Hebrew text of Isa 59:20–21 says the deliver will come "to" Zion (the LXX has "on behalf of"); Paul says he will come "from" Zion (the beginning, as in Acts 1:8). For Paul, Zion is no longer the *telos*. Again, the tenor of Romans shows that Paul locates this action in Jesus. Once again there is no reference to any ongoing significance for geographical Zion as the locus of promise. Nothing in the tenor of the argument to that point in Romans would suggest Zion having ongoing geographical significance for Paul, or anticipated new (positive) theological significance, a possibility he had effectively blocked in the allegory of Gal 4.

of fact: the place where he met with the apostles (Gal 1:18); and the destination of the gift he intended to convey (Rom 15:25, 1 Cor 16:3). There is one exception: the allegory of Gal 4 in which Paul equated the theological significance of Jerusalem to that of Arabia! The land that had formerly preoccupied him as a Pharisee, along with its central city and temple, just does not figure in his writings.

Arguments from silence are of course inconclusive. But these are loud silences. Surely we could expect references to land in letters from this former Pharisee who was "extremely zealous for the traditions of [his] fathers" (Gal 1:14; cf. Phil 3:4–6). But there are none. Paul has ceased to refer to *the* symbols of his former faith with any of the interest that formerly preoccupied him.

None of this is to distance Paul from his people and their Scriptures. His gospel is unintelligible apart from the history and heritage of Israel. He viewed the Jewish narratives and categories as having reached their surprising *telos* in the life, death, and resurrection of Jesus. But there is a "cosmic" hermeneutic at work in the ways Paul employed the Jewish Scriptures.

When Paul builds an appreciative argument from the Old Testament for the significance of Christ, he always starts with Abraham (Rom 4 and 9, Gal 3), not Moses. When Paul argues from Moses/law/Sinai, it is to contrast the experience of redemption under Moses and under Christ (1 Cor 10, 2 Cor 3). For Paul the argument seems to carry the sentiment of Gen 12:1–3 ("and all nations on the earth will be blessed through you") more than the sentiment of Exod 19:3–6 ("and so you will be for me a treasured people").[5] Paul's vision of what Christ had accomplished by his death and resurrection was cosmic (Rom 8:20–23; Eph 1:9–11; Col 1:15–20): it could not be nationally or geographically contained.

Am I putting Paul in a place Jesus alone deserves? Paul's story was after all his rendition of Jesus' story. But the Gospels do not show us Jesus as a translator of Israel's story. Rather, Jesus appears in the Gospels as the one in whom Israel's decisive chapter is being written (e.g., Matt 1:17; 4:15–17; Mark 1:1–3; Luke 1:67–79; 4:21). They reveal Jesus the

---

5. N. T. Wright among others has suggested that the logic of Rom 3–8 turns on the exodus experience of Israel. See Wright, "New Exodus," 27–28. If so, the point is that this new exodus takes place in one person on behalf of Jew and Gentile alike, and that it ends not in Jerusalem but in a redeemed cosmos. Paul's most sustained argument from Moses is 2 Cor 3, where he claims that in Christ the Corinthians' experience of the glory of the Lord surpasses that of Israel and even Moses.

prophet and Messiah who stood with his people even as he subverted their expectations of him and of their God. In this sense, Jesus was the story waiting to be translated: a Jewish Messiah carrying Israel's story up to a Roman cross, there abandoned by all but women, thieves, and centurions; a Jewish Messiah who commissioned his disciples to proclaim the good news of his resurrection from Jerusalem, Judea, and Samaria to the ends of the earth, without a hint anywhere that anyone need ever return in pilgrimage.

The story of Jesus was pregnant with significance. This is what Paul expounded and translated for the world. This message of cosmic reconciliation eclipsed the localizing of redemption to any particular geography.

UNPACKING THE IDEA OF TRANSLATION AND PAUL'S ACCOMPLISHMENT

What then do I mean by "translate"?

Paul's forebears and contemporaries had viewed their story as bound to the traditions and geography of the nation.[6] Paul placed this story on a global stage. I would suggest that Paul was amplifying what he had learned of Jesus' novel exposition of the "kingdom of God" (1 Cor 15:3–8, 24; Col 4:11). Jesus, it seems, confounded historic and contemporary expectations of this kingdom. Jesus undermined the expectation that the kingdom of God belonged to Israel in the ways they had assumed.[7] Paul went further, radically "de-Israelizing" Israel's story in the light of the cosmic accomplishments of their own Messiah: Jew and Gentile were placed on the same non-Jewish common ground (Eph 2:11–22; 3:6).

What Paul did with this story was startling to Jew and Gentile alike (1 Cor 1:22–23). He continued to tell the story within Jewish categories of thought (e.g., Adam, Abraham, Moses, Exodus, law, righteousness,

---

6. For a treatment of land in biblical theology, see Brueggemann, *Land*, 175–83. Brueggemann more than once derides those who claim Paul has no interest in the land. However, he concludes his treatment of Paul by saying that the apostle's interest in "land" is in fact an interest in the ongoing idea of inheritance now located in Christ with the promise of resurrection to a new creation, not an abiding interest in geographical Israel or Jerusalem.

7. Treatment of the radicalness of the kingdom in the Synoptic tradition is of course well-ploughed ground. See for example the extensive discussion and exposition in Wright, *Victory*, 145–472.

temple, new creation, Spirit). But he did not call Gentiles to embrace a Jewish way of life; indeed he explicitly rejected this possibility (Gal 2:14–16; 5:3). Paul framed the story in ways that were intelligible to educated inhabitants of the Greco-Roman cities (Acts 17:23–28). But he did not reduce the story to the categories of the popular intellectualism of his day.[8] His story and way of life required a response. But he never required converts to adopt his culture or language. He reframed the story and its implications for their lives in the terms of his listeners' own worlds, whoever they were: *their* language, *their* customs, *their* sources, and *their* categories. That, I would argue, is translation of a worldview. I would go further: that is arguably a translation unsurpassed both in content and methodology. But I am running ahead of myself.

Was this a first? Paul's novelty is perhaps made clearer by comparison.

Many before Paul had imposed worldviews; Alexander for example.[9] Some had sought to transplant ideas into new contexts; like Plato in Sicily. Some had welcomed new concepts as supporting or augmenting the existing intellectual and social status quo; recall Cicero's and other Romans' love of Greek philosophers and poets. Much later, Mohammed represents a translation of sorts,[10] but one that still requires conformity to a singular culture, language, and geography.[11]

---

8. Considerable work has been done on Pauline innovations (see the works by Judge, Malherbe, Meeks, Winter, and Forbes among many others). In the following terms, Paul makes a novel use of a traditional category or metaphor (often subverting its traditional intent): e.g., lord, gospel, body, *ecclesia*, grace, righteousness, glory, power, strength, wisdom, knowledge, and boasting. In others he exalted less prominent or even despised terms, e.g., transformation, service, weakness, and love. He also employed new metaphors for society, e.g., building, gift. It is similarly instructive to note the vocabulary he largely avoided: leader, virtue, courage, status, and ambition.

9. Alexander's accomplishments were extraordinary and long-lasting. His legacy was the spread of Greek language and culture, often involving hybridization with the cultures of conquered peoples. The story, the worldview, and the legacy, however, never displaced the assumption of a superior culture (Greece).

10. See Walls, *Cross-Cultural*, 27–48, for a discussion of the attributes of Islam that work against the kind of translation that has proven a hallmark of Christianity.

11. At his point the question may arise: What about Buddha? Is Buddha (fifth century BCE) the one figure who can claim priority to Paul as a translator of a worldview? I have no expertise on the life of Buddha, nor on Buddhism in any of its forms. Nonetheless some general observations are possible that may put the comparison in perspective. The teachings of Buddha are almost entirely personal. They offer little by way of reframing social relations. Rather they present a personal way of life and a contemplative religion

To be translated, a worldview needs a story to retell, not simply ideas to reconceptualize and transfer. Worldviews all have stories.[12] But I am suggesting something more: a worldview is not really a *world*view without a world *story*—without a "worldstory," a worldview is just a "*local*view," even if "local" is *very* big.[13] In a sense, no one could have translated a worldview, because no worldview had a worldstory. Except one.

Israel's worldview rested on a worldstory: "through you all the nations of the earth will be blessed" (Gen 12:3). This worldstory carried explicit and implicit critiques of other worldviews and stories. Some holders of Israel's story had to live out their worldview in foreign soil (most famously Joseph, Moses, and Daniel). It is unclear to what extent these figures and their biographers understood the story of their own people as in some way a story for the world held in trust by Israel. The visions of the prophets did extend to the inclusion of the nations in the ultimate blessing of Israel and the earth, but in the sense of the nations coming within the orbit of Israel's symbols (e.g., Isa 2:2–4).

Paul's letters assume a worldstory that had been held in trust by Israel (Rom 3:2). This worldstory turned on Jesus of Nazareth and his resurrection. Paul recognized in Jesus and his accomplishment not only the Jewish Messiah, but the "worldperson," the "Second Adam" (Rom 5, 1 Cor 15) who would fulfill the worldstory when he brought "all things in heaven and on earth together" (Eph 1:10). Having grasped the world dimension of the story, the cultural tie had to be cut. His language was unequivocal: "circumcision counts for nothing" (Gal 6:15); "I count it all

---

(in itself a remarkable innovation), but not a view of the world carried by a story of and for the world. Indeed, at heart, Buddhism is world-denying, not world-affirming. Traditional forms of Buddhism suggest that the hope of humans lies in escape from the world through enlightenment; they seem to advocate disengagement from all story, all culture, from everything that is physical and social about being human. Buddhism is a philosophy, a set of ideas for individual adoption. It is an extraordinary innovation. But Buddhism has no original or necessary grounding in culture; no story of the world for the world. Popularized forms of Buddhism prevalent in the West today are viewed by some as a basis for humanitarianism and environmentalism. It could be argued that in being co-opted to these causes, Buddhism has come to share in the syncretism of classical and Christian ideas that characterizes the West.

12. For a discussion of worldview and story in relation to a critical realist epistemology, see Wright, *People of God*, 31–80.

13. I am of course being playful with my terms. *Weltanschauung* or "worldview" generally refers to a view *of* life and/or *of* the world rather than an encompassing view of life *for* the world. I do not literally mean that there are no worldviews, only "localviews."

loss" (referring to his Israelite identity and achievement; Phil 3:8); "the middle wall of partition has been torn down" (Eph 2:14); "there is neither Jew nor Greek" (Gal 3:28); "Hagar stands for Mount Sinai in Arabia and corresponds to the present city of Jerusalem" (Gal 4:25).

For Paul, the story could not be about incorporating Gentiles into Israel. Rather Jew and Gentile together are being made into a new humanity living toward the resolution of a shared story (Eph 2:14–22). Neither Roman citizenship nor Israelite heritage could any longer define what it is to be human. Being human had been redefined by a man raised to heaven and the promise of being transformed into his likeness (1 Cor 15:45–49).

Given the likely priority of his letters in the New Testament corpus, Paul is the first person whom we know to have made these connections on this scale. This is not to minimize the imagination and contribution of Peter and others recorded in the first half of Acts. But their proclamations remained tied to Israel. Peter's vision from heaven climaxed in his realization that the Gentiles were no longer unclean. This was a significant breakthrough. But the man who would be called to give an account on Mars Hill needed, and found, far more. It was Paul who accepted the calling to carry the story to the peoples of Athens, Ephesus, and Corinth—peoples who knew neither the background to the story nor understood the culture that had carried it. It was Paul who recognized that the story had to be taken to them because it was in fact their story: "what you worship as unknown I am going to proclaim to you" (Acts 17:23). How he did so is one of the great stories of personal transformation, dedication, and genius.

THE COST OF TRANSLATION TO PAUL

Consider the deconstruction of Saul. Paul, the former Pharisee, radically reconfigured "in Christ" his lifelong devotion to the marks of covenant: Christ's faithfulness superseded Saul's own devotion to law; God's yes in Christ to the covenant promises superseded Saul's own devotion to the restoration of land and temple. The architecture of Saul's thought remained in place, but the realization of its *telos* in Christ, together with his calling to the Gentiles, began in Paul a process of theological reimagining and intellectual innovation for the task ahead.

The debates continue over the extent of Paul's education within Hellenism as a youth growing up in the Roman colony of Tarsus.

Whenever, however, and how much he learned, we will never know.[14] But his letters and Acts show a brilliant mind conversant with the shape of classical and Greco-Roman thought, and an ex-rabbi who (now) worked (often freely) from the Septuagint more than from the Hebrew text. How did he bridge these two worlds?

As Paul walked to the Areopagus we can imagine a message forming in his mind:[15] he began with an idol (had any Jew ever positively expounded such a source?); he nimbly exploited the theological disputes between the Stoics and Epicureans in his audience; he drew on the traditions known via Epimenides, Aratus, and/or Cleanthus (including a hymn to Zeus no less!); he wove in Jewish cosmology and the prophetic tradition; and he ended with a play on the founding motto of the Areopagus.[16] This unprecedented juxtaposition of ideas and cultures cannot have been a whim of the moment. Extempore speeches like that are built on great learning, considerable innovation of thought, rhetorical skill, and subtlety of mind. Profound intellectual translations are built on considerable familiarity with and reflection upon the traditions one is bridging.

The Corinthian letters reveal a masterful critique of Greco-Roman popular intellectualism couched in startling and unprecedented self-disclosure.[17] Paul knew how rank and status worked in Corinth. He knew the complicity of education and rhetoric in the machinations of men who loved their own honor and ambition above all else. He knew how the courts worked. He understood patronage and the complexities of balancing deference and boasting. He turned the tables on standard Stoic metaphors and phrases. And all the while he articulated a radically alternate worldview grounded in the story and traditions of his ancestors but now recast in the light of the crucifixion and resurrection of Jesus.[18]

---

14. See the still apt and judicious conclusions of Judge, "Boasting."

15. I do not mean to minimize the hand of Luke in Acts 17. The recorded speech is surely not verbatim and most likely crafted to suit Luke's intent. Nonetheless it just as surely reflects the brilliance of the original.

16. See the works of Hemer, *Hellenistic History*, and "Speeches." For a summary treatment, see also Strom, *Reframing*, 120–22.

17. Thinking particularly of the Corinthian correspondence, Edwin Judge notes: "There is in my view no writer of antiquity who exposes himself so ruthlessly to direct human contact and reveals himself to others with such candor and directness as does St. Paul" ("Radical Critic," 193).

18. See my *Reframing* for the evidence for Paul's familiarity with, and innovation within, the Greco-Roman context.

This surely shows a brilliant mind and a life of great intellectual labor. It may well be that Paul did what no one had ever done. There was no model. There was no methodological precedent. Neither Jewish nor Greek. The works of Philo were a major achievement in synthesis, but I suggest they do not match the finely wrought argument for transformation that pervades the letters of Paul.

We should not minimize the scope or the cost of this endeavor. This was a commitment of a life, not merely a mind. Paul's translation did not endear him to any but a small group of converts, and even *they* viewed him with mixed regard (note particularly the Corinthian correspondence). Paul's translation left no part for Jewish nationalism. It ostracized him from his own people and especially from those who continued to assume the priority of Jerusalem and all that it entailed (Gal 1–2). The story dislocated him from his sense of personal and cultural identity (Phil 3). Unlike his compatriot Josephus, Paul did not find a new home outside Israel; he did not transfer his hopes to a new nation, empire, or ruler. His gospel critiqued the structures of Greek and Roman social and intellectual life. He refused the kinds of patronage his education and citizenship could secure. Eventually it could not help but antagonize Rome given that the story of Augustus/Rome was proclaimed in decree, coinage, and inscriptions as *the* worldstory. Paul's gospel was a scandal to Jews and foolishness to Greeks (1 Cor 1:23), and perhaps ultimately sedition to Rome.[19]

To return to the theme of this collection: Paul the ex-Pharisee— formerly zealous for his people, his city, and his temple in the face of Roman oppression and hubris—had ceased to be concerned with the land of his ancestors. Why? The story he now told was a *worldstory—the* story for the world. The central figure was a *worldperson—the* person for the world. The *telos* of his good news was the reconciliation of *all things—* heaven and earth, Jew and Gentile—under this worldperson. No nation, land, city, or temple could convey or contain the cosmic reconciliation that Paul believed the God of Israel had accomplished through their own Messiah. The hope of a renewed land had been absorbed and eclipsed in the reconciliation of the cosmos (Rom 8:20–23; Col 1:15–20).

---

19. See for example the treatment of Col 1:15–20 by Walsh and Keesmaat, *Colossians*, 82–95. There is of course considerable debate as to the extent to which Paul's letters should be read as subversive of the claims and ideology of Rome.

THE BREADTH OF PAUL'S LEGACY

If the argument holds to this point, then the claim needs to be extended in terms of the legacy of translation as an intellectual achievement and model. I think we can argue that Paul, more than any other figure, was the architect and pioneer of something we take for granted in virtually every arena of local, national, and global life—the assumption that cultures can be transformed by the translation of ideas modeled in a life given at one and the same time to service and to subversion.

This is not to minimize later translators, nor to suggest that the complexity of Western ideas somehow all traces its way back to Paul. It does not. But it is to make a claim for the source of an idea: *The idea that a story, a way of being, a complex of ideas, a worldview, needs to be translated out of its cultural soil for the people to whom it (also) rightly belongs; and the concomitant idea that this translation needs to be done free from any obligation of identification with the original national, cultural, or geographical context of the story.*

Today the language of culture, worldview, paradigm, and transformation is standard fare in commercial, political, and social theory and commentary. It has long passed into the vernacular. Some of these terms are recent arrivals. None derive from Paul—though following Edwin Judge I again note the innovations he crafted through his highly original use of several Greco-Roman terms and metaphors. My argument is not that Paul coined all this, nor even that he prefigured it. My argument is that our preoccupation with change is the outworking of a collision of ideas—of Judaism and classical thought—for which Paul more than anyone else is responsible.

The shaping of Western intellectual and social life defies any single explanation. Nonetheless history is never flat; it has a way of throwing up disproportionately influential figures, ideas and moments. That is my claim: that Paul's passionately embodied ideas brought two iconic worlds together in a way unprecedented in method and scope, and perhaps unsurpassed in influence.

The story of Jesus was pregnant with significance. This is what Paul expounded and translated for the world. In doing so, Paul not only passed on the greatest story of all, but also bequeathed an extraordinary epistemological and methodological legacy. To turn one of his lines of thought, the renewal of Paul's own mind put into effect a transformation of the patterns of this world that continues to disturb conformity.

This reading of Paul might suggest lines of conversation with wider audiences. If the argument holds, then, like his gospel, Paul's story and method belongs to the world, and it remains uniquely placed to inform that world, to bless it, and to subvert it. The need remains for translators.

PAUL'S GOSPEL NEEDED THE WORLD

This argument begs to be taken further: the more we consider Paul's achievement, the more reasonable it seems to suggest that the translation is not only *of* the message but, in some important sense, that the act of translation *is* (at least part of) the message. It does not seem too great an imposition on Paul (albeit clearly anachronistic) to say that his vision of the gospel is the foundation of all translation. Paul's use of "mystery" (e.g., Rom 16:25; Eph 1:9; 3:3–9; Col 1:26–27) to describe the gospel suggests a hermeneutical trajectory, not only in terms of his use of the Jewish Scriptures, but also in terms of his sense of the intellectual dimensions of his calling. He had "to make known the mystery hidden from ages past" to peoples who knew nothing of the story. Without those peoples, there could be no translation, and the gospel would not be what it is.

Notwithstanding the intersections between the ancient Jewish writers and the cultural and religious traditions of their neighbors, Israel and her covenant were largely self-contained. Ultimately Israel existed for the nations; but Israel did not need the nations to know what Yahweh had done or would do. The Exodus would seem the exception. If the Exodus is the defining memory of God's self-revelation and redemption, then in some sense Israel needed Egypt. But the nation's self-understanding based upon their memory of the Exodus shaped an identity of standing over against the nations. Something perhaps began to shift in this self-understanding through the experience of exile. The visions of Ezekiel and Daniel "require" the nations. Certain strands in Ezekiel's visions hint at a broader anthropology. Daniel's visions portray a global and cosmic history. Perhaps "worldstory" is the stuff of apocalyptic. Something about these prophets seems to lean toward what Paul was to do. A hint at least.

Jesus, and particularly Paul, abandoned the self-contained self-understanding of Israel. The gospel could not be known adequately apart from its encounter with foreign peoples, ideas, and cultures. It needed the world. The gospel *required* "foreign" soil, as redemption required incarnation. Its genius was its need, as well as its ability, to be translated. The message was and is *inherently* incarnational, cruciform, and resurrectional—it requires flesh and opposition (creation and fall) to create new life (redemption). In the words of missiologist Andrew Walls,

> The essentially vernacular nature of Christian faith ... rests on a massive act of translation, the Word made flesh, God translated into a specific segment of social reality as Christ is received there ... Christian faith must go on being translated, must continuously enter into vernacular culture and interact with it, or it withers and fades. Islamic absolutes are fixed in a particular language of original revelation. For Christians, however, the divine Word is translatable, infinitely translatable. The very words of Christ himself were transmitted in translated form in the earliest documents we have, a fact surely inseparable from the conviction that in Christ, God's own self was translated into human form.[20]

As much as Paul's articulation of the gospel rested on the themes and figures of the Jewish story that had carried it, the brilliance of his translation *required* the intellectual and social architecture of classical Greece, the clashes of Hellenistic thought and culture, and the pervasive ideology of *Romanitas*.[21] Without these there would be no letters to the Romans, Corinthians, or Ephesians. There would have been no exposition of Christ as cosmic. There would have been no embodiment of ideas capable of subverting the givenness of hierarchy, dualism, and imperialism. And, given the likely chronological priority of Paul's letters, one might speculate that there may never have been the Gospels as we know them.

It has ever been so.

The brilliance of the creeds and of Augustine required Neoplatonism and the myths of *Romanitas*. Luther and Calvin needed the Aristotelian revival and the Renaissance. Edwards and Schleiermacher needed the Enlightenment. Each was a translator. Each translation required its intellectual and cultural context. The shape of ideas and culture in every era of the West has always depended upon the legacies of the translators of Jesus and of (the translations of) Paul, and vice versa; even if only by reaction. Each turn in the history of ideas and culture has enabled and

---

20. Walls, *Cross-Cultural*, 29.
21. See the brilliant older treatment of Cochrane, *Classical*.

triggered new vistas of exposition, whether by accommodation or by critique.

Today's swirl of culture and ideas is no more foreign to the gospel than was the swirl of culture and ideas in the first century. Our context is equally vital for this gospel to find and give new life. Humanity is cultural. Incarnation is cultural. Redemption is cultural. Translation is cultural. Paul said: "Be imitators of me as I am of Christ" (1 Cor 11:1). We might well say, "Be translators of Paul as he was of Christ." In imitation of Paul's brilliant original translation, the gospel requires fresh exposition and enlargement for and by every era and culture.

The transposition of land to cosmos offers a window into the far-reaching intellectual legacy of Paul. This most unlikely *theologos* and *philosophos* could not have foreseen the implications or eventual impact of his thought. By bringing his strikingly original rethinking of Judaism into dialogue with Hellenistic thought and empire, Paul triggered a seismic shift in metaphysics, epistemology, anthropology, historiography, and political thought. As a translator, Christ, not land, was Paul's message and his hermeneutic.

3

Paul's Answer to the Threats of Jerusalem and Rome (Phil 3)

MARK KEOWN

INTRODUCTION

PHILIPPIANS 3 IS SHROUDED in controversy. Three questions in particular are raised. First, is it original to the letter or a separate letter fused with others to form the final extant form of Philippians?[1] Secondly, who are the opponents of Paul mentioned in 3:2 and 3:18? Thirdly, are the opponents in these verses the same people in both cases? The passage is also embroiled in the controversies over Paul's understanding of the law. Different answers to these questions have led to diverse interpretations.[2] In addition, as is often the case in contemporary biblical scholarship, seeking resolutions to these questions has tended to obscure and complicate the meaning of the passage.

The claims of a composite letter lack any substantive warrant, and indeed, a number of recent studies have demonstrated the theological coherence of the letter—most especially, the links between this passage and Phil 2:5–11.[3] Thus I will proceed on the basis that Phil 3 is an integral part of the epistle, and will suggest a reading of the chapter that has

---

1. See for example the recent commentary of Reumann, *Philippians*, 3, 13–18.

2. This essay will not deal in depth with these questions or other introductory questions concerning Philippians. For this writer's views see Keown, *Congregational Evangelism*, 37–70.

3. See the discussion in Hansen, *Philippians*, 15–19.

important implications for Paul's relationship to Judaism, Jerusalem, and the land.

I will argue that in Phil 3 Paul deals with two distinct threats to his beloved Philippians. The first is the external threat of the Judaizers and Judaism, i.e., "Jerusalem." The second threat is more present: that of paganism found in Philippi and in Paul's context, i.e., "Rome."[4] The chapter is not tightly structured to give a symmetrical patterned response to these threats. Generally speaking, however, Paul deals with the problem of the Judaizers and Judaism in 3:2–11 and that of Rome in 3:18–21.[5] In this view, the section 3:12–17 is transitional relating to both situations, Paul urging the Philippians to live according to his example and the pattern of the cross in the face of both sets of opponents. A suggested structure for the chapter and this essay follows:

1. Warning and response to the Judaizers and Judaism (3:2–11)

    a. Believers in Christ and not "Israel," the people of God (3:3)

    b. Paul's superior credentials under the system of Judaism (3:4–6)

    c. The futility of "Judaism"; knowing Christ by faith is all that matters (3:7–11)

2. Transition: Paul's example of perseverance in the Christ-pattern and his appeal to the Philippians to emulate him (3:12–17)

3. Warning and response to Greco-Roman paganism (3:18–19)[6]

4. Hope, a new kingdom, the return of Christ, bodily transformation, and cosmic victory (3:20–21)

The aim of this essay is to draw out Paul's argument. Here we will find that Paul deals adeptly with threats of both Jerusalem and Rome. As he does, he gives hints into his Christ-defined perspective on land,

---

4. "Jerusalem" and "Rome" are used in this essay as ciphers for Judaism that rejects Jesus as Messiah and/or argues for a Christianity that upholds Jewish law and tradition; and Roman thinking that rejects or distorts the gospel.

5. There is overlap in Paul's argument. For example, 3:10–11 is antithetical to the theology of the "enemies of the cross." These verses can also be placed with what follows as they transition into identification with the pattern of the cross that undergirds the appeal of 3:15–17. Philippians 3:20–21 serves not only as a conclusion to his response to the "enemies of the cross" but culminates the whole letter. Similarly, 3:8–11 speaks to both Jewish and pagan distortions of the gospel.

6. I have used "paganism" here for want of a better term. It merely means Greco-Roman cultural and social norms as opposed to those of the gospel.

Jerusalem, Zion, temple, law, salvation, incorporation into the people of God, election, the return of Christ, and the eternal state.

WARNING AND RESPONSE TO THE JUDAIZERS AND JUDAISM (3:2–11)

In 3:2 Paul warns the Philippians about certain opponents. He describes them as "dogs, evil workers and mutilators of the flesh." The identity of these opponents is disputed, with three main perspectives. First, Klijn and others argue that these are Jews in general.[7] This is unlikely since these opponents appear to be seeking to directly afflict the church in Philippi in which there is little evidence of a strong Jewish presence.[8] That being said, this view correctly notes that Paul's response, in effect, challenges the whole religious edifice of a Judaism that has rejected the Messiah Jesus.

Secondly, it is argued that these are pneumatic false teachers blending Jewish ideas with such ideas as a hyper-spirituality, Gnosticism, divine man theology, libertinism, and/or an over-realized eschatology.[9] This too is unlikely since Paul counters their teaching with a contrast of faith and law, making it doubtful that they are ethically libertine while remaining law-bound.

Thirdly, some contend that these opponents are Judaizers, actively seeking to convince Gentile believers in the Pauline churches of the need for circumcision and adherence to the Law of Moses.[10] This is the majority position and is almost certainly correct since Paul's response refers to circumcision and law obedience, recalling his arguments in Galatians and Romans in particular.[11]

---

7. For example, Klijn, "Paul's Opponents," 278–84; Houlden, *Paul's Letters*, 34, 103.

8. See Keown, *Congregational Evangelism*, 56–57.

9. See for example Köster, "Purpose," 317–32; Schmithals, *Paul and the Gnostics*, 65–122. Gnilka, "Die antipaulinische Mission," 258–76, sees them as divine man missionaries. This accords with an Ephesus provenance.

10. See for example Fee, *Philippians*, 293–94; Keown, *Congregational Evangelism*, 59–62.

11. See for example Williams, *Enemies*, 153–59; De Vos, *Conflicts*, 267–71; Bockmuehl, *Philippians*, 184–89; Reumann, *Philippians*, 469–70; Witherington, *Friendship*, 87–91; Marshall, *Philippians*, 78–80; Barth, *Philippians*, 92; Smith, *Marks of an Apostle*, 63–67; Craddock, *Philippians*, 54–56; Mearns, "Paul's Opponents," 195–203; Jewett, "Conflicting Movements," 376; Müller, *Der Brief des Paulus*, 25, 145–46. Fowl, *Philippians*, 146, disputes that these are Judaizers directly challenging the church, arguing rather that they

While this is the case, although the opponents are Judaizers and not Jewish unbelievers, Paul's response in 3:3–12 is effectively his response to Judaism as generally understood in his time. It is his perspective, looking back on the way he viewed the world before his own experience of the risen Christ.

Since the early days of Paul's mission, these Judaizers had accepted Jesus as Messiah, but also urged Gentile believers to be circumcised and live in obedience to the Law of Moses, so seeking to bring new believers under the religious expectations of Judaism (Galatians; Acts 15:1). No doubt these expectations included the "boundary markers" of Judaism, including circumcision, Sabbath, food laws, ritual purity, and the festivals.[12] However, Paul's response here is not confined to such badges and "works of the law"; rather, he speaks of the law *per se* (e.g., 3:9), rejecting the whole edifice of *Judaism without Christ as a means of salvation*.[13] In view of Messiah's coming, membership of the people of God is now defined in, by, and through Christ. Here, Paul emphatically denies that any notion of salvation and inclusion in God's people, or retention within the people of God (i.e., covenantal nomism), is through circumcision or adherence to the law. Rather, it is through an ongoing faith relationship with Christ.[14] We thus have a window in these verses into Paul's view of Judaism, standing as he is now, as a believer that Jesus is the Messiah, and looking back at his previous Jewish understanding. For Paul, Judaism as a religious system has now found its fulfillment in Christ and is defined by relationship with Christ. This christological reframing means that the people of God have been redefined so that there is no salvation outside of Jesus.

In 3:3–11 Paul counters the teaching of these Judaizers focusing on the futility of seeking righteousness through obedience to the law and strongly emphasizing righteousness by faith alone for salvation. There are four parts to his argument.

---

are *social* Judaizers, with Judaism being an attractive place to stand for those threatened by the Imperial cult because it was tolerated by Rome.

12. See Sanders, *Paul, the Law and the Jewish People*; Dunn, "New Perspective," 183–206; Wright, *Climax*.

13. See O'Brien, "Was Paul a Covenantal Nomist?" 249–96.

14. This does not mean that Christian living is antinomian. It is no longer defined by "law" in the sense of a legal code imposed; rather, it is a Spirit-led living by the law of love. In such living, the law is fulfilled.

The first part is found in the four assertions of 3:3. In 3:3a he makes it clear that those who believe in Christ (cf., 3:9) are the true circumcision, a circumcision of the heart by faith (cf., Rom 2:25–29). Now, in light of the Messiah's coming, true Israel is comprised of those who believe in Jesus and not those identified through racial identity or identification with Judaism. This new people includes Gentiles such as the Philippians, and believing Jews like Paul. It stands in continuity with Israel by faith, now defined by faith in Christ (cf., Gal 3, Rom 4).

Secondly, he asserts that it is Christians, both Jew and Gentile, who worship in the Spirit (3:3b). Believers are the recipients of the long-awaited Spirit through Christ the Anointed One, and not the Jews *per se*. Believers in Christ are the temple of the Holy Spirit (1 Cor 3:16). This is not a *replacement* of Israel. Indeed, the one who defines this faith is Jewish (Jesus) and the community originates with Jews (e.g., Paul). Rather, this new people, including Gentile believers, is the *extension* of historic Israel, by faith in Christ. The religious system of Israel, in light of the coming of Israel's Messiah, is now defined by Christian worship directed not only to God the Father, but to his Son Jesus Christ (cf., 2:9–11). The Spirit is not limited to any geographical locale, whether it be land, Jerusalem, Zion, temple, synagogue, or church building. Nor is it limited to any ethnicity, whether Jew or Gentile. The new people of God in Christ, both individual and corporate, wherever located, is the temple of God in which his *shekinah* glory dwells (1 Cor 3:16; 6:19; 2 Cor 3:3; Eph 2:19–22; 2 Tim 1:14). This includes Paul himself in Rome under the shadow of the empire and his Gentile readers in Romanized Philippi. The Philippians do not need to go on pilgrimage to Palestine, to Zion, to a temple, synagogue, or indeed a church building, to experience the *pneuma* of God. In Christ, they worship and serve[15] by the Spirit whether gathered in *ekklēsia* or scattered in mission.

The third assertion is that there is only one in whom to glory or boast: Christ (3:3c cf., 1 Cor 1:31; 2 Cor 10:17). This is the language of worship rather than self-glory or boasting (cf., 3:2).[16] Believers are to glory and boast in nothing other than Christ and what he has done. He

---

15. The Greek *latreuō* means worship in the fullest sense including the vertical and the horizontal dimensions of worship of God and service. See *BDAG*, 586.

16. While the *kauch-* nexus of terms here means "boast," here it takes the sense of attributing glory to someone. As such, it carries the sense of worship of, i.e., "glory in Christ Jesus." Cf., NIV, NASB (1995), ESV. Cf., Swanson, *Dictionary*, s.v. καυχάομαι (3016).

is the focus of worship; God is known through Christ and not through the law except that it leads to Christ and God. While the law is holy, righteous, and good (cf., Rom 7:12), it is now fulfilled and completed in Christ and they now glory in him alone.

The fourth and final assertion is that Paul takes no confidence in the flesh (3:3d). This is an important statement launching what follows. For Paul, trusting in one's ability to obey the law for salvation and inclusion in God's people is a version of self-reliance. Reliance on law whether to get in or stay in the new covenant people of God is in effect a self-confidence that renders grace obsolete (cf., Gal 5:4). Thus, Paul repudiates any idea of physical descent, circumcision of the flesh, or self-confidence in works-righteousness as determinative of being in the newly formed people of God around Christ. Paul's emphasis is on his identity as a true Jew and his adherence to law.

The second element of his response to the threat of the Judaizers is found in 3:4–6. Here Paul presents his CV in terms of Judaism, with seven credentials all carefully chosen to emphasize that he is not only a Jew, but one who is able to match his opponents against the backdrop of Judaism. The first four demonstrate that he is not only a true Jew in every sense: (1) he was circumcised on the eighth day as expected in the Abrahamic covenant (Gen 17:10–12); (2) he is an Israelite and so a member of the elect people of God formed in Jacob; (3) like King Saul, his namesake, he is from the favored tribe of Benjamin;[17] (4) he is a genuine Hebrew, raised a Hebrew, and a Hebrew speaker.[18] The final three speak of his superior credentials: (5) he is a Pharisee, and so an esteemed Jewish religious leader, and interpreter and teacher of the law (cf., Acts 22:3; 23:6; 26:5; Gal 1:14); (6) he has been a persecutor of the church and so a zealot for Israel's traditions and against any threat to them (1 Cor 15:9; Gal 1:13, 23; 1 Tim 1:13; cf., Acts 7:58—8:4; 9:4–5; 11:19; 22:4, 7–8; 26:11, 14–15); (7) he is faultless in living the law as defined in Second Temple Pharisaic Judaism.[19] In his ironical challenge to his opponents he states that, if anyone should have confidence before God for salvation

---

17. Aside from Saul, Benjamin was a favored son of Joseph, the tribe supported Judah in the division, and Jerusalem was in its bounds; see Hansen, *Philippians*, 224.

18. See O'Brien, *Philippians*, 371.

19. Paul is not stating that he is perfect in his obedience (sinless), but that he lived out the requirements of the law, including sacrifice and penitence, with great rigor; cf., Thurston and Ryan, *Philippians & Philemon*, 122.

and inclusion in God's people through obedience to the Law and the religious system of Judaism it is himself.

Thirdly, in 3:7–11, Paul radically writes off these claims of superiority. All that matters is relationship with Jesus Christ as Lord through faith;[20] it is faith rather than law obedience in any sense that saves and sees a person incorporated into God's people.[21] His renunciation of his own credentials is analogous to Christ's self-emptying in Phil 2:6–8.[22] This desire to fully identify with the Christ-pattern of suffering, death, and resurrection laid out in the Christ hymn of 2:6–11 is picked up in 3:10–11. Paul wishes to live out the pattern of full identification with Christ in this age, in his desire to know the resurrection power of God to sustain him in his life and ministry, to fully associate with Christ's suffering and death, and ultimately to experience the resurrection from the dead.

Thus far, Paul has dealt with the threat of the Judaizers. In so doing, he also demonstrates the poverty of a Judaism that rejects the Messiah Jesus. In continuity with historic Israel by faith, Israel is now found in Christ. It is made up of those, both Jew and Gentile, who believe in Jesus as Messiah and Lord. It stands in continuity with Israel by faith in God from its history (Rom 4; cf., Heb 11). Nevertheless, in this "Israel by faith" there is no interest in Jewish law, the land, Jerusalem, Zion, the temple, or the covenants. What was formerly significant in "Israel after the flesh" has been set aside for "Israel by faith." The trajectory of Paul's teaching here moves away from ethnicity, nomism, and geographical centricity toward a christocentric, universal, and cosmic definition of faith.

---

20. This is so whether we take *pisteōs Christou* subjectively as the faithfulness *of* Christ or objectively as faith *in* Christ (as the next clause "through faith" [*epi tē pistei*] indicates. See the debate between Dunn and Hays in Hays, *Faith*, 249–97.

21. The position taken here argues that incorporation into the people of God (ecclesiology) is *coterminous* with salvation (soteriology) and forms one component part of Paul's theology of salvation. For Paul, to be "saved" means being "in Christ" and so included in the people of God by faith.

22. Some reject that this is in Paul's mind here. However, while the analogy is not perfect, the manner of self-renunciation does recall the pattern of Christ's self-humbling in Phil 2:6–8.

TRANSITION, PAUL'S EXAMPLE OF PERSEVERANCE IN THE CHRIST-PATTERN AND HIS APPEAL TO THE PHILIPPIANS TO EMULATE HIM (3:12–17)

In 3:12–14 Paul speaks of his determination to live out his Christian life and ministry according to the Christ-pattern. He uses an athletic metaphor: he runs, overcoming all struggles, and surges toward the goal of victory (cf., 1 Cor 9:24–27). The prize is the ultimate goal, the resurrection from the dead and eternal life. The passage is transitional with a twofold function. First, it looks back to what precedes and speaks against any presumption of election on Paul's part. As such, it ensures that the Philippians do not fall into the mistake made so often in Israel's history, of excessive confidence in election. While he is justified by faith and not by law, this does not presuppose that he can sit back and live a life of leisure confident of his salvation. Rather, he continues to serve Christ living by faith, living by the Spirit, proclaiming the gospel and doing the works of faith.

Secondly, it points forward to what will follow, where he urges emulation of his own example and reminds the Philippians of the hope of salvation when the savior Christ returns and their bodies are transformed for eternal life. While Paul rejects false overconfidence, there is a sense of assurance for his readers. If they continue in their faith, not diverted by the Judaizers or pagan opponents, pressing on with all their being, the goal of eternal life is assured (cf., 1:6; 2:13). It picks up the imperative passages through Philippians calling for gospel living citizenship, perseverance, proclamation, love, humility, unity, obedience, and the working out of salvation (cf., 1:27—2:4; 2:11–16).

Considering this section against the question of the land in Paul's thought yields further points of interest. Paul speaks of his "forgetting what is behind." O'Brien argues that the immediate context demands that Paul here speaks of his glittering career as an apostle.[23] However, the transitional function of the passage takes us back further not only to Paul's achievements in Christ,[24] but to his earlier list of Jewish credentials.[25] Indeed any forgetting of present credentials before God is analo-

---

23. O'Brien, *Philippians*, 428–29.
24. The present tense of *epilanthanomai* (forget) extends to the present.
25. Bockmuehl, *Philippians*, 13; Thurston and Ryan, *Philippians and Philemon*, 126; Martin, *Philippians*, 209.

gous with his example given in this chapter.[26] Unlike the Judaizers, Paul has left behind such things as claims before God and false or limited theology.[27] Rather, he presses on as an Olympic athlete to win the prize of the upward call of God in Christ Jesus. The context for this fervent endeavor is not limited to any geography; it is cosmic. The call is from the heavenly Jerusalem, not from Jerusalem, Zion, or the temple (see further below on vv. 20–21). While these ideas are not spelt out in the text, the trajectory of Paul's thought is clearly in the direction of Christology ("in Christ Jesus," 3:14) rather than in the land or the earthly Jerusalem.

In 3:15–17 Paul appeals to the Philippians to emulate this attitude of perseverance. They are not to slip back from faith into confidence in the law, and so the flesh. They are not to assume their salvation with an election presumption. Whatever their claims, they are not to consider themselves above others and superior in any way. Rather, they are to take up the appeal of the letter to this point, and live the Christ-pattern found supremely in the cross (2:6–8).

The pattern of the cross undergirds all of Philippians. Christ's self-emptying and humbling, his incarnation and service, his suffering to the point of death, all function as a pattern for the Philippians to emulate. 2:5–11 functions as the theological center of the letter, with positive and negative examples of this pattern resounding through the text.[28] The Philippians are to live out their faith with humility, love, selflessness, sacrifice, suffering, and service for the gospel.

Paul here subtly draws them in with the appeal to the mature. He places confidence in God to enable all to see the truth of what he is saying. He appeals to them to live up to the pattern of the cross. He urges them to imitate his own example, which he has laid out through the letter, and which itself is an emulation of Christ (1:7, 19–26; 2:16–18; 3:4–8,

---

26. Hansen, *Philippians*, 253, sides with O'Brien here, but does acknowledge 3:5–6. Both fail to see the analogous relationship of Paul's pre-Christ past and his Christian past. This is the very point Paul is making.

27. Clearly Paul has not completely left Judaism and its theology behind, as Christ is its culmination and the lens through which he now reads it. The absence of the language of land in his letters suggests that he now reads this as a limitation of God's purposes on earth preferring a cosmic focus.

28. These include the Philippians themselves from their own history (cf., 1:5–7; 4:10–19); the Romans, positive and negative (cf., 1:14–18); Paul (1:7, 19–26; 2:17–18; 3:4–6, 12–14); Jesus (cf., 2:6–8); Epaphroditus and Timothy (2:19–30); the Judaizers other false teachers (cf., 3:2, 18–19); Euodia and Syntyche (4:2–3); other churches who have not supported Paul (4:10–14).

12–14; cf., 1 Cor 11:1; 2 Cor 8:9; Rom 15:4). He broadens his appeal beyond his own example to others who take up the *typos* of the cross— supremely Timothy and Epaphroditus (1:1; 2:19–30). Verse 17 speaks of a pattern of living that will be contrasted in 3:18–19. Paul repeats in both verses his favorite metaphor for Christian living, *peripateō*, contrasting two modes of living. They are to live out the pattern of the cross and not of the enemies of the cross that he will define in what follows.

WARNING AND RESPONSE TO GRECO-ROMAN PAGANISM (3:18–19)

Against the backdrop of his appeal for the emulation of a cruciform life in 3:15–17, Paul now contrasts this life with that of enemies of the cross. In 3:18 the antithesis is emphasized with the repetition of "live" (*peripateō*, lit. "walk"). There are four main possibilities for the identification of the enemies of the cross.[29] First, some argue that these opponents are Judaizers, the same group as in 3:2.[30] If so, Paul is speaking ironically and sarcastically as in 3:2. The problem here is that Paul's language, while possibly targeted at the Judaizers, seems more likely to focus on a pagan licentious perspective. In particular, the clause "their god is their stomach" fits more neatly as a comment on the licentiousness of the Greco-Roman world.[31]

Others claim that they are false teachers with a libertine viewpoint.[32] That is, people who have accepted Christ but propagate a syncretistic perspective of the faith based not on Judaism as with the Judaizers, but on fusing faith in Jesus with a Greco-Roman way of life. These could be libertines (cf., Corinth), antinomians, Gnostics or proto-Gnostics, Epicureans, and/or pneumatics with an over-realized eschatology (cf.,

---

29. Within these four there are countless variants.

30. Silva, *Philippians*, 179–82; O'Brien, *Philippians*, 26–35; Williams, *Enemies*, 217–28; Mearns, "Paul's Opponents," 201–02; Müller, *Der Brief des Paulus* 25, 145–46; Martin, *Philippians*, 221–27.

31. Some contend that *koilia* ("belly") need not refer to the literal stomach or eating. For example Klijn, "Paul's Opponents," 283, suggests it means "self-interest"; Williams, *Enemies*, 224, argues it merely means "things that will ultimately perish." However, Fee, *Philippians*, 372, rightly sees here a "metonymy for the craving after sumptuous fare, or perhaps for surfeiting."

32. For example Jewett, "Conflicting Movements," 377–82 (from an Ephesus provenance); Beare, *Philippians*, 133–34; Craddock, *Philippians*, 64–68; De Vos, *Conflicts*, 271–75; Fee, *Philippians*, 374–75.

2 Tim 2:18). This appears to be closer to the direction of Paul's response, especially "their god is their stomach."

A third possibility is that Paul is speaking with a double voice, writing cleverly to address both sets of enemies: Jewish and Greco-Roman false teachers.[33] However, this suffers from the same objection as the first view.

The fourth option is that Paul is speaking broadly of enemies with a Greco-Roman perspective, including not *only* "believers" and false teachers who claim faith in Jesus while distorting the gospel, but also unbelievers who reject the gospel. Many scholars reject that pagan unbelievers could be in view.[34] However, in Philippians Paul has already referred twice to contexts where pagans resist the gospel. First, in 1:12–26 he speaks of being in a Roman prison among unbelievers.[35] Secondly, in 1:28–30 he refers to active present opponents of the Philippians. In 1:30 he notes that the Philippians are experiencing the same kind of resistance he himself experienced in Philippi (Acts 16:11–40) and currently suffers in Rome. While some seek to argue that these opponents in 1:28–30 are false teachers, this is hardly likely as there is no evidence of Paul suffering opposition from false teachers in a previous visit to Philippi, or concurrently in Rome.[36] Rather, he faced, and now faces, opposition from those who found his teaching counter to Roman culture. It is likely then that these enemies of the cross include those in Philippi who from the beginning had found in the nascent Christian movement a threat to the imperial cult and the Greco-Roman pantheon (cf., Acts 16:21; 1 Thess 2:1; Phil 1:28–30). They reject the cross and a cruciform life. It is the same form of pagan opposition to the message of a crucified Messiah, as found in 1 Cor 1:23 where this message is "foolishness."

---

33. This was my own view in *Congregational Evangelism*, 61, which I have now modified.

34. See for example Marshall, *Philippians*, 100; Hansen, *Philippians*, 30; Fowl, *Philippians*, 170–72; Fee, *Philippians*, 374, who notes they are "believers"; however, the text says nothing of the sort.

35. The reference here is not to the Roman Christians ("brothers") afflicting Paul but to those who imprisoned him.

36. The opponents in 1:14–18 are not false teachers (cf., Houlden, *Paul's Letters*, 34, 65) as they preach Christ. The issue is not the content of the gospel, but their motive. See Fee, *Philippians*, 167; Oakes, *Philippians*, 86–88; Smith, *Marks*, 67–69; De Vos, *Conflicts*, 26–65.

Thus, these "enemies" are most likely to be both pagans who reject the gospel of a crucified Messiah and "believers" who fatally compromise the gospel in the direction of a Greco-Roman mindset. Thus, the pattern of Phil 3 begins to emerge. In vv. 2–10 Paul deals with Judaizers and Judaism, and the Jewish corruption or rejection of the gospel. In vv. 18–19, albeit much more briefly, Paul deals with the threat of Greco-Roman paganism to the gospel. The chapter deals consecutively with the threat of the two great opponents of his day, Jerusalem and Rome.

Both sets of enemies find their hope in their own religious perspectives. For the Jews and Judaizers, the hope is in Torah and the Jewish religious system. For pagan libertines, the hope is in the gods of the pantheon, the imperial cult, and their religious system. For those who have formed a syncretistic blend of Christian faith with elements of Judaism and Greco-Roman thought, sacrificing the cross and what it stands for, their hope is in this new system that adds to the complete sufficiency of the cross for salvation and life. For Paul, this is anathema (cf., Gal 2:21)!

In 3:19 Paul speaks of the hopelessness of life for pagans and those who distort the gospel in the direction of licentiousness. Their destiny, unlike the Christian destiny of eternal life, is eternal destruction. Their god, unlike the Christian God, is their stomach: literally their gluttony, and figuratively their self-centered desires to satisfy the flesh. Their glory (*doxa*) is not God (cf., 1:11; 2:11; 4:20), but their shame. Shame here has both present and future dimensions: their shameful conduct now, and the shame of eternal rejection in the future. They focus on life in the present rather than on eternal matters (cf., 3:12–14).

HOPE, A NEW KINGDOM, THE RETURN OF CHRIST, BODILY TRANSFORMATION, AND COSMIC VICTORY (3:20–21)

We now come to the climax of the chapter where Paul answers the challenges of Jerusalem and Rome. In these two verses Paul sharply contrasts the present and future status of believers and that of these enemies. It is a glorious statement of the hope believers have in Christ. The shift to the first-person plural "our" (*hēmōn*) in the emphatic first position emphasizes the contrast.

There are four aspects to 3:20–21: (1) the present reality of heavenly citizenship (3:20a); (2) the hope of Jesus' return (3:20b); (3) the hope of bodily transformation (3:21a); and (4) the power that transforms believers and subjugates all things to Christ (3:21b).

The Present Reality of Heavenly Citizenship (3:20a)

The statement uses a *hapax*, *politeuma*, recalling *politeuomai* in 1:27, where the readers are to live as citizens worthy of the gospel of Christ. The word can mean citizenship but is better rendered "state" or "commonwealth."[37] It is the language of kingdom, empire, or republic.[38] In the Roman colony of Philippi, and especially if Paul is writing, as is likely, from Rome, this is powerful, subversive language in the face of the might of the empire. In the context of a chapter that initially focuses on Judaizers and Judaism, this heavenly hope also stands in stark contrast to the hopes of those who find the religious and political center of the world, both present and future in Jerusalem.

The locale for this reign is not Jerusalem or Rome, but heaven (*ouranos*), from where the resurrected man-God, Christ, rules. Christian believers in this present world, then, have their socioreligious political identity not in any earthly Zion, but in the heavenly kingdom, while living on earth under the lordship of Christ. Paul does not use here the language of "the Jerusalem above" of this heavenly setting, but his reference to "the Jerusalem that is above" in Gal 4:25–26 correlates with the reference to heaven here. The present city of Jerusalem is now fulfilled in this new heavenly Jerusalem that transcends all earthly *politeuma*. It is the people of God in Christ who are the true circumcision, and not Israel, who claims to be the circumcision, by descent or by law observance (3:2). It is believers in Jesus Messiah who truly worship by the Spirit, not Jews who worship God through the Jewish religious cult without regard for Messiah Jesus.

In the same breath Paul is saying that believers in Christ no longer have their identity in Rome nor should their primary allegiance be to Caesar or to Zeus/Jupiter and the Greek and Roman pantheons. Rather, their identity is found in the heavenly "empire" under the rule of the one true Lord, Jesus Christ.

It is not insignificant that Paul uses the full name of Jesus here: "Lord Jesus Christ [Messiah]." "Lord" (*kyrios*), while having strong OT

---

37. Strathmann, "πολίτευμα," 515–35; O'Brien, *Philippians*, 459–60; Witherington, *Friendship and Finances*, 98–99.

38. The contemporary term "commonwealth" is inadequate as it essentially refers a loose collective under an essentially impotent monarch. The *politeuma* here is God's people under the cosmic Lord Jesus. It carries the notion of reign; cf., Schenk, *Philipperbriefe*, 324. Thus it is the language of *basileia*.

antecedents and speaking in some sense of the divinity of Christ, perhaps more pointedly here speaks of Christ as Lord over all lords, especially, in Romanized Philippi and from Rome, Caesar. "Christ" speaks of Jesus as the long awaited king of Israel. Yet he is more than this; this Roman-crucified, itinerant Jewish peasant is in fact Lord over all lords, subjugating to himself all rule, spiritual and temporal. Politically this is subversive and cuts to the heart of all worldviews—in this context, both Jewish and Roman.

The Future Hope of Jesus' Return (3:20b)

In 3:20b Paul speaks of the return of Christ, although not explicitly. His words tell us that the resurrected Christ is currently in the heavenly dimension. The antecedent of the phrase "from where" (*ex hou*) is the "heavens," and expresses the expectation that Christ will return from heaven to earth. "We await" is *apedechomai*, meaning "await eagerly."[39] Paul and the writer of Hebrews use it exclusively of eagerly awaiting *the return of Christ* (Rom 8:19, 23; 1 Cor 1:17; Gal 5:5; Heb 9:28). This is an intense longing for the Parousia and the consummation of the age. Thus, we have here believers on earth, whether in Philippi, Rome, or elsewhere (Jerusalem?), desperately yearning for the return of Christ.

Significantly, for our discussion, nothing is said of *where he will return to* except earth itself. The Philippians in Macedonia and Paul in Rome both await the same event with the same hope. Land, Jerusalem, Zion and temple are not mentioned. If we look at other references to the return of Christ in Paul,[40] none of them mention land, Jerusalem, Zion, or the temple. Neither do other NT references to the return of Christ,[41] although it can be argued that Luke envisaged Jesus returning to the Mount of Olives in Jerusalem (Luke 21:27; Acts 1:11). The key point for this discussion is that there is nothing at all to suggest that the land or Jerusalem plays a role in *Paul's* understanding of the second coming.

The Future Hope of Bodily Transformation (3:21a)

In 3:21a Paul turns to what will happen at Christ's return: all believers will experience the transformation of their bodies. Paul describes the

---

39. *BDAG*, 100.
40. 1 Cor 15:23, 52; 1 Thess 4:16; 2 Thess 1:7–10; 2:8.
41. Matt 24:30; 26:63–64; Mark 13:26; 14:62; Rev 19:11–21.

human body as a "body of humiliation" (*sōma tēs tapeinōseōs*), which will become like Christ's body, a "body of his glory" (*tō sōmati tēs doxēs autou*). Both genitives are attributive and should be translated "lowly body" and "his glorious body."[42] "Lowly body" is the body subject to death and decay. "Glorious body" is a body like Christ's, incorruptible, immortal, and imperishable. Unlike the enemies of the cross, who are trapped in false empires concerned for legalistic observance or satisfaction of gluttony and who will face destruction, Christians who live by faith and the Spirit will be transformed.

Critically, neither is there any hint of believers being transformed and then *leaving earth for heavenly existence*. The only possible hint of this in Paul is in 1 Thess 4:17, where living believers at the second coming are caught up to meet Christ in the air, to be "always with the Lord." What happens here is heavily debated, with some arguing that this is a rapture, and others a second coming after which believers will be taken to heaven permanently or for an interim period.[43] Others argue that the Greek *apantēsis* should be interpreted in its technical sense of believers meeting Christ and then welcoming him to earth as reigning king for eternal existence on a renewed earth (cf., Acts 28:15).[44] Neither interpretation can be conclusively established, as the details are scanty. Whichever is correct, Phil 3:21 speaks of a transformation, saying nothing categorical about departing earth. Similarly, in 1 Cor 15:42–57 Paul speaks about the raised body in continuity with the seed of the "natural body." He speaks of the transformation as a "change" (*allassō*) in which the perishable becomes imperishable, and which occurs in a flash with no reference to leaving earth. In Rom 8:19–23 the creation awaits its redemption from corruption and death. This would seem to be that same event. Either way, in Paul this is a cosmic moment that appears to transcend any geographical center such as Jerusalem or Rome.

The Power that Transforms Believers and Subjugates All Things to Christ (3:21b)

The final part of Phil 3:21 emphasizes the power by which this occurs. This is the same power that Christ exercises to subject all things, includ-

---

42. Wallace, *Grammar*, 86–87.
43. Wanamaker, *Thessalonians*, 175.
44. Martin, *1, 2 Thessalonians*, 152.

ing all enemies of the cross, to himself as Lord of the cosmos, to whom ultimately every knee will bow (Phil 2:9–11). This recalls 1 Cor 15:27–28, where things will be made subject to Christ and Christ will hand over to God the Father all things so that God will be all in all. Again, in neither of these references is there a sense of leaving earth for eternity or of the centrality of the land of Israel. Rather, all, including spiritual forces inimical to God and human rejection of God, will be made subject to Christ. God will be all in all, including all people, nations, and worlds. This is tremendously comforting to the believers suffering at the hands of their highly Romanized pagan persecutors in the Roman colony of Philippi (cf., 1:28–30) and also being threatened by Judaizers (3:1–2). Both sets of enemies will be defeated!

CONCLUSION

In Philippians 3 Paul deals with the two great threats to his converts: Judaism without Christ, and the imperial cult and gods of Greece and Rome.

First, he warns his converts of the threat of Judaizers, who preach Jesus as Christ and Lord to be sure, but also urge Gentile converts to be circumcised and come under Mosaic Law. Paul deals with them strongly, outlining his credentials as a Jew, renouncing them, and affirming that righteousness is found through faith in Christ and not the Mosaic Law. He speaks of his commitment to experience the fullness of life in Christ and in the Spirit, and suffering, death, and resurrection. It is this that motivates him. For this he presses on, humbly and determinedly. He urges the Philippians to emulate this pattern of life.

Secondly, he warns of the threat of libertines who reject a crucified Christ, living licentiously and materialistically. Such people will face destruction. Unlike these, believers are to live as God's kingdom citizens throughout his world awaiting eagerly the return of their Lord. They will then receive their prize, eternal life and the transformation of their bodies.

Throughout this discussion Paul shows absolutely no interest in the land, Jerusalem, Zion, or the temple. Rather, his focus is christological and his vision is cosmic. Land and related concepts barely rate a mention here or elsewhere in his letters. They are apparently among those things he has "left behind" as he presses on toward his goal. His rejection of

Judaism implicit in the first half of the passage includes anything that limits his focus on Christ and his "world"-view.

Philippians 3 then gives at least tacit support to those who argue that, for Paul, "in Christ" is the fulfillment of the promises of Israel. Paul's interest does not lie in land, Jerusalem, Zion, temple, or law. Rather, the new Joshua has come not only for Palestine, but for the whole world (Rom 4:13). God and his people are found where Jesus Christ is trusted as savior and Lord. Paul's worldview, then, transcends any limitation to a particular piece of land, a building, or a nation. God is found with his people in all places and at all times.

This is not the end of the discussion, however. It does not rule out that the climax of world history will revolve around the geographical nation of Israel and Jerusalem, and that Jesus might indeed return to the Mount of Olives. It does not rule out an attempt to build the temple. However, for Paul the temple is now the people of God. It does not rule out premillennialism, although if Paul does hold to a millennium he gives absolutely no indication of it in his eschatological teaching. However, where Israel and the land are concerned, while this may be eschatologically significant in a historical sense, Paul gives no indication of any soteriological significance. Salvation is found in Christ alone for Jew and Gentile alike, a remnant by grace in continuity with true Israel by faith. Paul's interest is not historical Israel; rather, his interest lies with Israel by faith in Messiah Jesus, both Jew and Gentile. His concern is not the land of Palestine *per se*, but the whole world.

4

"Here We Have No Lasting City" (Heb 13:14)

The Promised Land in the Letter to the Hebrews

PHILIP CHURCH

INTRODUCTION

THIS CHAPTER IS A brief survey of land terminology in the Bible, culminating in a discussion of land in the Book of Hebrews, the only book in either the Old Testament or the New that actually refers to the "promised land" (Heb 11:9)—although is it conceivable that the notion might be present elsewhere without the specific vocabulary. Hebrews also contains an extended discussion of God's rest in a context where the land of Canaan is in view. This chapter is an attempt to understand what one early Christian theologian had to say about the promised land.

LAND TERMINOLOGY IN THE BIBLE

When discussing land terminology in the Bible we are presented with two problems: a variety of terms are used, and the terms are used in a variety of senses. For reasons of space we cannot survey the whole field. Consequently, we will look at some key terms for "land," in both the Old and New Testaments, followed by a review of how the New Testament uses land terminology apart from in Hebrews. Finally, we will take a closer look at Hebrews.

The Old Testament

The most important Old Testament word for land is the Hebrew *erets*, which appears over 2,500 times, with a variety of senses. In Gen 1 this word is used both for the *earth* that God created along with the heavens (Gen 1:1), and for the *dry land* (which God named *yabbashah*) as opposed to the sea (Gen 1:10). Later in Genesis, when Abraham bows down to the *ground*, he bows down to the *erets* (Gen 18:2). In Exod 23:10–11 the people are commanded to work their *land holdings* (*eratsim*) for six years and to let them rest for the seventh. In this context *erets* is somewhat like our expression "private property" (although this expression is anachronistic in the context since the people were not free to dispose of their ancestral land).

The same word is also used for land in the sense of sovereign territory. It can refer to the land of Egypt and the land of Canaan (Gen 47:13); in Amos 7:12 it is the land of Judah; in 1 Sam 13:19 it is the land of Israel; and in Zeph 2:5 it is the land of the Philistines. It is also the "land of the living," as opposed to the dwelling place of the dead (Ps 27:13).

In Jer 2:7 it is *Yahweh's land*—the sense that is most significant for this chapter. There are too many references to enumerate, but Brueggemann is clearly right when he suggests that, when it carries this sense, "land is a central, if not *the central theme* of biblical faith."[1] Yahweh's land is the land promised to the patriarchs and given to the people of Israel after their wilderness wanderings. It is the land from which they were exiled for their sins, and to which they returned after the exile. Almost the entire Old Testament is taken up with this theme.

Several other words for land appear alongside *erets*. Sometimes land is viewed as an inheritance. The Hebrew word *nakhalah* appears about 220 times (with nearly half of these in Numbers and Joshua). Again there is a variety of senses: the inheritance is the entire land of Canaan given by God to Israel (Deut 4:21), as well as the inheritance of individual tribes (Judg 18:1), and also of families within their tribes (Num 36:2).

The semantic range of *erets* overlaps to some degree with the word *adamah*, which appears about 220 times. This word can refer to a pile of dirt (2 Kings 5:17); to arable land for farming (Gen 2:5); to private property (Gen 47: 20–22); to the place where people live (either the entire world in Gen 12:3—where God promises that all the tribes of the

---

1. Brueggemann, *The Land*, 3.

adamah will be blessed through Abraham—or to a more limited place such as the territory of Judah in Isa 19:17); and also the promised land, from which God threatens to expel his people (Josh 23:14) and to which he promises to restore them (Ezek 20:42).

Another significant Old Testament idea connected with the land is the notion of rest. The key verse, Deut 25:19, combines with all these ideas, when Moses anticipates the time when Yahweh would give them rest from all their enemies in the land that Yahweh would give them as an inheritance. This rest is further elaborated in two other important texts. In his prayer at the dedication of the temple, Solomon recalls God's promise to give the people rest (1 Kings 8:56); and in the account of the same prayer in 2 Chronicles Solomon asks Yahweh to go to his resting place in the temple (2 Chr 6:41). Not only do the people rest but Yahweh also rests; and he does so in the temple—an idea implied in Exod 15:13–17, where God is said to have brought his people to his "dwelling place, the sanctuary his hands established, where he will reign forever." The implication is that the land implies the city of Jerusalem and the temple—the pinnacle of the land.[2]

The New Testament apart from Hebrews

In the New Testament we encounter the same terminological range, although the statistics are more manageable. Nevertheless, while the land is mentioned less often in the New Testament, it is important in ways the statistics do not always indicate. The exile was viewed as a matter of history in the early decades of the first century. God's people were in God's land, Jerusalem was the capital, and the temple was functioning as the religious and economic center. However, there was a serious issue. The return from the exile was supposed to mean that Israel would enjoy sovereignty in the land, and would be a light to the nations (Isa 49:6). But they were subject to their Roman overlords. Thus, there was an important sense in which the exile, when viewed more theologically, was not yet over. The situation reflected in Neh 9:36–37 still applied: "Here we are, slaves to this day—slaves in the land that you gave to our ancestors to enjoy its fruit and its good gifts. Its rich yield goes to the

---

2. Davies, *The Gospel and the Land*, 152, suggests that "since the texts dealing with the Temple always implicitly and usually explicitly, implicate the city, just as Jerusalem became the quintessence of the land, so also the Temple became the quintessence of Jerusalem."

kings whom you have set over us because of our sins; they have power also over our bodies and over our livestock at their pleasure, and we are in great distress."[3]

God's people in God's land were in great distress, and were looking for a Messiah to deliver them from the Romans and restore their national sovereignty (Luke 2:25, 38; 24:21; Acts 1:6). This was *the* issue in the early decades in the first-century Roman province called Palestine.[4]

Given this perspective, it is surprising the New Testament says so little about the land. The Greek word *gē* appears about 250 times with many of the connotations of *erets* in the Old Testament. However, the key Old Testament concepts of the land as God's land and as the inheritance of the people of Israel fade into the background, seldom being mentioned.

The Gospels contain several geographical references to the land. The expression "land of Judah" appears in Matt 2:6 and "land of Israel" in Matt 2:20–21. In Matt 4:15 we read of the land of Zebulun and of Naphtali. In Luke 4:25 Jesus refers to the severe famine all over the land in the time of Elijah. In John 3:22 Jesus and his disciples go into the Judean "countryside" (*gē*). But the notion of the promised land, the inheritance of God's people, and the idea of rest from their enemies (surely a hot topic in the cafés and bars of Jericho, Jerusalem, and Capernaum!) is conspicuous by its absence apart from a couple of hints at the beginning of Luke in connection with the hopes of Zechariah, Simeon, and Anna (Luke 1:67–79; 2:25, 38), and at the end in the Emmaus story (Luke 24:21).

There are a handful of references to the land in Acts. In 1:8 Jesus deflects the apostles' question about the sovereignty of Israel, explaining that with the empowerment of the Spirit they would be his witnesses to the ends of the earth (*heōs eschatou tēs gēs*). While at one level Jesus is turning their attention away from their preoccupation with "national" interests, at another level Luke is announcing the plan of his second volume, as well as the importance of the Gentile mission that will occupy him throughout.

Luke makes a similar announcement through Peter in Acts 3:25, where, addressing the people of Israel (3:12), Peter cites God's promise that all the families of the earth (*pasai hai patriai tēs gēs*) would be

---

3. Unless otherwise noted Bible quotations in this chapter are from the NRSV.
4. These ideas are developed by Wright, *People of God*, 268–79.

blessed through "Abraham's seed." The implications of the quotation for the Gentile mission are not developed here, although they are not far from the surface in v. 26, where Peter explains that God's servant, Jesus (whom we should understand here as "Abraham's seed"), had been sent to them (Israel) first (*prōton*), giving them the opportunity to repent. The "international" implications of the coming of Jesus are thus implied in these two texts, very early in the history of the primitive church.

In Acts 7:3–4 Stephen refers to God's promise to Abraham and to Abraham's move to "this country [*gē*] in which you are now living." In Acts 7:47 Stephen refers to Solomon having built God's house. But he immediately introduces a qualification from Isa 66:1, which refers to the temple as God's "resting place." He explains from this text that God dwells not in "houses built by human hands," but in heaven. In Stephen's mind there had been a fundamental shift with regard to the temple: it was not God's resting place after all. In Acts 13 Paul gives a brief summary of the history of Israel up to the time of David, which includes a reference to the annihilation of the inhabitants of Canaan and God's gift of the land to Israel as an inheritance (13:19). Apart from these references, the word for "land" appears in Acts only in a general sense to refer to the "earth" or the "world."

There is not one reference to the land of Israel in the writings of Paul, James, Peter, or Jude, or in the Book of Revelation. This also applies to Rev 20:1–6, the text said to refer to the "millennium." Some read this text as referring to the time when the temple will be rebuilt and Jesus will rule the world from Jerusalem. Strikingly, however, the words "land," "temple," and "Jerusalem" are absent from these verses.[5]

Another way of finding New Testament references to the idea of land is to note allusions to the key texts in Genesis where God promised land to Abraham, as well as numerous descendants, and blessing to all the nations of the earth (Gen 12:1–3; 15:1–19; 17:1–8). In Luke Mary refers to these promises (1:55; while she does not mention "land," it can be inferred) so does Zechariah in his prophecy (1:73).[6] Stephen too, in

---

5. Rev 20:9 refers to "the camp of the saints and the beloved city," both metaphors for the community of believers. See Beale, *Revelation*, 1026–28.

6. The references to the promises to Abraham in Mary's song and Zechariah's prophecy could be read as veiled references to Rome and to the end of the exile (in the manner discussed above).

Acts 7:17, refers to the historical fulfillment of the promise to Abraham in the events of the Exodus.

Paul refers to God's promises to Abraham several times (notably in Rom 4, 9; Gal 3–4). Paul clearly understands both the promises of numerous descendants and of blessing to the nations to be fulfilled in the inclusion of Gentiles in the people of God. Curiously, however, Paul never mentions the land promise. The land is not mentioned in Rom 9–11 where, if it was important to Paul, one would expect it.[7] He refers to an "inheritance" in Gal 3:18, but the context does not imply a land inheritance.

In Rom 4:13, however, he makes the striking claim that God had promised that Abraham and his descendants would inherit not just the land but the whole world (*kosmos*). Nowhere does the Old Testament claim that God promised the world to Abraham, although Paul may have been thinking of Gen 28:13–14, where the Abrahamic promises are reiterated to Jacob, and the territory extended to the four points of the compass, without limit. In any event Paul has evidently interpreted the land promise to Abraham not as a promise that his descendants would inherit a slice of real estate at the eastern end of the Mediterranean, but rather a promise that Abraham's descendants (both Jew and Gentile) would inherit the entire world. The Old Testament land promises thus find their New Testament fulfillment not in a return to a geographical territory, but in the kingdom of God spreading out to encompass the entire world.[8] Preoccupation with the land since the coming of Christ truncates the Pauline theology of inheritance to something far less than is indicated by God's purposes expressed in the New Testament.[9]

---

7. In Rom 11:26 Paul cites Isa 59:20, where the Hebrew text refers to a deliverer coming *to* Zion. The LXX, probably cited by Paul, refers to a deliverer coming *for the sake of* (*heneken*) Zion. Significantly, however, Paul modifies the LXX text to claim that the deliverer will come not *to* Zion, or *for the sake of* Zion, but *from* (*ek*) Zion. Paul is referring to what God did in Christ in Jerusalem in the recent past for the salvation of the Gentiles; and also to the spread of the gospel from Jerusalem to the entire world, which will ultimately culminate in the salvation of "all Israel." This text says nothing about a return to the land in the so-called endtimes. See Walker, *Holy City*, 140–41. Horbury, "Land, Sanctuary and Worship," 221–22, connects the preposition "from" to Ps 110:2, where the Lord extends his sceptre "from Zion." This seems to me to be foreign to the context of Rom 11:26.

8. This idea is latent in the response Jesus gives in Acts 1:8 to the disciples' question concerning the sovereignty of Israel.

9. Similarly, in Eph 6:1–3 Paul refers to the promise attached to the commandment to honor parents in Exod 20:12 and Deut 5:16. But when Paul supports his call to chil-

THE LAND IN HEBREWS

In Hebrews we breathe a different air. Here is the only reference to the "promised land" (Heb 11:9) in the entire Bible, and it is in a context that indicates that Canaan is being referred to; moreover, Heb 3–4 discusses the entry of God's people into his rest. In at least some of the verses in these two chapters, this rest is evidently rest in the promised land. We will now look at these texts more closely.

There are many things about Hebrews that we wish we knew but about which we are left to make educated guesses. The book was formerly considered to have been written by Paul, but this is almost universally denied today.[10] Many other suggestions have been made about the author, but we should let the matter rest with Origen, who wrote, "as to who actually wrote the Epistle, God alone knows the truth of the matter."[11] Neither do we know who "the Hebrews" were, but many scholars see some connection with Rome or Jerusalem.

It used to be said the book was addressed to Jewish Christians tempted to revert to Judaism. However, this theory is increasingly discredited. One reason for its falling out of favor is that Heb 10:2 could indicate that the Jerusalem temple was still standing when Hebrews was written, indicating a date no later than the late 60s CE. If so, it would be anachronistic to speak of Christianity and Judaism as two different religions. At that time Christianity seems rather to have existed as a party within Judaism, as witnessed by Paul's frequent visits to synagogues in his travels, and indeed his synagogue sermon in Acts 13.[12]

The people addressed in Hebrews had faithfully endured persecution (10:32–39), and perhaps there was more persecution on the horizon (12:1–4). That the author encourages them not to give up meeting

---

dren to obey their parents, from the authoritative Torah, he abbreviates the Torah text. Whereas Moses commanded children to honor father and mother "so that your days may be long in the land that the Lord your God is giving you," Paul exhorts children to obey parents "so that it may be well with you and you may live long on the earth." The limitation of the promise in the Torah to the promised land is removed in the NT, where the promise refers to the whole earth, wherever the followers of Jesus live.

10. Attridge, *Hebrews*, 1–3. For a recent defense of Pauline authorship see Black, "Pauline Authorship (Part 1)," 32–51, and "Pauline Authorship (Part 2)," 78–86.

11. Cited by Bruce, *Hebrews*, 20.

12. It is easy to overstate the case here. The attitude of the author of Hebrews to the Jewish cultus, is evidence that, to his mind at least, there were significant differences between Christianity and Judaism. See Bauckham, "Parting," 142–48.

together (10:25) and to obey and submit to their leaders (13:17), along with his heavy dependence on the details surrounding Jewish worship ritual, seems to indicate a conservative Jewish-Christian enclave that was part of a larger Christian congregation. Because they seem to have become discouraged, the author sent a written homily encouraging them to persevere.

Land and Rest in Hebrews 3–4

Foundational to this appeal to persevere is the idea of God's rest in Heb 3–4, couched in terms taken from Ps 95. This Psalm explains why a former generation was excluded from God's rest (the promised land). It is quoted in Heb 3:7–11 and applied to the readers in 3:12—4:11. These chapters focus on the warnings to the Old Testament people of God about the failure of the wilderness generation to enter the land, and exhort the readers of Hebrews to persevere, striving to enter God's rest. Before this, in an introduction to the two chapters (3:1–6), the author establishes a continuity between the old and the new people of God. The implications of this are that the rebellious people referred to in the psalm, the first and subsequent readers of the psalm, the recipients of Hebrews, and other readers of Hebrews are *all* successive generations of the one people of God.[13] There is only one people of God, to whom this psalm applies every day that is called "today" (3:13).[14]

Psalm 95 falls into two parts. In vv. 1–7a God's people are invited to come and worship in the temple. The second part (7b–11, quoted in Heb 3) is a solemn warning to the same people to heed the voice of the God they are worshipping. This warning is supported by the example of the wilderness generation who rebelled against Moses' leadership. This rebellion, recounted in Num 14:1–35, resulted in the entire generation that left Egypt apart from Joshua and Caleb, being excluded from God's rest in the promised land.[15] Clearly, the two references to God's rest in Heb 3,

---

13. Enns, "Creation," 272, writes: "It is already assumed on the basis of 3:1–6 that Israel and the Church are in an analogous situation. What once applied to Israel now finds its full meaning with respect to the Church."

14. Note the repetition of "today" taken from the Psalm (Heb 3:7), and applied to all readers of Hebrews in Heb 3:13, 15; 4:7.

15. The psalm mentions the rebellion at Massah and Meribah, suggesting that either Exod 17:1–7 and/or Num 20:1–3 could be seen in the background. Coming as they do at the start and at the end of the wilderness wanderings, they probably sum up everything in between. Numbers 14:1–35 has even more points of contact with the psalm.

one in the psalm quotation (3:11) and one in the author's interpretation of the psalm (3:18), refer to the promised land.

In Heb 3:12–19 the author argues that his readers must learn from the failure of the wilderness generation. The people of God from that generation were excluded from God's rest because of unbelief; similarly, unless the people of God in the (then) present generation persevere, they could be excluded from their participation in Christ. Here participation in God's rest in the promised land in the Old Testament is used as an analogy for participation in Christ in the New Testament, with the implication that Christ has taken the place of the land.

The application of the psalm is further developed in Heb 4, which contains no less than seven references to God's rest (vv. 1, 3, 4, 5, 8, 10, 11). In addition, in v. 9 the Greek word *sabbatismos* appears, usually translated "Sabbath rest." A careful wordsmith like the author of Hebrews is likely to have chosen this new word (which he might have even coined) to convey something different. It is likely that 4:9 should be read, "so then there remains a 'Sabbath celebration' for the people of God." [16]

We now need to identify the referent of the expression "God's rest," which the readers are to strive to enter. As we have seen, the referent in Heb 3 is the promised land, but what of Heb 4? There are two options. It could refer to either (1) a state of rest, or resting (possibly salvation); [17] or (2) a resting place, that is, the eschatological goal of the people of God.

While the Hebrew word translated "rest" in Ps 95:11 and the Greek word used in the Greek Psalter and in Heb 3–4 can both refer to either a state of rest or a resting place, [18] it seems clear that in Ps 95 it refers

---

Hofius, *Katapausis*, 124–27, has argued that this is the true background of the Psalm, followed by Laansma, *Rest Motif*, 262–64.

16. The Greek word *sabbatismos* only appears here in the NT, and is usually translated "Sabbath rest," but is more likely to refer to a Sabbath celebration. See Laansma, *Rest Motif*, 276–77. Laansma suggests that "God's ... resting place [κατάπαυσις] is where he enjoys his on-going σαββατισμός" (p. 283). God's people will ultimately join in the *sabbatismos*, and indeed may be considered to be there already (Heb 12:22–24). The word *sabbatismos* is not found in any ancient Greek literature earlier than Hebrews, leading to the suggestion that the author may have coined it.

17. As suggested by Kaiser, "Promise Theme," 147–48.

18. The Hebrew word is *menukhah*. For a place of rest see, e.g., Gen 49:15; Num 10:23, and for a state of rest see 2 Sam 14:17; Jer 45:3. The Greek word is *katapausis*. In the Greek OT *katapausis* refers to a state of rest in such texts as Exod 35:2 and 1 Kings 8:56. In the NT *katapausis* only appears in Acts 7:49 (where it refers to the temple as God's resting place) and Heb 3–4. Laansma, *Rest Motif*, 277–83, argues that it means "resting place" in both Ps 95 and in Hebrews.

to a resting place (as it also does in Heb 3:11, 18). In Heb 4 it seems to refer most often to a resting place. This is certainly the case in 4:1, 3, 5 (quotations from and allusions to Ps 95), and 8 (entry to the promised land under Joshua).

The verb "to rest" in 4:4 obviously refers to cessation from activity (a state of rest), leaving only 4:10–11 to consider. In 4:10 "those who enter God's rest also cease from their labors as God did from his." Here entering God's rest and ceasing his labors are distinguished, conveying the idea that when we enter God's resting place we stop working. 4:11, following on from that, seems also to refer to a resting place rather than a state of rest ("let us therefore make every effort to enter that rest"). That Heb 4 refers to a *place* rather than a *state* of rest is supported by one other consideration: it is God's rest we are encouraged to enter, not ours. If we were encouraged to enter "our rest" we could understand it as a state of rest, but God's rest is not easily understood in this way.

God's rest is therefore best understood in this chapter as the resting place that God entered at the creation (Gen 2:2; see Heb 4:4). It is this that the author encourages his readers to strive to ensure they are not excluded from. This is the eschatological goal of the people of God, which we will now attempt to define more closely.[19]

The Eschatological Goal of the People of God

Kaiser, taking his cue from his classification of Ps 95 as a "Millennium Psalm," suggests this goal is the promised land in the millennium.[20] We need to test this reading of Hebrews, however, for if it is valid then it can be argued that Hebrews supports a Christian Zionist understanding of the land.

---

19. Beale, *Temple*, 28–80. suggests that in Gen 1 the entire universe is understood as a temple built by God in which he rests after the creation. The Jerusalem temple was understood as a microcosm of this "temple-universe." While there is no space to develop these ideas here, I would argue that they are reflected in Hebrews, with the claim that ultimately God's people enter God's rest in the new creation. See also Horbury, "Land, Sanctuary, and Worship," 209, who suggests that the rest of Ps 95 is "not just the land in general, but Zion and the sanctuary in particular."

20. Kaiser, "Promise Theme," 148–50. Kaiser applies the ideas of this so-called "Millennium Psalm" to believers, and suggests that they will enter God's rest in the promised land in the millennium. I have not encountered this psalm classification in any other scholar. The usual designation is "Enthronement Psalm," celebrating God's reign.

The main point of Hebrews is that Jesus has taken his seat at the right hand of the throne of God (8:1–2, see also 1:3, 13; 10:12; 12:2), a throne that in Jewish and early Christian thought is considered to be located in the heavenly temple.[21] Hebrews also makes it clear that there is a sense in which Jesus has blazed a trail for us to follow. He is the "pioneer" of our salvation, crowned with glory and honor, through whom God is leading many heirs to glory (2:9–10); he is our "forerunner" who has entered the heavenly temple on our behalf (6:19); and he is the "pioneer and perfecter of faith" who has sat down at the right hand of the throne of God, to whom we are to direct our attention. Evidently, we will ultimately go where he has gone.[22]

This idea is supported by two texts where the readers are encouraged to enter the presence of God, and one text that envisages the readers to be already there. Hebrews 4:14–16 repeats the idea that Jesus has entered the heavenly temple, and then encourages the readers to approach the throne of grace (in the heavenly temple). And 10:19–25 makes it explicit that we have confidence to enter the "sanctuary" (of the heavenly temple). Finally, 12:22–24 claims we have *already* "come to Mount Zion and to the city of the living God, the heavenly Jerusalem," where the angels worship.

These texts express the "already" of the standard New Testament eschatological tension. The recipients of Hebrews were still on earth, but there is a sense in which they could even then enter the heavenly throne room (4:14–16; 10:19–20); and there is a sense in which they were considered to be already there (12:22–24). But this "already" has its counterpart in the "not yet," seen in the way the author encourages his readers to persevere to the goal of their heavenly calling—the "rest" of Heb 3–4.

These positive expressions of our ultimate goal tell us where we are heading, and where in a sense we have already arrived. A negative expression comes right at the end of the book, where the readers are encouraged to follow Jesus "outside the camp," since they have "no lasting city" (Jerusalem), seeking rather the "city that is to come" (13:13–14).[23]

---

21. See *1 En* 14:8–34; 4Q405 20 II 21–22 8; Rev 4:1–11.

22. Laansma, "Cosmology," 137–38.

23. 4QMMT (4Q394 8 IV 10–12) identifies Jerusalem as "the holy camp," and claims that "outside the camp is outside Jerusalem" (4Q394 3–7 II 16–18). This is not to suggest any connection between Hebrews and Qumran; nevertheless, it indicates a contempo-

The ultimate goal of the people of God is God's rest. God's rest is not in the promised land, Jerusalem, or the temple. Rather, it is in the world to come, the city to come, the heavenly Jerusalem, and the heavenly temple where God dwells and where Jesus is enthroned.

The Promised Land in Hebrews

We are now ready to consider the one text in Hebrews that refers to the promised land (Heb 11:9). Hebrews 11 chronicles the faith of several figures in the history of Israel, including Abraham, whose career is recounted in vv. 8–19. Abraham lived as an alien in the promised land along with Isaac and Jacob,[24] but they knew it was not their ultimate goal. They were looking for "a city with foundations" whose architect and builder was God, seeking not an earthly country, but a "better country, that is, a heavenly one," and the city God had built for them (11:16); that is, the same heavenly Jerusalem the readers are encouraged to seek in 13:14. According to Hebrews, the promised land was not an end in itself even for the patriarchs. They knew it was only an interim goal on the way to the heavenly Jerusalem.[25]

This is confirmed by 4:8, which refers to the conquest of Canaan under Joshua: "If Joshua had given them rest, God would not speak later about another day." If rest in the land of Canaan was the ultimate goal of the people of God, why would God refer to yet another goal? As Walker suggests, here the author "effectively denies that the historical entrance into the promised land gave the people rest at all."[26]

CONCLUSION

The author is clear where his readers are to look, and it is not to the promised land in which Abraham lived as an alien. Neither is it Jerusalem or the temple. To suggest, as Kaiser does, that God's rest in Hebrews is the

---

rary identification of Jerusalem with "the camp," an idea to which the author of Hebrews seems to have subscribed.

24. Referring to Abraham's life as an "alien" Burge, *Jesus and the Land*, 100, remarks: "Abraham walked in the Land as if it were a Diaspora."

25. Burge, ibid., 98, suggests that the reference to "Salem" rather than "Jerusalem" in Heb 7:1 is part of the author's strategy to deflect interest from the earthly Jerusalem. He also notes that in all four references to a "city" in Hebrews (11:10, 16; 12:2; 13:14) the referent is the heavenly city.

26. Walker, "Apostles' Writings," 89.

promised land in the millennium, imports into Hebrews ideas foreign to the author. His sights are set much higher than that. It is nothing less than rest with God in the new creation.

Hebrews sounds a warning to Christians against thinking of the promised land in utopian terms, and against support for Zionism on Christian theological grounds. While it is the only New Testament book to refer to the "promised land," it does so to negate it in favor of the eschatological goal of the whole people of God in their successive generations. The promised land was not the ultimate goal of Abraham, Joshua, or the wilderness generation, nor should it be for twenty-first-century followers of Jesus. Our ultimate goal, and that of the people whose faith is recounted in Heb 11, is in the world to come (11:39–40).[27] The promised land, Jerusalem, and the temple are simply way stations on the journey to the ultimate goal of the entire people of God. To be overly preoccupied with these is to lose sight of our heavenly calling (Heb 3:1).

---

27. Significantly, specific details of the deeds of the faithful people in Heb 11 ends with Rahab at the entrance to the promised land (Heb 11:31). After Rahab the author hurries to the end declining to deal in detail with any of the other individuals he names. Thus, all these faithful people exercised their faith outside the land of Canaan. Moreover, Rahab was saved because she went "outside the camp" (Josh 6:23), as we are called to do (Heb 13:13–14). See Mosser, "Rahab outside the Camp," 383–404.

5

The Kingdom of God and the Land
The New Testament Fulfillment of an Old Testament Theme

Alistair Donaldson

INTRODUCTION

When we turn from the Old Testament to the New it almost seems that we are entering a different story. In reality we are not. We are actually entering the Bible's grand story of redemption at its most crucial moment, the moment when Jesus Christ, Israel's longed for Messiah, comes into the world. This event, according to the opening words of Luke's Gospel, is not unrelated to the past, but inextricably linked to it by way of fulfillment (1:1); the coming of Jesus; his life, death and resurrection, was *the* realization of Israel's prophetic hopes and promises. Thus the New Testament continues and expands the story that began in Gen 1. This realization of the promises implies that things in the world are no longer what they were. What was anticipated has eventuated, and as the implications of this unfold, the New Testament reveals more and more about the person and work of Jesus and the ways in which he fulfilled Old Testament hopes.

While the church generally recognizes that Jesus fulfills many aspects of the Old Testament, one aspect that is often overlooked or dismissed by many is that of "land"; a constant theme in the Old Testament, yet one that is barely noticeable in the New. Does the coming of Jesus as "fulfiller" have any bearing on how we understand the Old Testament promises of land for Israel? This is not just a theoretical question. How we answer this question is vital in order for us to form a biblical understanding of, and response to, the current Israeli/Palestinian conflict; a conflict that, among its many and complex issues, is a struggle over the land.

The Old Testament contains so many references to the land that Walter Brueggemann considers land to be "a central, if not *the central theme* of biblical faith."[1] Contrasting this Old Testament abundance of land references, Peter Walker notes that scholars struggle to find in the New Testament more than a handful of references that "unambiguously refer to the land of Israel."[2] "At the same time," Naim Ateek points out, "the expressions 'the kingdom of God' or 'the kingdom of heaven' are frequently on the lips of Jesus and are recorded more than a hundred times in the Synoptics alone."[3]

This dramatic shift in focus provokes us to ask two questions: Why the sudden dearth of land language in the New Testament, and what does this near silence suggest concerning the significance of the land from a New Testament perspective? The same questions can be asked from another angle; the New Testament's sudden scarcity of "land" language, is amplified by the equally sudden, and frequent use of the term "kingdom of God/heaven"—a term not seen in the Old Testament. This abrupt movement from the Old Testament's focus on land to the New Testament's emphasis on the kingdom suggests that we might frame the question this way: *Does the notion of the kingdom of God in the New Testament supersede the land in the Old Testament, and can this be established from the New Testament?*

DEFINING THE KINGDOM

To adequately respond to this question we must first clarify the referent of the expression "kingdom of God." The sudden appearance of this phrase in the Synoptic Gospels without explanation when first used (e.g., Mark 1:15),[4] implies it was familiar terminology in the first century

---

1. Bruggemann, *The Land*, 3.

2. Walker, "Apostles' Writings," 82. See also Waltke, "Kingdom of God," 21, who notes that while "'land' is the fourth most frequent word in the Old Testament, it is never used in the New for Canaan."

3. Ateek, "Zionism," 201.

4. In time Jesus did teach about the kingdom, e.g., Mark 4:26, "the kingdom of God is like ..."; Matt 13:47, "the kingdom of heaven is like ..." However, the notion of the

world. Mark Strom has noted that "Jewish writers after the Old Testament had used this term regularly to describe the coming time of salvation associated with the appearance of the Messiah."[5] If we go further back and consider the Old Testament we will find that—despite its lack of the exact phrase[6]—we can clarify what the hearers of the kingdom announcement in the Gospels might have understood by the term.

The Kingdom in the Old Testament

A major emphasis throughout the Old Testament is that God is king. He was king of Israel (Deut 9:26). The Psalmist writes that he is "enthroned as king forever" (Ps 29:10) and his rule is "over the nations" (Ps 22:28). The extent of his kingship is seen in Isa 66:1, "Heaven is my throne, and the earth is my footstool." Riddlebarger writes, "Clearly, the picture of a throne is meant to convey regal authority and rule."[7] Isaiah, however, portrays the cosmic scope of that rule with his use of "heaven" and "earth"—all creation is God's palace; "the throne room of the King of kings."[8] Evidently these Old Testament writers understood that God ruled as a king, thus it seems reasonable to propose that where God is acknowledged as king, there must be a kingdom that is God's.

This kingdom is first portrayed in the opening chapters of Genesis. Here God is presented as a ". . . king presiding over 'heaven and earth,' . . . Humanity is created like God, with the special role of representing or imaging God's rule in the world."[9] In the same way that ancient kings would place images of themselves in outlying regions of their realm, God places humanity within his realm as his image to represent his kingship; to exercise dominion and rule over the non-human creation as God's vicegerents (Gen 1:26–28) to work it and care for it (Gen 2:15).[10] Alexander

---

kingdom and the term itself seems to come as no surprise to the original hearers. The NT has no record of anyone explaining the expression.

5. Strom, *Symphony*, 157.

6. The LXX ascribes *basileia* (Hebrew *mĕlûkâ*) to God (e.g., Ps. 21:29 LXX). See also "your kingdom" three times in Ps. 145:11–13 NRSV). Dumbrell, *Search for Order*, 185, gives several references in the literature of Second Temple Judaism.

7. Riddlebarger, *Amillennialism,* 104–6.

8. Kline, *Kingdom Prologue*, 27.

9. Middleton, *Liberating Image*, 26.

10. Ibid., 59. Beale, *Temple*, 81–82. Middleton and Beale use the term "vice-regent," which could imply a layer of rule between God and humanity. "Vicegerent" more accurately describes someone acting directly on behalf of a sovereign.

reminds us that the "concept of royalty underlies the expression 'image of God'" in an ancient Near Eastern context.[11] The notion of the kingdom of God is without doubt present within the Old Testament writings from the beginning and continues on in the convictions and writings of the Old Testament people of God.[12] Thus while Waltke notes that, "[t]he expression 'kingdom of God' . . . never occurs in the Old Testament, and its equivalents are relatively rare and late terms in the progressive revelation of the Bible," pointing out that "[i]n the Old Testament the phrase 'kingdom of the Lord' occurs in various forms in only fifteen isolated texts,"[13] he can also propose that, "Israel's history from the creation of the world (Genesis 1) to the fall of Israel (2 Kings 25), is all about what the New Testament calls 'the kingdom of God.'"[14]

The Kingdom in the New Testament

Reign or Realm

The New Testament story of the life and ministry of Jesus further explicates this theme. Anthony Hoekema, informed by this later understanding, states that

> [t]he kingdom of God . . . is to be understood as the reign of God dynamically active in human history through Jesus Christ, the purpose of which is redemption of God's people from sin and from demonic powers, and the final establishment of the new heavens and the new earth . . . The kingdom must not be understood as merely the salvation of certain individuals or even as the reign of God in the hearts of his people; it means nothing less than the reign of God over his entire created universe. "The Kingdom of God means that God is King and acts in history to bring history to a divinely directed goal."[15]

The semantic range of *basileia* includes the concepts of "rule" and "reign," as well as "territory,"[16] all of which must be held together as indicated

11. Alexander, *Eden to the New Jerusalem*, 76.
12. Glasser, *Announcing*, 20–23.
13. Waltke, "Kingdom of God," 15.
14. Ibid.
15. Hoekema, *Bible and Future*, 45. The final sentence quotes Ladd, *Presence*, 331.
16. BDAG 168–69, s.v. βασιλεία, glosses, "the act of ruling" and "territory ruled by a king." See also Marshall, *Kingdom Come*, 43.

by Hoekema's claim that it is, "the reign of God over his entire created universe." Rule, despite being the principal nuance throughout the Old Testament's use of king/kingship language, requires a locality in which to be administered.[17] Thus Hoekema directs his readers to the final consummation of the kingdom/rule of God over his entire created universe in the renewed heavens and earth. Earth (land) is a vital aspect of the eschatological form of God's kingdom.[18] The Kingdom of God is more than a heavenly ideal or a spiritual principle; it is a living and earthed reality that requires a place (i.e., a land), in which God's kingly rule is both administered and experienced by his people in tangible ways.

Synonyms of the Kingdom

The conversations recorded in Matt 19:16–25 provide important insights that advance our understanding of these aspects of the kingdom of God. The pericope records a conversation between the rich young man and Jesus, followed by explanatory dialogue between Jesus and his disciples. The young man had asked Jesus how he could have *eternal life*; a term Wright suggests may be appropriately understood as "the life of the age to come" rather than simply "existence without end"[19]—indicating that *eternal life* implies a quality of life. We should hear the young man's question as, "How can I experience the blessings of the life of the age to come, now."[20] Jesus, responds in a manner that displeased the young man and then turns to the disciples and explains that "it is easier for a camel to go through the eye of a needle than for someone who is rich to enter the *kingdom of God*" (v. 24; cf. Mark 10:23; Luke 18:24). The disciples respond, "Then who can be *saved*"? To this question Jesus begins his summing up of this series of questioning by saying, "Truly I tell you, at the *renewal of all things* . . ." (v.28). Interestingly, in the Lukan account of this conversation, Matthew's "at the renewal of all things" is paralleled by "in *the age to come* eternal life" (Luke 18:30). While it seems evident that Jesus heard the young man's question about eternal life as a question

---

17. Compare ibid., 43.

18. Ladd, *Presence*, 195, concurs: "There should . . . be no philological or logical reason why the Kingdom of God may not be conceived of both as the reign of God and as the realm in which his reign is experienced."

19. Wright, *Acts*, 205. See also Bruce, "Eschatology," 364.

20. Marshall, *Theology*, 194–95, 205: Wright, *Surprised*, 205, "Heaven's rule, God's rule, is thus to be put into practice in the world, resulting in salvation in both the present and the future . . ."

about the kingdom,[21] the disciples heard it as a question about salvation. The concurrence of all these terms within a single conversational moment makes apparent the synonymy of *eternal life*, *kingdom of God*, *salvation*, *renewal of all things*, and *the age to come*, and clarifies that their point of reference is indistinguishable. None of these terms can be differentiated from the other.

Ladd also notes the close association of these terms, "In the Gospels the eschatological salvation is described as entrance into the kingdom of God (Mark 9:47; 10:24), into the age to come (Mark 10:30), and into eternal life (Mark 9:45; 10:17, 30; Matt 25:46). These three idioms are interchangeable."[22]

LAND, KINGDOM, AND COSMIC RESTORATION

Discovering the analogous and interchangeable nature of these terms is essential to a proper understanding of the kingdom of God. This understanding makes clear that the kingdom of God/eternal life/salvation, in its final and future eschatological expression, will involve humanity and all creation (Rom 8:21) living and flourishing under God's loving reign with the decaying effects of sin removed, and God dwelling with them on the renewed earth (Rev 21:3). This reversal of the present state of affairs restores the manner of life to what it was before the intrusion of sin (Gen 3); or as Plantinga describes it, the "vandalism of shalom"[23]— the marring of God's very good creation through sin. In the kingdom/eternal life/salvation a flourishing, fruitful, and creative harmony of life is re-established between God, humanity, and the earth (i.e., *shalom* restored[24]). Thus *shalom* (life as it ought to be) also functions as a synonym for the kingdom. Following a similar line of thought Plantinga also says,

---

21. Marshall, *Theology*, 498: "Entry into the kingdom of God is the same as coming to life . . ." See also, Wright, *Victory*, 301: "He came with a question: 'What must I do to inherit eternal life?' This was, of course, the question of the kingdom: what must I do to have a share in the age to come . . ."

22. Ladd, "Kingdom," 610. See also Bruce, "Eschatology," 364: "Sometimes Jesus uses 'life' or 'eternal life' . . . as a synonym for 'the kingdom of God'; to enter the kingdom is to enter life. This links the kingdom with the new age . . ."

23. Plantinga, *Not the Way*, 7.

24. Ibid., 10. "The webbing together of God, humans, and all creation in justice, fulfilment, and delight is what the Hebrew prophets call *shalom*. . . . In the Bible, shalom means universal flourishing, wholeness, and delight. . . . Shalom, in other words, is the way things ought to be."

"In fact, 'the coming of the kingdom of God' is just the New Testament way of spelling shalom."[25] This same idea can be seen in the parallelism of Isa 52:7 where the announcement of "*shalom*" is analogous with the kingdom language of "Your God reigns,"—and with "salvation" and "good news."[26]

By God's good purposes human beings were intended to live on earth, and their God given vocation was to function as its royal stewards (Gen 1:27–28; 2:15); a mandate nowhere rescinded in Scripture. Any valid concept of salvation, eternal life, or kingdom must therefore include a full reversal of the effects of sin (Gen 3)—i.e., a complete restoration of what was distorted; including the human ability to be what God created humanity to be and to fulfill this mandate. It seems entirely reasonable, therefore, and indeed necessary, to have the earth or "land" as an integral element of our understanding of salvation and kingdom. Land is essential in order for humanity to have a place in which to function once again as stewards of creation according to God's mandated way of life. A creation/un-creation/re-creation[27] or creation/fall/redemption[28] motif undergirds the narrative flow of Scripture.

With this arrangement in mind it is by no means insignificant that Rev 21–22—a vision of the consummated kingdom in the renewed heaven and earth—reverberates with the scenery of Eden, where a kingdom model is portrayed as God's people, in God's place, under God's Rule.[29] This threefold state of kingdom, including the land element, is seen to be renewed in Rev 21:3 as a loud voice proclaims, "Look! God's dwelling place is now among the people, and he will dwell with them. They will be his people, and God himself will be with them and be their God" (TNIV). Here God has come to be with his people where they are—on

---

25. Plantinga, *Engaging*, 103.

26. The promised messianic child of Isa 9:6, the one who would establish *shalom* with justice and righteousness, is named *śar šālôm* ("Prince of Peace"). Thus kingly language is linked to the concept of *shalom*. See Geddert, "Peace," 604. Geddert asserts that *eirēnē* ("peace") "in the teaching of Jesus and the Gospel writers can be fully appreciated only in light of the Hebrew concept of *šālôm*." While *eirēnē* in "classical Greek literature means little more than absence of war" in the NT, "it incorporates the full breadth of meaning conveyed by the Hebrew *šālôm*."

27. Clines, *Theme*, 80–82. Clines applies this framework to Gen 1–11. I have applied it to the Bible as a whole.

28. Wolters, *Creation Regained*, 12.

29. Goldsworthy, *Gospel and Kingdom*, 47.

land/earth. This earthly location of the restored kingdom is confirmed from Rev 21:2 where the Holy City, the New Jerusalem, is depicted as coming "down out of heaven," and also from Rev 5:10 where those ransomed by the blood of Christ are "to be a kingdom and priests serving our God, and they will reign on earth."

This vision of a comprehensive eschatological redemption including the restoration of all creation (Acts 3:19–21; Eph 1:9–10; Col 1:19–20; 2 Pet 3:10–13; Rom 8:19–23) to its God-intended state and potential is perhaps one of the most crucial elements in the formation of a biblical understanding of kingdom, of biblical hope, and of a New Testament view of the land. Sadly, the study of the "last things" in popular eschatology, particularly with its emphasis on the continued significance of the land as defined by Old Testament boundaries,[30] appears to have been developed in a manner radically disconnected from the "first things" of Scripture.[31] It is as though Gen 1–11 records a history wholly unrelated to the entire biblical narrative that follows. The Biblical story, beginning in Gen 1 with God's creational intent, the cultural mandate for humanity to rule over and tend God's "very good" world, the impediment of that intent through sin, and God's continuing love for his entire creation, lies at the heart of eschatology, and implies the enduring significance of land.[32] While *the* "land" is highly significant in the Old Testament, it must ultimately be understood in the light of the whole of Scripture and the progressive unfolding of God's redemptive work, including the Christ event and the final consummation of the kingdom; that is, Eden regained, creation freed "from the shackles of sin and evil and a reinstatement of creaturely living as intended by God."[33] This work of God, as we know from Scripture, is motivated by his love for his entire creation, and his desire to restore it from the effects of sin and liberate it from its bondage (John 3:16; Rom 8:21). As Col 1:19–20 maintains, creation-wide restoration is the very purpose for which Jesus Christ, Israel's Messiah died: "For

---

30. Defining the exact boundaries of the land is, however, very difficult due to significant variation in the way these boundaries are delineated in Genesis through Joshua. See Katanacho, "Christ Is the Owner of Haaretz," 427. It is also worth noting that in Gen 28:13–14 God promises Jacob the land where he lay, and explains that his offspring will spread west, east, north, and south without limit, and that through them all families of the earth will be blessed.

31. C. J. H. Wright, *Salvation*, 58.

32. Middleton, "New Heaven and a New Earth," 73–97.

33. Wolters, *Creation Regained*, 75.

in him [Jesus] all the fullness of God was pleased to dwell, and through him God was pleased to reconcile to himself all things, whether on earth or in heaven, by making peace through the blood of his cross."

God's kingdom is much larger than a small parcel of land known as Israel/Palestine. "Indeed, the Old Testament's use of the term land with reference to Canaan is resignified to encompass the whole earth in Matthew 5:5 and Romans 4:13."[34] It is also clear in Eph 6:2–3: "Honor your father and mother ... so that it may be well with you and you may live long on the earth" (NRSV). The Decalogue promise (Exod 20:12; Deut 5:16) is of a long life "in the land that Lord your God is giving you." The Ephesians text removes the restriction, thus widening the promise of a long life in the land to encompass the whole earth. A similar widening also appears in our Lord's prayer that God's kingdom come and God's will be done, not "in the land," but "on earth" (*gē*, again unqualified, Matt 6:10). This larger vision of the land, and/or kingdom, and its intrinsic cosmic restoration hope must inform our understanding of the land and its role within the entire salvation-historical narrative.

THE NEW TESTAMENT VIEW OF LAND AND THE ABRAHAMIC COVENANT

Undeniably the land was part of God's covenant with Abraham (Gen 12:1–3), indeed "all the land of Canaan" was promised to Abraham and his descendents as an everlasting possession (Gen 17:1–8).[35] However, it is equally true that Israel's gift of land was conditional on covenant fidelity; failure to live according to God's law would see her expelled from that land (Lev 18:26–28; 20:22–26; Deut 4:25–27). The end goal of the covenant with Abraham was not to have one people group in restored relationship with God and settled in Canaan.[36] Rather it was that through this one people in the land that blessing—the restoration of *shalom*, God's rule and fruitfulness of life—would be the experience of all na-

---

34. Waltke, "Kingdom of God," 21.

35. Preston, *Israel*, 35, shows that *ôlām* (forever) "must not be pressed to mean endlessness when applied to the land," listing a number of "forever" aspects of Israel's way of life that are no longer literally applied, e.g., circumcision (Gen 17:13), Passover (Exod 12:14), Aaronic priesthood (Exod 29:9), offerings (e.g. Exod 29:28), and Sabbath (Exod 31:16).

36. Walker, "Apostles' Writings," 87: "God's rule over the promised land is now extended through Christ to the whole world, and his true 'people' are a worldwide community, not an ethnic group associated with a particular land."

tions in all lands.[37] "This universal vista that is intrinsic to the Abrahamic covenant is central to our biblical understanding of salvation—indeed to our whole Christian understanding of the gospel and of mission."[38] The covenant with Abraham, which the church inherits through being in Christ (Eph 2:11–22; Gal 3:29), forms the basis for all that follows in Scripture. It is the initial redemptive movement towards the restoration of the world from the decaying effects of sin and the establishment of the renewed world; the kingdom of God.

Given the role of land as a means to achieving God's global purposes within the Abrahamic covenant we may propose, as analogous to the "creation/un-creation/re-creation" model, the following suggestion for the narrative structure of the redemption story: kingdom (Gen 1–2), kingdom distorted (Gen 3–11), land as kingdom anticipated (Gen 12 through the rest of the Old Testament), kingdom restored now but not yet fully realized (New Testament).

The land becomes part of the middle section, consistent with the form of the Abrahamic covenant—a temporary[39] means for the accomplishment of the final clause and goal of the covenant promise, that is all nations blessed. The New Testament, consistent with the form of this covenant promise, widens the land element of this promise to its full intent and takes the whole world into the promised blessing. "For the promise that he would inherit the *world* [*kosmos*] did not come to Abraham or to his descendants through the law but through the righteousness of faith (Rom 4:13)."[40]

37. In Gal 3:8 Paul calls this covenant the *gospel* and does so in a cultural context where gospel implies kingship. Gospel in the New Testament is the gospel of the kingdom. The Abraham covenant is a kingdom promise, therefore the land acts as a go-between to achieve that end.

38. C. J. H. Wright, *Salvation*, 59. See also Glasser, *Announcing*, 59.

39. Walker, "Apostles' Writings," 87: "The land, like the Torah, was a temporary stage in the long purpose of the God of Abraham. It is as though, in fact, the land were a great advance metaphor for the design of God that his people should eventually bring the whole world into submission to his healing reign. God's purpose now goes beyond Jerusalem and the land to the whole world."

40. Paul substitutes the covenant promise of "all the land of Canaan" (Gen 17:8) with the idea that Abraham would inherit the world (*kosmos*). "[Paul] is asserting that behind the promise of a particular land to Abraham there lay God's prior purpose to use this as a means of blessing 'all the nations of the earth'" (Walker, "Apostles' Writings," 87). See also Kline, *Kingdom Prologue*, 339: "in the New Testament there are clear indications of a positive kind of the shift to the second level of meaning of the land promise. Indeed, with surprising abruptness the New Testament disregards the first level meaning [i.e.,

Moreover, the author of Hebrews maintains that while Abraham lived in the promised land like a stranger in a foreign land, he did so while anticipating something more than that land (Heb 11:8–16). His hope extended beyond the land as he "looked forward to the *city that has foundations* whose architect and builder is God"; he "desired a better country, that is, a heavenly one ... indeed he [God] has prepared a city for them."[41] For Abraham, Canaan was *not* the ultimate fulfillment of the promise. Interestingly, in a picture of the climax of God's cosmic redemptive work, Rev 21, speaking concerning the new heavens and earth, picks up on this image of a *city that has foundations* (21:14) and gates. The gates and the foundations of this one city, symbolize the oneness of the people of God; the New Testament's multi-national people and the Old Testament's particular people brought together into one new people of God (Eph 2:15–16),—a global people encompassing far more than the boundaries of the land of promise.

If the New Testament's depiction of the people of God being extended from Old Testament ethnic Israel to include people from all nations is accepted, should we not expect a similar pattern with the territory occupied by ethnic Israel also expanded to include all lands—the world for which Christ died? The fulfillment that Abraham longed for, while he "made his home in the promised land like a stranger in a foreign country" (Heb 11:9, TNIV), was the full restoration of *shalom* for the whole world—that is, the kingdom of God, with people from every tribe, language, people, and nation (Rev 5:9)—in its ultimate form in the age to come.

O. Palmer Robertson writes, "In the process of redemptive history, a dramatic movement has been made from type to reality, from shadow to substance. The land which once was the specific locale of God's redemptive working served well within the old covenant as a picture of Paradise lost and promised. Now, however, in the era of new-covenant fulfillment, the land has expanded to include the cosmos."[42]

Israel's possession of Canaan] and simply takes for granted that the second level, cosmic fulfillment is the true intention of the promise."

41. See also Heb 13:14, where any "continuing city" (on earth) is negated in favor of the "city that is to come."

42. Robertson, "New-Covenant Perspective," 139.

JESUS, LAND, PEOPLE OF GOD, AND KINGDOM: RESTORATION HOPE

Some Christians read the Old Testament prophetic oracles of salvation, including those that promise the restoration of the people of God to land and kingdom, and conclude that this is yet to happen. They are looking for God to fulfill these longings. Many believe this restoration began with the return of the Jews to the land and the declaration of the state of Israel in 1948.[43] But, this is to read the Old Testament as though Jesus Christ had not come into the world, and as though the New Testament had not been written, for the New Testament shows that these oracles of salvation find their fulfillment in Christ and his church.

Jesus, Fulfiller of Restoration Promises

That this is the case is clear from 2 Cor 1:20a, "no matter how many promises God has made, they are 'Yes' in Christ" (TNIV). No promise is excluded. And no understanding of the significance of the promised land should circumvent this clear statement of Christ as fulfiller of *all* God's promises.[44] So, when the land promise found partial fulfillment in the conquest under Joshua, this was only an "anticipatory portrayal of the consummated kingdom-land . . . the new heavens and earth."[45] And in standard New Testament "already-not yet" eschatology, this consummation is inaugurated in the life, death, and resurrection of Jesus. As Peter proclaimed on the Day of Pentecost, "Fellow Israelites, I may say to you confidently of our ancestor David that he both died and was buried, and his tomb is with us to this day. Since he was a prophet, he knew that God had sworn with an oath to him that he would put one of his descendants on his throne. Foreseeing this, David spoke of the resurrection of the Messiah" (Acts 2:29–31); his exaltation to the right hand of God (verse 33).[46]

---

43. LaHaye and Ice, *Charting*, 84: "God is moving his chosen people—Israel—into place for the future fulfilment of His prophecies relating to the nation. He has already brought the Jewish people back to their land (1948) and has given them Jerusalem (1967)."

44. Baker, *Two Testaments, One Bible*, 210–13, writes, "It is abundantly clear that the New Testament understands Jesus to be the supreme fulfilment of the promises of the Old Testament, both in what he does and who he is" (213).

45. Kline, *Kingdom Prologue*, 338.

46. In Acts 13:32–34 Paul similarly claims that the OT promises are fulfilled by the resurrection of Jesus. The author of Hebrews repeatedly claims that Jesus has sat down

Whereas the Old Testament kings ruled over the land, the resurrected Jesus, exalted to the right hand of God, rules over renewed creation, the age to come, i.e., the kingdom of God now experienced in part through the gift of the Spirit as the deposit on our inheritance (Eph 2:13–14).

Israel's prophetic voice provided the nation with the grounds of their hope for land restoration and the coming of a Messianic king; however, the realization of that hope came surprisingly in Jesus Christ.[47] Luke's opening chapters are unambiguous in declaring Jesus as the "consolation of Israel" and the "redemption of Jerusalem" (Luke 2:25, 38) and yet at the same time it was because "God so loved the *world* that he gave his one and only son, so that *everyone* who believes in him may not perish but may have eternal life (John 3:16)." And, as we have already seen, eternal life is to be equated with the kingdom of God.

In a similar vein, Jesus redirects the focus of the disciples when they ask, "Lord, is this the time when you will restore the kingdom to Israel (Acts 1:6)?" They are to be his witnesses in Jerusalem, Judea, and Samaria to be sure, but the gospel must also be proclaimed to the ends of the earth (Acts 1:8).[48] Further, on the road to Emmaus while two disciples are engaged in a discussion of the events surrounding Jesus and his death, Jesus himself appears, and speaks to them. They

> . . . express this same hope (that Jesus would have been the one to "redeem Israel," Luke 24:21), their doubts are answered as the risen Jesus explains that the suffering and resurrection "on the third day" of Israel's Messiah are written in the Scriptures. This may allude to a general pattern of suffering and glory in the Old Testament, or to the sign of Jonah in the whale for three days, but

---

at the right hand of God (Heb 1:3; 8:1; 10:12–13; 12:2) in fulfillment of the command to the Davidic king in Ps 110:1.

47. Beasley-Murray, *Jesus and the Kingdom*, 25: "[t]he hope of Israel is not for a home in heaven but for the revelation of the glory of God in this world, when 'the earth shall be full of the glory of the Lord as the waters fill the sea' (Hab 2:14). . . . In the person of the Messiah God's purpose in history finds its embodiment."

48. While Jesus acknowledges the disciples' question of timing in v.7 he redirects their inappropriate focus on the sovereignty of Israel to the task of kingdom mission to the ends of the earth. They were still thinking in terms of a Jewish national kingdom, rather than the restoration of the world to which Jesus was sending them (3:21). See Wright, *Acts*, 7–8. Johnson, *Acts*, 35, comments: "the disciples'. . . needed to see the expanding horizons of the Lord's work of rescue, repair, and restoration, embracing not only Israelites, but all peoples in a triumphant conquest of grace."

the only clear prophecy that speaks about something happening on the third day is Hosea 6:2: "on the third day he will restore us." If this passage from Hosea is indeed what underlies this teaching, then a prediction that ostensibly concerned the restoration of *Israel* has now been applied by Jesus to his *own* resurrection ... "the resurrection of Christ *is* the restoration of Israel of which the prophets spoke."[49]

Jesus as Israel and Land

Much has been written of the many ways the New Testament asserts that Israel's identity is summed up in Jesus.[50] For example, the Old Testament referred to Israel as God's vineyard,[51] but Jesus applied this imagery to himself with the seemingly audacious claim of John 15:1, "I am the true vine,"—thus implying the existence of a less real or less authentic vine.[52] Israel's history is relived and her identity and purpose found in the life of Christ.[53] Jesus is claiming to be *the* true Israel. He then extends the metaphor with the analogy of those who abide in him being the vine's fruit-bearing branches. The land and the expected fruitfulness of its people, is now centered in the person of Jesus Christ. "This implies that the disciples belonging to Jesus as the 'branches' of the vine (vs. 5) denotes not only a personal relationship and fruitfulness but also their incorporation into the great community of the people of God."[54] The people of God

---

49. Walker, "Land and Jesus," 107.

50. Holwerda, *Jesus and Israel*, 27–58; N. T. Wright, *Victory*, 517; Walker, *Holy City*, 45; Chapman, *Promised Land*, 159–60; Riddlebarger, *Amillennialism*, 37; Snodgrass, "Use," 37; Strom, *Symphony*, 200; C. J. H. Wright. *Knowing Jesus*, 44.

51. See Isa 5:3–7; Jer 2:21, 12:10; Hos 10:1. See also Ps 80:8, 14. New Testament parables assume and further develop this metaphor, e.g., Matt 20:1–16; 21:28, 32; 21:33–41; Mark 12:1–12; Luke 20:9–19.

52. Ridderbos, *John*, 515, notes that "'the true' emphasizes distinction from or even the contrast with persons or things that have received the same predicate.... Jesus, by calling himself the true vine ... applies to himself this redemptive-historical description of the people of God."

53. N. T. Wright, *Victory*, 531: "He [Jesus] believed that Israel's destiny was reaching its fulfillment in his life ... that he should summon Israel to regroup, and find a new identity, around him."

54. Ridderbos, *John*, 516. See also Beasley-Murray, *John*, 272: "That the Vine is *Jesus*, not the church, is intentional; the Lord is viewed in his representative capacity ... that in union with him a renewed people of God might come into being and bring forth fruit for God."

are now those who are *in* Christ, *the true Israel*. These are the children of God (Gal 3:26), Abraham's offspring, and heirs according to the promise (Gal 3:29). And a significant part of the promise was the promise of land. To be *in Christ* is therefore now the "place" of inheritance and where the blessings of life—i.e., the kingdom of God—are experienced. Wright concurs, noting that, "by incorporation into the Messiah, all nations are enabled to enter upon the privileges and responsibilities of God's people. Christ himself takes over the significance and function of the land kinship qualification."[55] Similarly, Burge writes, "God the Father is now cultivating a vineyard in which only one life-giving vine grows. Attachment to this vine and this vine alone gives the benefits of life once promised through the land."[56]

Is it not surprising then that Jesus tells the Samaritan woman of John 4 that since he is the living water of eternal life, worship is no longer limited to locations such as Jerusalem or the mountain in Samaria where her ancestors worshipped (John 4:20–23). The significance of temple, city, and land is noticeably diminished.

Consistent with this shift in focus away from the land, in Rom 5–8 Paul weaves the account of Israel's Exodus through to the promised land as corresponding to Christian salvation and the renewed creation. Walker explains,

> The four stages of redemption (from Egypt, through the red sea, via Sinai to the promised land) are now transposed in four successive chapters into a Christian key. The argument proceeds from redemption from sin (ch. 5), to baptism (ch. 6), to the issue of law (ch. 7) and on to the renewal of the cosmos (ch. 8). On this view, the analogue of the promised land is the whole *kosmos* renewed in Christ. The goal of redemption is not limited to the promised land but is widened out to include the renewal of God's whole creation.[57]

Since encountering the risen Christ and recognizing him as Israel's Messiah, Paul now understands land in the fullest sense of the promise as being nothing less than the kingdom of God fully revealed in the renewal of all creation.

---

55. C. J. H. Wright, *God's People*, 111.

56. Burge, *Jesus and the Land*, 55. Davies, *Gospel and the Land*, 217: "To be 'in Christ'... has replaced being 'in the land' as the ideal life."

57. Walker, "Apostles' Writings," 86.

Not only does Jesus take on Israel's identity, and mission, the New Testament presents him as embodying many aspects of Israel's story and life.[58] For reasons of space I simply list those Old Testament realities that find fuller meaning in Christ: Adam (1 Cor 15:45), the seed of Abraham (Gal 3:16), Exodus (Matt 2:15), Moses (Acts 3:22; Heb 3:1–6), law (Matt 5:17), manna as bread of life (John 6:32–35), Sabbath rest (Matt 11:28; Heb 4:1–11), sacrifice (John 1:29; Heb 10:12), tabernacle/temple (John 1:14; 2:19–21), prophecy and prophet (Matt 5:17; Heb 1:1–2), priest (Heb 4:14), king (Acts 2:22–36), Son of God (Matt 2:15; 3:17), fulfiller of the covenant promise (Gal 3:29), vineyard/vine (John 15:1–5), water (John 4:7–14), light of the world (John 8:12; 9:5), shepherd (John 10:11), and indeed Israel itself (John 15:1). What seems entirely unreasonable is to understand all of these Old Testament images as finding their fullest meaning in Jesus Christ, and then to think that the land promises alone are excluded. "In sum, the theme of 'land' is 'Christified' in the New Testament,"[59] and we can agree with Wright that, "the whole world is now God's holy land, and God will reclaim it and renew it as the ultimate goal of all our wanderings."[60]

CONCLUSION

I have argued that Eden is a pattern of the kingdom rule of God, that the global destructive effect of sin demands a global solution, and that the solution is portrayed in the Edenic imagery of Rev 21–22. The initial redemptive moment was formulated in the Abrahamic covenant in which a particular land and a particular people are the first steps in God's plan to achieve this global restoration. Even Abraham recognized that the promise of God extended beyond "the land" to the city to come, the heavenly Jerusalem that of a renewed cosmos (Heb 11: 8-10; 13:14). The New Testament uses the land theme as analogous to the salvation that will ultimately be experienced in the new creation. Christ is the one who fulfills Israel and her hopes for kingdom and land restoration. And the people of God have come to include gentiles as co-heirs of the promises through belonging to Christ. Finally, Jesus is the locus of the blessings of life once offered by the land (John 15). Thus he redefines the national

---

58. Baker, *Two Testaments, One Bible*, 211–13.
59. Waltke, "Kingdom of God," 22.
60. N. T. Wright, *Simply Christian*, 222.

and religious symbols of Israel with reference to himself. Indeed all of God's promises find their "Yes" in Jesus Christ.

We can therefore confidently affirm that the Kingdom of God in the New Testament takes over from and fulfills the land motif of the Old Testament, at the same time extending it to its fullest potential and promise. This can indeed be established from the New Testament.

6

"Exile away from His Land"

Is Landlessness the Ultimate Punishment in Amos?

Tim Bulkeley

ALTHOUGH THE INDIVIDUAL SPEECH units in Amos are (in the main) clear, and are sharply argued, there is no strong consensus on understanding the themes or structure of the book as a whole, except that it addresses with particular force issues of social and economic injustice.[1] This paper will endorse a suggestion by Snyman that "land" is a major *leitmotiv* in Amos.[2] Yet, since in many ways the shadow of invasion and exile hangs over the book, attention will be focused particularly on how Amos views land and asking whether or how loss of land is the ultimate punishment in Amos.

The book of Amos uses a rich vocabulary for land. The two most common words will be discussed in more detail below, but a brief summary of other terms used in the book from this semantic field will help to underline its thematic significance. The majority of the terms used refer to land as agricultural space.[3] The first of these to appear in the book is *navah*, "pasture or settlement" (1:2); *gannah*, "orchard," and *kerem*, "vineyard," are used together of productive land (4:9; 9:14), while *kerem* is used alone in 5:11 and 17 as well. 5:17 is interesting since vineyard

---

1. Gitay, "Amos's Art of Speech," 499–502; Hayes, *Amos*, 124.

2. Snyman, "Leitmotiv," 527–42.

3. Though, as I shall argue below, the most frequently used term *eretz* may often refer to land as political space, it can and does also refer often to land as agricultural space, as for example in Amos 7:2.

occurs there along with city places (*rehob*, "square," and *chuts*, "street") linking the two main genres of land mentioned in the book. The root *chalaq*, which speaks of land as an apportioned "lot" (discussed further below), provides three examples: *chelqah* (twice in 4:7) where the co-text makes clear that these "lots" are land that is expected to be agriculturally productive, and *cheleq* (in 7:4), with the verb used in 7:17 of the priest Amaziah's land being apportioned to others.

Along with these terms for agricultural space, another set of terms referring to city spaces, *'ir*, "city" or "town," is itself used eleven times in Amos (3:6; 4:6–8; 5:3; 6:8; 7:17; 9:14) and, in addition to the passing reference to squares and streets (5:17), there is a specialized vocabulary for military installations. The term *armon*, "citadel," is also used eleven times mainly in the first three chapters (1:4, 7, 10, 12, 14; 2:2, 5; 3:9–11; 6:8) and *'oz*, "stronghold," twice (3:11; 5:9). The two terms are similar in meaning and clearly used in parallel in 3:11,[4] while in 5:9 *'oz* is used in parallel with the rare term *mibtsar*, "fortification." The term *armon* is itself typical of the book, with a third of all its biblical occurrences here. These citadels are in Amos highly associated with foreign peoples (six uses refer to the citadels of foreign nations in chapter 1, and a further two occurrences also in 3:9 mention Philistine and Egyptian citadels). In Israel they are directly associated (by possessive pronoun suffixes) with the people being punished in 3:10, 11; as is the mention of fortifications already noted in 5:9. In this political domain *gebul*, "border" (so "territory," 1:13; 6:2), should also be included.[5]

However, even without considering this more specialized vocabulary, an analysis of the frequency of the two main words for "land" in Hebrew, suggests the importance of this theme in Amos. These two terms, *eretz*, "territory, country, land," and *adamah*, "soil, earth," are both common in the Hebrew Bible, used respectively some 2500 and 250 times. Looking at figures for the usage of these words, and comparing their frequency per one hundred words in the different books

---

4. The commonest meaning of *'oz* is "strength." So NRSV renders it with "defense" in 3:11 and "strong [person]" in 5:9. However, in both places in Amos *'oz* is used in parallel with a word suggesting a military building—in 3:11 *armon*, "citadel," and in 5:9 *mibtsar*, "fortification." Therefore, at least in this book, the suggestion in *HALOT* (strengthened from KB) that it may carry the sense "stronghold" seems evident.

5. For completeness I should mention that *maqom* place is used twice, once as a broader synonym of "city," and once in the construction *kol-maqom* as simply "everywhere."

of the Bible, gives interesting results (see the tables below). Land is clearly a significant theme in many of the prophets; and thus among the books with the highest frequencies for *eretz* are Habakkuk, Zechariah, Joel, Jeremiah, Isaiah, Amos, Micah, Zephaniah, and Ezekiel. Genesis, Deuteronomy, Joshua, and Psalms have a similar frequency; these four books each clearly have land as a theme, though this is least evident for Psalms where it is only individual psalms that give special importance to "land."[6] For *adamah* the Prophets are again prominent among the books with the highest frequencies, while Genesis and Deuteronomy again feature prominently. However, in this case Amos has the highest frequency of any book in the Bible—to a quite striking degree.

Table 1 shows the figures for *eretz*, and Table 2 those for *adamah* (in each case the books are ranked from the most frequent usage downwards):

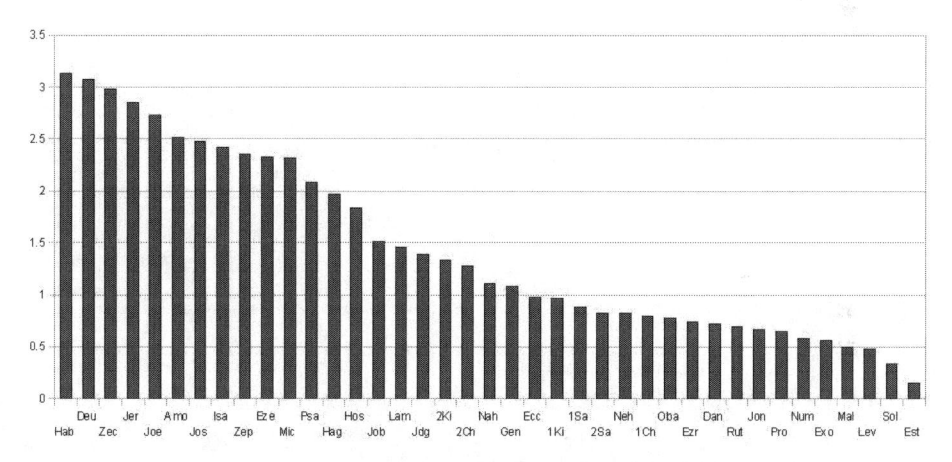

Table 1: Bible books by frequency of *eretz* per 100 words

---

6. The book of Psalms is perhaps a special case as, despite interesting readings of the work as a whole, it is more a collection of works than a unified work. Land as territory is for example thematic in Ps 47, the agricultural gifts of the soil are also celebrated in a number of psalms, and Ps 67 brings both ideas together strikingly.

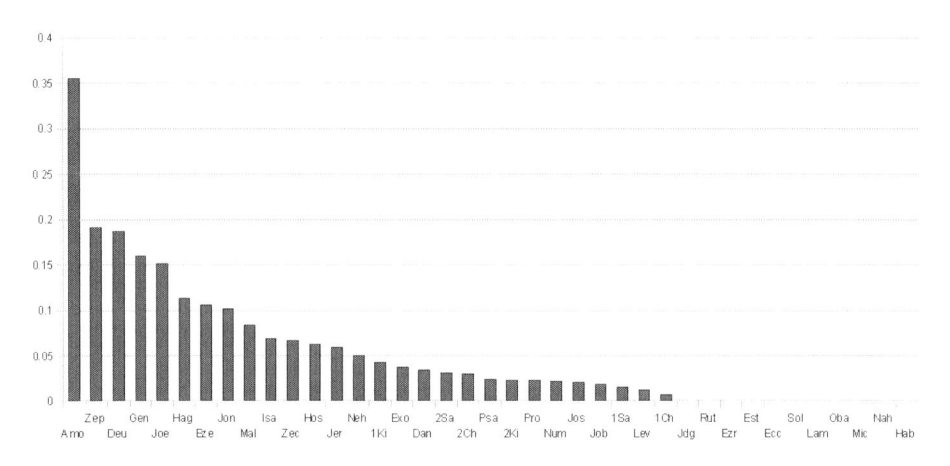

Table 2: Bible books by frequency of *adamah* per 100 words

Since *adamah* is not a highly frequent word, it may be better to consider the frequency with which *both* words occur; Table 3 shows the figures for each book (taking the occurrence of the two words *eretz* and *adamah* as a percentage of the total words used in the book):

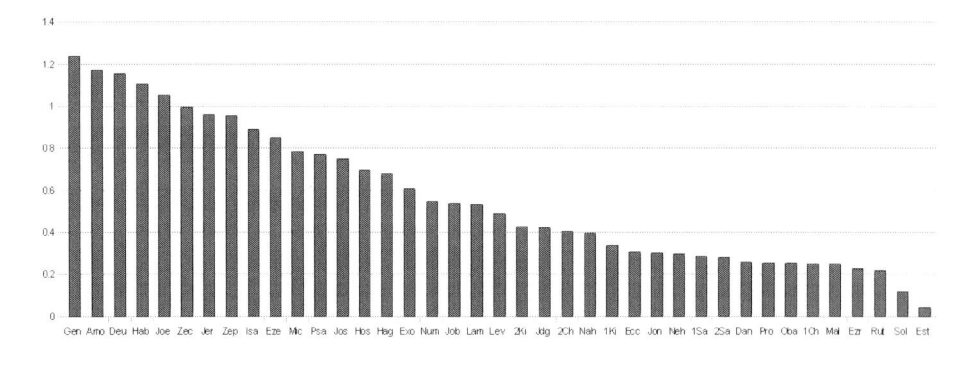

Table 3: Frequency for both words considered together

Here too the relatively important place "land" plays in Amos is evident; only Genesis shows greater use of these two words considered together than Amos does. Genesis focuses strongly on the relationship that first humanity as a whole and then Israel in particular have with land and with a promised land; so despite the length of Genesis it has a very high frequency of use of both of these terms.

Such a simple study of word usage strongly suggests that "land" is of thematic importance in Amos. Indeed, Snyman has argued that this concept provides a *leitmotiv* for the book. He argues for this claim by tracing the terms *eretz* and *adamah* through the book, and presenting the earthquake mentioned in 1:1 as a metaphor for exile away from the land. He organizes his understanding of land as a *leitmotiv* under a number of headings: "the land granted," "the land lost in a coming exile," "living conditions in the land," "the land turning against the people," "the land lost to Israel in exile," "the land regained in Amos 9:11–15," and "the land in the doxologies of Amos."[7]

There is one other factor to be considered before looking more closely at the development of this theme: in Amos the land is not merely a material possession but also one of a small cast of actors in the story of the book.[8] The one-verse superscription of the book (1:1) only names one actor, Amos, who receives visions. Even the claim that these visions come from Yahweh (making God a second character in the book) is only implicit. It is also suggested, but perhaps not said (depending on one's interpretation of *'al*), that Israel (and potentially Judah, and their kings) will receive the implied messages. By contrast the next verse, the brief motto (1:2), introduces three characters who speak and act: someone unnamed (usually presumed to be the prophet) who "says"; Yahweh who roars; and the pastures who "mourn."[9] Thus dramatically, at the start of the book, we hear the land introduced as one of the three (or four) primary "characters."

In Amos, land is considered within a theological framework that considers Israel to be a chosen people who have been given shares in this land in preference to others. The judgment on Israel (2:6–16) comes as

---

7. Snyman, "Leitmotiv."

8. By this metaphor I want to draw attention to the people or things that are said to act or to respond in the telling of the book—thus distinguishing them from mere objects that are acted upon. Such a distinction has been important to the "Earth Bible" project (see, e.g., Marlow, "Other Prophet," 75–83). My colleague Tim Meadowcroft has, however, raised interesting questions about such metaphors (Earth Bible Team, "Voice of the Earth," 23, responding to Meadowcroft, "Some Questions for the Earth Bible"). When present in texts they are still useful rhetorical markers.

9. In my commentary on Amos (Bulkeley, *Amos*, "Amos 1 (Temp EV) 1") I rendered this verb "wither" in this verse because "withering" seemed better to fit the subject "pastures" (though see my notes on *'abal*). I am now convinced by Hayes, in her monograph study of this metaphor, that the more natural translation "mourn" does indeed reflect the literary and rhetorical intent of the verse, see Hayes, *Earth Mourns*, 10–35.

the climax to the series of oracles against the nations in chapters 1 and 2. Here, talk of deliverance from Egypt and the discussion of the Amorites (who were removed to make way for Israel), begins and ends with mentioning the Amorites. This talk climaxes in the gift of "the land of the Amorite" (2:10) thus highlighting this aspect of the divine favor. That Amos' theology is grounded in election and promise is underlined again in 3:1–2: "you only have I known from all the families of the *adamah*." And notice also in the next verse the question: "do two walk together unless they have agreed?" As Gitay claims, this could well be a reference to Yahweh and Israel as the parties who have agreed to walk together.[10]

So, the climax of the first block of material in the book—the highly rhetorical series of oracles against various nations (1–2), and also the opening of the next section (3:1–2 cf. 3:3)—both in different ways highlight election, promise, and land. Talk of "land" leads us through this book, but it is understood not as neutral space, nor even as mere human territory, but rather it is always thought of as a divine gift. This is underlined later by the choice of the root *chalaq*: the first two forms of noun from this root at 4:7 and 7:4 suggest both its sense of the land as agricultural space, but also as divine gift; and the mention of land being apportioned (*chalaq*) to others in 7:17 also indirectly supports this by echoing the claims in Num 26 and Joshua that the promised land be apportioned according to God's plan.[11]

The catalog of unheeded warnings that run from 4:6–11 concern the land and its fertility: a famine due to drought (4:6–8) and the rhyming wind and worm (*beshidaphon ubeyeraqon*) in 4:9, then pestilence like Egypt's (4:10) and death like Sodom and Gomorrah's (4:11). The climax of this series focuses on the threat of God's decisive intervention. It first echoes God's interventions in Israel's story towards the end of the series, then expresses this threat in sharp focus in 4:12–13. There, finally Yahweh threatens to intervene personally (4:12). The next verse responds to this threat with a hymn to Yahweh as creator and sustainer of the land (4:13). The simple participial phrases "maker of mountains, creator of wind" invoke Yahweh as creator; meanwhile the revealing of his thoughts in connection with the cycle of day and night, and "treading the high places of the land" play a more ambiguous role. They remind

---

10. Gitay, "Amos's Art of Speech," 295.

11. Num 26:53, 55, 56; 31:36; Josh 12:7; 13:7; 14:4, 5; 15:13; 17:2; 18:2–10; 19:9, 51; 22:8, 25, 27; cf. Deut 10:9; 12:12; 14:27, 29.

hearers that the creator has an ongoing function in sustaining creation, but also warn (subtly, but in the context, powerfully) that this creative sustenance could be undone or withdrawn.[12]

The central section of the book follows this hymn.[13] It opens with a call to hear a funeral song, which is about the hearers (5:2):

> Fallen, never to rise again,
> is the Maid of Israel;
> left on her land,
> with no one to raise her.

Here Israel, personified as a young woman[14] is abandoned "on her land," fallen and with no one to raise her. Here too, the possession of the promised land becomes questionable and the death of "Israel" is raised as a possibility.

Verses 4–6 progress this "story," as the failure to seek Yahweh now leads explicitly to exile. The land is emphasized through the rest of this central chiasm. The list of sanctuaries in vv. 5–6 mentions Bethel (where, in the patriarchal stories, Yahweh reiterated the promise of the land to Jacob—Gen 28:13–17); Gilgal (where, in the story of the "conquest," twelve stones were erected to mark the entry into the land); and Beersheba (where, in Gen 26, the divine promise first made to Abraham was repeated to Isaac, and where he and Abimelech king of Gerar swore a treaty together; this is where he had a well dug, marking a new connection to the land, and from where also Jacob/Israel left the land for Egypt). Thus, by mentioning together these particular locations, the text underlines the thought of the land as promised gift of Yahweh, and opens the possibility of losing this gift. Again the focus on land is underlined when the location of the perversion of justice in the accusation that follows in v.7 is "the land."

The hymn fragment (5:8–9) is clearly the center of a chiastic section 5:1–17[15] and can be seen as the center of the book.[16] As well as proclaim-

---

12. Bulkeley, "Worship and Amos," 14–20.

13. In calling this the "central section" I am following (at least the broad lines of) the structure suggested by de Waard and Smalley, *Amos*; this is largely supported by Dorsey, "Literary Architecture," 305–30; and Dorsey, *Literary Structure*.

14. Concerning this image both here and beyond in the Hebrew Bible see Turner, "Daughter Zion," and the references there.

15. As proposed by de Waard, "Chiastic Structure," 170–77.

16. De Waard and Smalley, *Amos*; Dorsey, "Literary Architecture"; Dorsey, *Literary Structure*.

ing Yahweh's greatness as creator, it focuses on the potential destruction of the land. Notice the pouring out of the waters of the sea across the land, and the mention of the destruction of citadels and fortresses that bracket the mention of God's name. In v. 11, as well as cities, the prominence of vineyards reminds that the land itself has become the locus of punishment.[17] In the climax of this section, vv.16–17, mourning reaches both city dwellers and also the countryside.

After a section concerned primarily with worship, chapter 6 deals with politics, and chapter 7 returns to the theme of land. The first vision concerns locusts that consume all the produce of the land (7:2) echoing the warning described in 4:9.[18] The second vision involves Yahweh calling for fire that consumes both "the great deep" and the land (7:4). As we noticed above the choice of *cheleq*, "allotted portion," to describe the land seems significant—particularly when paralleled with the quasi-mythical *tehom rabbah*, "great deep" (implying that the land upon which Yahweh brings consuming fire is the very "portion" he granted to Israel).

The narrative (7:10–17) plays a prominent role in the second half of the book. The focus of the narrative is on the disparity between Amaziah the priest of Bethel and Amos the prophet of Yahweh. In the main this disagreement is about the nature of prophecy and of the call to serve Yahweh.[19] But the priest and the prophet also seem at odds concerning the importance of different elements in the coming catastrophe as foretold by Amos. According to the priest there are two related matters of concern: the death of the king and the exile (7:11); in this way Amaziah casts exile as a political event. Amos by contrast seems to see exile as primarily the loss of the land that was God's gift. This difference is clearly seen in the words used by each protagonist. Amaziah speaks first of land as territory (*eretz*) and mentions it in the same breath as its king (7:10–11);[20] though when repeating Amos' message he uses *adamah* and the focus is on the people carried off rather than on the land itself. Amos, however, says that Amaziah's land (*adamah*) will be apportioned with a

---

17. Snyman, "Leitmotiv," 533–35.
18. Cf. ibid., 535.
19. Bulkeley, "Amos 7,1—8,3," 515–28.
20. The choice of *eretz* rather than *adamah* here might be simply stylistic, except that mentioning "land" and "king" together does highlight the potentially more restricted sense of *eretz*.

cord (*bahebel techullah*), echoing the apportioning of the promised land in Josh 17 and 19 (Josh 17:5, 14; 19:9, 29).

So, at the start of this narrative in vv. 10 and 11 the two words *eretz* and *adamah* are nuanced and distinguished. Snyman claims: "[T]hat the two terms ארץ and אדמה function as synonyms can be seen throughout the book. It seems as if the two terms are used inter-changeably in the various units of the book."[21] However, although the book of Amos often uses the two terms as synonyms, sometimes deliberately—at least here and in chapter 9 (see below)—it also plays on the distinctiveness of each. So here, for most Israelites, the truly terrible thing in this coming invasion and exile is not the loss of king or sovereignty (Amaziah's *eretz* land as political territory), but the loss of their land—that is the *adamah* of which Amos speaks. As Amos underlines in his judgment on Amaziah, their connection to the ancestral, gifted land will be broken. Here *adamah* recurs again at the climax of Amos' speech (7:17), for there we read: "your (Amaziah's) land shall be parceled out by line; you yourself shall die in an unclean land, and Israel shall surely go into exile away from its land." While we might wish that the character Amaziah was more troubled by the prostitution of his wife, and the deaths of his children, probably the logic of the rhetoric demands that we understand these threats as escalating in significance for him, for the implications get closer and closer to the man himself. It is probable that the tail of the speech carries its sting, and here the focus is on land. Amaziah (proud to be the royal priest of the national shrine) will die in an "unclean" land, after his own inheritance in the gifted land has been shared out by others (as Israel once allocated Yahweh's inheritance). And in a line that is an echo of Amaziah's accusation ("Israel will surely go into exile from its land"), now Amos himself confirms this future reality, using the same words: "Israel will surely go into exile far from her land."

Chapter 8 returns to considering the land (*eretz*) as a political entity, in which oppression takes place (8:4) and therefore punishment (8:8,[22] 9, 11). This leads to the terrible final vision in 9:1–4. In this vision there is no escape from Yahweh, whether in the temple, or the underworld, in

---

21. Snyman, "Leitmotiv," 529

22. In this verse I followed the traditional English renderings in my commentary, but I would now be more inclined to follow the LXX and render the opening words "shall the land not be troubled," highlighting more the thematic echo of Amaziah's accusation than the somewhat difficult imagery of an earthquake.

the sky or the most fertile forest, even at the bottom of the sea, or indeed carried away into exile by enemies, in response to which the worship song (9:5–6) affirms that indeed it is "the lord Yahweh of armies" whose touch causes the whole land's turmoil (9:5), who is at home in both sky and land, and uses the sea to water, or flood, the land. After this triple repetition of *eretz* in the hymn, its use again in the next verse of the "land of Egypt" is a reminder of less cosmic, more political senses of land.

In 9:8–9 both words are used; in v. 8 the *adamah* offers a last glimpse of hope: "although the sinful kingdom will be destroyed, the house of Jacob will not totally be destroyed from the *adamah*." While in v. 9 the sifting avoids allowing a single pebble to return to the *eretz*, again it seems to me the text may be exploiting the different nuances of the two terms. The people will not be totally destroyed from the face of the land (*adamah*), yet no one will return to the political entity the land (*eretz*) of Israel.

At the very end of the book restoration is promised in vv. 11–15. After restoring a range of things previously imposed as punishments this reaches its climax in 9:15: "I will plant them up on their land (*adamah*), and they shall never again be plucked up out of the land (*adamah*) that I have given them, says the Lord your God."

CONCLUSION

The book of Amos uses the land as its *leitmotiv*. Its central section (5:1–17) both holds out the possibility that the coming judgment is not the final end, yet also sees it as an end for Israel (5:1–17). The book opens with warnings of a coming invasion (in chapters 1–4), but in its second half presents exile and loss of the promised land as the final consequence of injustice and oppression. Yet, behind this loss of national life and of land, there is a yet more terrible punishment revealed. In chapter 8 the coming of the "end" is signaled (8:1–2), temple worship is silenced (8:3) and the description of the collapse and exile of the land (8:8) culminates in a thirst, not for water but for the word of Yahweh (8:11–13).[23] As earlier in chapter 4, the warnings had culminated in Yahweh's arrival to "meet" Israel in judgment, so now at the close of the book it is his withdrawal of favor (seen among other ways in the loss of the land that he promised) that is the real punishment. In the final vision (9:1–4),

---

23. All of this because of the injustice and oppression vividly illustrated in 8:4–6.

even exile (9:4)—like flight to the most unlikely parts of the cosmos (9:2–3)—cannot protect Israel from this terrible God. Thus following the final hymnic fragment (9:5–6), verse 7 questions whether the two great signs of Yahweh's gracious choice of Israel (deliverance from Egypt and gift of land) are indeed unique.

Thus while the book of Amos knows and argues from God's election of, and gift of the land to, Israel (e.g., 2:9–10; 3:1–2), this gift cannot be separated from the requirement on Israel to act appropriately as the chosen and gifted people. Time and again Amos castigates injustice and oppression (2:6–8; 3:9–10; 4:1; 5:7, 11, 24; 8:4–6), and particularly systems that overlook such breaches of God's holy requirements (2:7–8; 5:10, 12–13 cf. 14–15; 6:3). The consequence for Israel of such breaches is to lose its status with Yahweh (5:18–23; 6:8–14; 8:7–14; 9:7) and therefore the land itself (5:27; 7:17; 8:12; 9:4).

So, we may conclude that in Amos land is conceived of both as the space promised and gifted by Yahweh to Israel and as the political space ruled by Jeroboam, which is spoiled by oppression and greed. This land will be invaded, and national life ended. This will mean that others will divide out the promised land by lots. For Amaziah, priest of the national shrine at Bethel, loss of land comes as the ultimate punishment as it does time and again for Israel as a whole. The restoration envisaged in the final verses of the book also culminates in Israel being (once again) planted in her land. Yet loss of land itself is not in this book the real punishment. Rather it is the sign of the real terror, loss of Yahweh's favor and even his word.

7

A "Fifth Gospel" Less Torn and More Legible?
On Recent Attempts to Retrieve Herodian Galilee

Bob Robinson

THE PAST FEW DECADES have seen a rich proliferation of studies of the region of Herodian Galilee. These studies, ranging across fields as diverse as archaeology political, and social science studies, socioeconomics, and historical sociology, have contributed greatly to a more substantial understanding of the religiocultural milieu of Galilee than has been possible on the basis of the literary sources alone. The research has centered on three major debates: the extent to which Herodian Galilee was Hellenized (and Romanized), the appropriateness of conflict models derived from social-scientific methodology for understanding Galilee, and the kind of Judaism found there.

HOW HELLENIZED (AND ROMANIZED) WAS HERODIAN GALILEE?

Which of the many kinds of late Second Temple Judaism were present in Herodian Galilee? To what extent was that Judaism Hellenized—if at all? And, in particular, how widespread was Gentile presence and influence, especially Greek and Roman? During the middle decades of the twentieth century (and with some notable earlier examples) there was speculation that Galilee was ethnically diverse and significantly Hellenized as the result of successive waves of Gentile influence, both Greek (following Alexander's conquest) and Roman (following the conquest by Pompey of Jerusalem in 63 BCE). This supposedly rendered Galilee only marginally Jewish or even, in the description of Funk, "semi-pagan."[1] In 1988, Burton Mack could confidently describe Galilee as "complex in cultural mixture" and with an "open" attitude towards cultural exchange between traditional Jewish villagers and more recent arrivals of Hellenized Jews.[2] And, as recently as 2007, Arnal could write simply that "'Galilee of the Gentiles' supported a multiethnic populace with multiple social and cultural ties to a diverse range of urban centers."[3] Typical of such centers were Sepphoris, Tiberias, and Hippos (on a prominent hill on the eastern edge of the Sea of Galilee, and currently under excavation).[4] The renovated Sepphoris, a city with an estimated 8,000–12,000 inhabitants, was set out on a typically Hellenistic grid with prominent civic markers, and contained typically Greek features: aqueducts and baths, open spaces, basilicas, an acropolis, and—though probably later than the time of Jesus—a sizeable theater. Tiberias was newly built in 19 CE on the shores of the Sea of Galilee; it had some 6,000–12,000 inhabitants and included a stadium.

However, a number of factors count against the thesis of a Hellenized Galilee populated with Gentiles and Jews who were less observant than those living further south in Judea. Even if the cultural impact of cities such as Sepphoris and Tiberias as a Hellenizing force is acknowledged, critics point out that Greco-Roman style urbanization was only in its infancy under Antipas.[5] In his *Greco-Roman Culture and the Galilee of Jesus*, Mark Chancey employs standard archaeological criteria to demonstrate a clear contrast between the limited urbanization seen in a few urban centers with the continuing rural character of Galilean culture: "Hellenistic culture was the culture of cities, not villages, and Galilee as yet had no major cities..."[6]

---

1. Funk, *Honest to Jesus*, 58.
2. Mack, *Myth*, 62.
3. Arnal, "Galilee, Galileans," 517.
4. On Hippos, see the comments of Schuler, "Recent Archaeology of Galilee," 111–13.
5. A balanced account of the actual influence of the two centers is found in Horsley, *Galilee*, 174–81.
6. Chancey, *Greco-Roman Culture*, 33. Population studies may be also relevant here; see the conclusion of Jonathan Reed that "high population numbers are not a cipher for Hellenism" (Reed, *Archaeology*, 66). Some proponents of Gentile influence also point to the presence of the Roman military as a significant vector for Hellenization because

One undoubted contribution to a visible Gentile presence in Galilee was the emergence of a new social class around Herod Antipas and his immediate family—a group that the Gospels refer to as "Herodians."[7] The Herodian court at Sepphoris was notable for its ethnic diversity and assimilation to Gentile values. As client kings of the emerging empire, and among its most loyal propagandists, the Herodians were certainly Greco-Roman in cultural preferences. Nonetheless, these Herodians did show a certain respect for Jewish sensibilities. Despite Herod's "active propagation of the cult of Roma and Augustus"[8] his renovation of the temple mount in Jerusalem respected many aspects of Solomonic precedent. "Whether out of political shrewdness or genuine tolerance, Antipas . . . showed consideration for the Jewish population."[9] A further illustration is provided by the coinage allowed during the rule of Herod Antipas (4 BCE—39 CE). Chancey highlights the "selective adaptation of Greco-Roman numismatic practices" of Antipas (the symbolism that he used on his coins avoided, for example, the depiction of the human figure), whereas "coins minted in the second and third centuries reflect a wholesale adoption of Greco-Roman numismatic customs."[10] Chancey also describes and analyzes mosaics, frescoes, statues, and figurines and finds a similar pattern of a shift toward Hellenization beginning only in the second century CE. "At no point" do extant first-century statues, for example, "identify any Galilean communities as having idols."[11]

Chancey offers a further critique of the "Gentile Galilee" thesis as he differentiates between Hellenistic and Greco-Roman culture on the one hand and "paganism" (by which he means the worship of any deity other than the Jewish God) on the other hand. "One reason that the amount of evidence for gentiles in Galilee has been exaggerated . . . is

---

of the way in which road building often functioned as the first phase of urbanization. However, Chancey's discussion of "The Roman Army in Palestine" concludes that although Hellenization was indeed a byproduct of Roman military presence this did not take effect until the second century CE (see ch. 2 of his *Greco-Roman Culture* and ch. 4, "The Transformation of the Landscape in the Second and Third Centuries CE.")

7. E.g., Mark 3:6; 12:13; see discussion in Freyne, "Galilee and Judaea," 42–43.

8. Freyne, "Galilee as Laboratory," 156.

9. Schröter, "Jesus of Galilee," 43.

10. Chancey, *Greco-Roman Culture*, 192; see the whole of his ch. 6, "The Coinage of Galilee."

11. Ibid., 206; see the whole of his ch. 7. A similar point is made by Reed, "Archaeological Contributions," 49.

that evidence of Greco-Roman culture has been misinterpreted as evidence for paganism."[12] Inscriptions suggesting a pagan ethos are almost entirely lacking in Galilee proper—though not completely so. Chancey's argument is essentially negative: no Greco-Roman temple has been recovered at Sepphoris and "no pagan shrine has yet been discovered" anywhere in first-century Galilee,[13] and the few that have been found come from the territories of the surrounding pagan cities such as Tyre and Sidon on the coast, Banias in the north and Scythopolis/Bethsean to the south. However, more recent discoveries require a modification of Chancey's blanket statement. There certainly is a shrine at Hippos[14] and, if Bethsaida is to be identified with the et-Tell site, then that too had a small temple.[15] Nonetheless, as a whole, the evidence

> does not demonstrate that early Roman Galilee has a mixed population; in fact, it suggests the opposite case. In the first century C.E., its inhabitants seem to have been primarily Jewish, with only a few pagans. Not until the second century C.E. do we have strong evidence of large numbers of gentiles in Galilee.... The idea that Galilee's population included numerous pagans is unsupported by the region's history.[16]

Finally, mention must be made of the phrase "Galilee of the Gentiles." The description in Isa 8:23 of *galil ha-goyim* (Galilee of the Gentiles / nations—cf. the Septuagintal designation *Galilaia allophulōn*—Galilee of the aliens: Joel 4:4; 1 Macc 5:15) raises a number of issues and a variety of interpretive options. Chancey in a chapter title refers to "Galilee and the Circle of Nations"[17] and goes on to speak of Galilee as among the "district" of the nations.[18] For some scholars, however, the phrase has been a factor in their religiocultural definition of Galilee. This includes the assertion that Galilee was only marginally Jewish (in effect, "Galilee containing a number of Gentiles").[19] However, the most satisfactory explanation seems to be that the phrase replicates the early experiences

---

12. Chancey, *Myth*, 7.
13. Chancey, *Greco-Roman Culture*, 90; cf., 85, 98, 106–7, 115.
14. See Schuler, "Recent Archaeology," 112–13.
15. See Rami Arav, "Bethsaida," 161.
16. Chancey, *Myth*, 61–62; the same point is made in his *Greco-Roman Culture*.
17. Ibid., ch. 4.
18. Ibid., 170.
19. See discussion in Freyne, "Galilean Jesus," 291.

of the first settlers of the region, for whom the name Galilee denotes a potentially hostile or alien encirclement by Gentiles.

Discussion will return to the question of Galilean religious identity but the evidence seems to support the conclusion of Freyne that a depiction of Herodian Galilee as only marginally Jewish can be "exposed for what it was and still is today, namely, the product of a 19th-century overemphasis on the Hellenized and therefore enlightened, it is claimed, ethos of the region, and the devaluing of Galilee's Jewishness . . ."[20]

SOCIAL SCIENCE CONFLICT MODELS

A second major issue concerns the appropriateness of sociologically derived conflict models in the attempt to retrieve Herodian Galilee. What was distinctive about Galilean culture and do these distinctions require Galilee to be understood as "a society in conflict or harmony?"[21] The answer that emerges is not *whether* Galilee might best be described as a conflicted region—it certainly was in many ways—but, rather, what kind of conflict model or models might best describe it. Ought the social world of Herodian Galilee, as reconstructed in socioeconomic, political, and cultural categories, replace or merely complement those that center on the traditional categories of ethnicity and religion?

The issue is well illustrated by disagreements over the consequences of urbanization in Galilee. Some argue that the growth of towns and cities was not necessarily threatening and that it led to a beneficial symbiosis between old and new ways as a predominantly rural Galilee encountered embryonic urbanization. The encounter did not inevitably foster socioeconomic, political, religious, or cultural conflict unique to the region. For example, there are the (revised) conclusions of Eric Meyers that the lifestyle of rural upper Galilee (which had no larger urban centers of its own) had been exposed to town life, in particular the Gentile cities of Tyre and Sidon, yet without this exposure constituting a traumatic threat or change: "its incipient urbanism and its predominantly rural village culture could live in harmony. City and town were economically interlinked . . ."[22]

20. Ibid.
21. Moxnes, "Construction of Galilee," 74.
22. Meyers, "Jesus and His Galilean Context," 64. Batey arrives at a similar conclusion: "Sepphoris and the Jesus Movement," 407. Jensen even more strongly challenges the conflictual model. He offers detailed evidence that does seem to refute claims that the rule of Antipas impoverished rural Galilee. (Jensen, *Herod Antipas in Galilee*, 247).

But others argue that the consequences of urbanization were mainly or wholly negative and led to conflict, exploitation, incipient rebellion, corruption, injustice, and general rural-urban conflict. Reed, for example, offers evidence for the view that urbanization "placed an economic strain on Galilean peasants, added stress to families and challenged current values, and created new rural-urban dynamics"; it led to the "peasants' relative state of deprivation."[23]

Disagreement over urbanization is, in turn, usually symptomatic of a deeper conflict over the legitimacy and relevance of social scientific, agrarian, functionalist, and sociological models for understanding Herodian Galilee. Considerable influence has been exerted by the so-called "Lenski-Kautsky model," in which the social world of Herodian Galilee is reconceived in terms of acute social stratification, in the inevitable inequalities present in agrarian empires and in the dynamics of class struggles as understood by historical sociology.[24] Over against earlier analyses that drew mainly upon literary sources and the categories of ethnicity and religion, the newer macro-sociological categories around which discussions of conflict and Galilean distinctiveness are formed center upon socioeconomic, political, and cultural relationships including those of honor and shame.

None of these social-scientific methodologies has, however, commanded wide assent. Freyne does concede that Lenski's hierarchical model "corresponds generally with what we know of Roman Galilee, once certain adjustments are made to this ideal picture to account for local circumstances,"[25] although he rejects much of the social science approach because of his conclusion that proponents depend more on the presuppositions of particular social-scientific models than on careful review of the actual data, especially archaeological data. Elsewhere Freyne draws upon Sawicki,[26] and his own research, to conclude that advocates of the social-systems model rarely, if ever, allow "counterevidence from either the texts or archaeology to challenge the model," because their

---

23. Reed, *Archaeology*, 96–97; cf. the whole of his ch. 3.

24. Lenski, *Power and Privilege*; Lenski and Lenski, *Human Societies*; Kautsky, *Politics*. For examples that draw on this kind of approach see: Theissen, *Sociology*; *Social Reality*; Draper, "Jesus and the Renewal"; Horsley, *Sociology*; *Galilee*; *Archaeology, History, and Society*; *Jesus in Context*; Stegemann, Malina and Theissen, *Social Setting*; Crossley, *Why Christianity Happened*.

25. Freyne, "Galilee and Judaea," 42.

26. For example, Sawicki, *Crossing Galilee*, 64–67.

positions are "virtually predetermined by the choice of model and the manner of its application."[27] And although Levine considers that, "[u]sed carefully, social-scientific approaches contribute to our understanding of [the Galilean] context," she goes on to conclude that "[d]etermining how many of the sociological models are applicable to ancient Galilee and Judea, and how much of the argument is ideological rather than evidentiary is a difficult if not impossible task."[28]

When Levine assesses claims made about the supposed conflict between Galilean and temple-centered religion, she comments that "[e]vidence for these claims lies substantially not in texts or archaeological data but in social-science method and scholarly imagination."[29] Some who are sympathetic to the social-scientific method acknowledge the problem as well. For example, Crossley writes of his growing concerns about the ways in which model-based and macro-sociological approaches have been used by New Testament scholars.[30]

A detailed critique of social-science models is found in Sawicki's *Crossing Galilee*, in which she argues that only local data can reliably be used in models that attempt to retrieve cultures from the past. Her own reconstruction of first-century Galilee derives primarily from models constructed by what she calls the "Galilean built environment" as "read off of urban, village, and lakeside ruins, in doorsteps, highways, fortifications, and floor plans." Such models use an "indigenous Israelite logic of circulation and containment."[31] Sawicki considers some use of cross-cultural comparison in the retrieval of first-century Galilee to be warranted but she criticizes the use of sociological theories and models that are similar to the contemporary western background (gender-ideological conflict models) or are theories and models derived and refined by the study of cultures from other times and places (economic-conflict models or the Mediterranean "honor-shame" template). The same point is made by Levine: "When pan-Mediterranean claims derived from fieldwork in twentieth-century villages rather than detailed study of textual

---

27. Freyne, "Archaeology," 72; cf., 68–74.
28. Levine, "Theory, Apologetic, History," 59–60.
29. Ibid., 62.
30. Crossley, "Social-Sciences," 22–27. He writes of "the highly dubious generalizations about the ancient Mediterranean via the contemporary Middle East" (25).
31. Sawicki, *Crossing Galilee*, 7, 12; cf., 34.

or archaeological evidence drive conclusions, the understanding of [the Galilean] context becomes increasingly skewed."[32]

The kind of critique of social-science models offered by Freyne, Sawicki, Levine, and others is not a denial that rural Galilee was unaffected by the increasingly well-developed attendant features of urbanization, including monetization, manufacture, and market dynamics and, in rural areas, increased trade, increased cash cropping, and increased consolidation of rural holdings and consequent tenancy. There was also a more effective regime for tax collection—even if disagreement persists about the actual levels of taxation.[33] Moreover, the archaeological evidence for the monetization essential for any developing economy is well attested in both upper and lower Galilee. Such market exchange and rural trade offer a plausible alternative picture of Galilee to social-science conflictual models with their a priori assumptions of economic exploitation by urban elites and widespread impoverishment of peasants. As Freyne observes, there certainly was economic oppression but it had a specific and localized cause—the Herodians. "In order to maintain their elite lifestyle, the Herodians siphoned off the wealth of the land for their own benefit, without giving anything back in return.... During the long reign of Antipas, the upkeep of Sepphoris and Tiberias drained the countryside of its resources, natural and human, causing resentment and opposition."[34]

Urban-rural economic tension and even resentment can, therefore, be interpreted in a less ideologically driven way. Freyne's writings since 1995 have moved closer to a partial conflict model that draws on both archaeology and the modest employment of aspects of the social sciences. He sees the establishment of Sepphoris and Tiberias by Herod Antipas as an attempt by Herod to introduce an economic system derived from Hellenism and so the locus of conflict in Galilee is primarily to do with such Hellenism rather than economic exploitation. Tiberias and Sepphoris are opposed initially by the Jewish populace not because they exploit but because, as Rapinchuk puts it, they powerfully represent a different "worldview" not shared by the rural populace. That they exploit follows since these heterogenetic cities have no other way of exercis-

---

32. Levine, "Theory, Apologetic, History," 60.
33. Compare Downing, "Quest," 80, with Levine, "Theory, Apologetic, History," 65.
34. Freyne, "Galilee and Judaea," 47.

ing control and influence other than by coercion.[35] In a recent summary of "Distribution Maps of Archaeological Data from the Galilee," Aviam concludes that "[t]he archaeological remains consistently point not only to a vast majority of Jews but also to a clear isolation of Jewish villages in the Jewish region from Gentile villages around it."[36] This need not imply that Galileans had little or no commerce with Gentiles; it is clear both from Josephus and from archaeological evidence that Galilee was a significant center for the export of a range of agricultural, fishing, and other products.

In other words, the realities of Herodian Galilee can be understood without dependence on ideologically driven social-scientific models. The archaeological recovery of Herodian Galilee increasingly confirms the picture by Josephus of it as essentially rural and village-centered in character; only a small proportion of the population lived in Sepphoris and Tiberias or other centers that might be called "urban" (and Hellenized to some extent). In the words of Horsley, "the Galilee is best understood as a traditional agrarian society with peasants living in relatively autonomous villages."[37]

THE KIND OF JUDAISM(S) PRESENT IN HERODIAN GALILEE

A third major issue concerns the kind of Judaism(s) present in Herodian Galilee. The discussion helpfully divides between archaeology concerned with public space and activities, and the archaeology of private spaces. In terms of public space there is a growing consensus that, while the presence of Greek architecture and culture in Herodian Galilee need not be denied or even doubted, this presence is well described as a "veneer" over a culture that remained distinctively Jewish.[38] Freyne concurs: "Sepphoris, even after its later expansion, which presumably meant the introduction of non-Jewish population, continued to be a major center of Jewish learning for several centuries."[39]

---

35. Rapinchuk, "Galilee and Jesus," 204–5.
36. In Zangenberg, Attridge, and Martin, *Religion, Ethnicity and Identity*, 132.
37. Horsley, *Galilee*, 189.
38. Reed, "Archaeological Contributions," 49.
39. Freyne, "Galilee, Jesus, and the Contribution," 578.

Even "the oriental cities of the Decapolis and other gentile cities should not be viewed solely as purveyors of Greco-Roman culture but rather as eastern cities with a Hellenistic overlay that often facilitated the expression of aspects of Semitic religion and practice, including Judaism."[40] Archaeology also discloses that, for example, "music related items, along with other material finds of Sepphoris, demonstrate the flourishing of Judaism in an urban environment during the Roman and Byzantine periods, a time when paganism was still a prominent feature in many cities ... Both the Jewish and the Christian communities apparently found the syncretistic setting of the Hellenistic music culture a fertile ground and a vibrant catalyst for constructive symbiosis."[41]

Further confirmation of the Jewishness of Galilean ethnicity and religion is found in the material culture of private spaces. Reed points out that "[p]ublic architecture and visible inscriptions along with coins and statues were built either by political rulers or by local elites. Instead of looking to such public and visible space, there are artifacts found inside domestic space or controlled by private initiative that provide better evidence for the populace's identity ..."[42] A number of scholars (Reed himself, Freyne, Chancey, Jensen, and others) have drawn attention to the finding that domestic space in both urban and rural dwellings in Galilee disclose a material culture associated with distinctive Jewish religious identity.

These artifacts are: stone (or chalk) vessels believed to be impervious to ritual impurity; stepped, plastered or stone immersion pools (*miqva'ot*), sometimes shared by several dwellings; secondary burial with ossuaries in loculi tombs; and bone profiles that completely lack pig bones. In particular, the stone vessels "are so pervasive in the archaeological record, not just at every site but in every single house in well excavated sites like both Capernaum and Sepphoris, that they point to widespread purity concerns among the population who wished to live in such a way that acknowledged God." These *miqva'ot* and stone jars are "sparse along the coast and in Samaria and Transjordan,"[43] lending support to the conclusion that Galilee was overwhelmingly Jewish and

---

40. Meyers, "Jesus and His Galilean Context," 62.
41. Waner, "Music Culture," 446–47.
42. Reed, "Archaeological Contributions," 51–52.
43. Ibid., 52.

had never been as Hellenized as the coastal cities of Palestine or the Decapolis.

It seems reasonable to conclude that Herodian Galilee was predominantly—perhaps even thoroughly—Jewish. Argument for a pagan Galilee is poorly supported by the literary evidence "and receives no confirmation from the archaeological explorations."[44] The conclusion of scholars such as Chancey, Freyne, and Reed is unanimous: Herodian Galilee was predominantly Jewish.

The portrayal just outlined does, however, serve to qualify any picture that completely *excludes* the presence of Hellenism from Herodian Galilee. It appears that there was no rigid dichotomy between Hellenization and Judaism; they existed in a kind of tension. One reason is that, as Chancey puts it, Hellenization was not uniform or homogeneous across the ancient Mediterranean. "We scholars have been quicker to recognize the diversity in the *Judaism* of Hellenistic Judaism than in the *Hellenism* of Hellenistic Judaism."[45] Some of this diversity relates to conflict and resistance between Galilean Jewish particularity and a variety of intra-Jewish accommodating attitudes (most typically seen in a degree of acceptance of Hellenization).

SOME UNRESOLVED ISSUES

Nonetheless, there are still unanswered questions about the religious ethos and culture of Galilee. One question concerns the kind of Judaism found in Galilee in the first century CE: was it the religion of recent converts to Judaism who were perceived to be lax in their observance of the law? Or was it the Judaism of militant nationalism, hostile towards Gentile and Samaritan neighbors? Were there significant regional variations within Galilee itself? One question that might be asked about the methodology of Chancey (especially in his *The Myth of a Gentile Galilee*) has been whether Galilee was a homogenous region—to be studied as such—or whether it is better described as several sub-regions (upper and lower Galilee, and the area around the lake). Does the lake district, for example, imply a distinct economic, commercial and demographic profile, as Freyne, Reed and others conclude?[46]

44. Freyne, "Galilee and Judaea," 41; in more detail: Freyne, *Galilee from Alexander*, 101–45; see also the discussion by Chancey, *Myth*, 118–19.

45. Chancey, *Greco-Roman Culture*, 229.

46. See, for example, Freyne, *Jewish Galilean*, 50–53; Reed, *Archaeology*, ch. 5.

The question of regional variation is also raised by the role of *miqva'ot*. Lawrence's detailed discussion concludes that the archaeological evidence for *miqva'ot* shows uneven distribution: "*Miqva'ot* first appear in the second century B.C.E. at sites connected to the Hasmonean rule of Judea. For the rest of the Second Temple period, they are concentrated in Jerusalem and surrounding Judea, with *only a few* in the Galilee and Transjordan."[47] This is, of course, an example of the provisionality of archaeological findings. And, as Reed concedes, such material culture as the presence of *miqva'ot* reveals little or nothing of how people interpreted the practices involved especially if, as Reed concludes, such evidence might also suggest that the inhabitants were mostly transplants from the region of Judea.[48] In this case the evidence might not enable safe conclusions to be drawn about *Galilean* piety. But Freyne still concludes: "Assumptions about a Hellenised Galilee are neither wholly appropriate nor helpful, especially when it is meant to imply a hostile Galilee or a non-observant Jewish one."[49]

Nonetheless, the distinctiveness of Galilee as a whole—while still Jewish—clearly emerges. Demographic analysis by Reed leads him to conclude that, while Herodian Galileans had a different social, economic, and political matrix to that of the Jews of Judea (as revealed by a different archaeological profile), they shared a common ethnic and religious identity with them.[50] Levine also considers that, "it may have been the case that Galileans in Capernaum and Gamala had more in common with their Judean counterparts in Bethany and Jericho than they did with villagers in Nazareth or the inhabits of Sepphoris."[51]

Yet another issue concerns interregional conflict. Were Galilean Jews resentful of and in conflict with Judea and Jerusalem (with their privileged elite classes, priestly oligarchy, and exploitative temple demands)? Or were Galileans loyal to Jerusalem and its cultus? There was certainly some resentment generated by the fiscal and religious demands of the temple. Freyne, drawing upon Josephus, outlines the way in which "the Jerusalem priestly aristocracy lived a life of luxury, even when this

---

47. Lawrence, *Washing in Water*, 190 (emphasis added); the comparative rarity of *miqva'ot* in the countryside is also noted by Downing, "Quest," 80.

48. Reed, *Archaeology*, 55, 44–49; see also Chancey, *Myth*, 79–80.

49. Freyne, "Galilee as Laboratory," 153.

50. Reed, *Archaeology*, ch. 2.

51. Levine, "Theory, Apologetic, History," 63.

required violent action in the villages in order to ensure that offerings were paid to them rather than to country priests.... [T]he wealth of the temple itself was non-productive, and its benefits did not flow back into the country. Those who stood to gain most from the temple system, the aristocratic priestly families, were its immediate guardians who jealously sought to protect their privileged status..."[52]

But this resentment does not, in itself, vindicate social-scientific conflict models that depict Galilee and Judea as dominated, as Levine puts it, by "a system designed to separate male from female, rich from poor, Jew from Gentile, and Judean from Galilean, always to the advantage of the rich, male, Judean Jew."[53] Levine contrasts this with the positive social roles that religious institutions could and did play in Herodian Galilee. She notes that "[i]n terms of the Temple, both Josephus and the New Testament attest Galilean participation in pilgrimage" even if, as she also adds, "[p]olitically, Galilee appears to have been just as divided as any other location in the Roman Empire: some supported Rome and its client rulers; others did not."[54] Levine further suggests, in a critique of conflict models of Galilee, that "often either overlooked or underplayed in such conflict-model depictions of the Temple are the positive social roles religious institutions can play."[55] Reed also disputes the notion of exploitative temple domination and, with Levine and others, ascribes that approach to "the presentation of ancient Palestine solely with a sociology that is conflictual in orientation." He considers it "misleading to approach Jewish religion in the first century almost exclusively in terms of the Herodian Temple and the priestly oligarchy's exploitation of the Jewish peasantry." It is social-scientific modeling and not the material evidence that sees the culture in terms of "agonistic intergroup relations."[56]

Freyne argues that the traditional orthogenetic city of Jerusalem with the temple exerted influence because of belief shared with Galilee in its "great tradition." The Galilean world largely retained the central values of late Second Temple Judaism(s): land, temple, and the election of Israel, with these distinctives reinforced by a range of purity laws. Departure from the general thrust of the great tradition would have

52. Freyne, "Galilee and Judaea," 49–50.
53. Levine, "Theory, Apologetic, History," 59.
54. Ibid., 62.
55. Ibid., 69, a claim that she goes on to elaborate.
56. Reed, "Review."

been viewed as disloyal and unacceptable. Jerusalem seems largely (perhaps completely) to have retained Galilean loyalty—despite taxation and other economic pressures and regardless of whether these pressures were exerted by an ethnically mixed Herodian court, the Romans, or fellow Jews. The temple functioned as a source of unity between Galilee and Judea with no evidence yet uncovered of any serious alternatives to it as the cultic center for the religious life of Galilee.

Freyne concludes, therefore, that Galilean commitment to the Jerusalem temple was both longstanding and unwavering.[57] The Temple served as "the focal point" for Galilean loyalties and "the symbol of their identity," which enabled the Galileans to remain faithful to traditional Judaism even in the presence of Hellenizing and other Gentile influences.[58] In a comment that is critical of social-scientific modeling, Levine notes that "[d]espite the fact that Galileans worshiped in the Temple and the Temple as a place of pilgrimage served to undermine socioeconomic and regional boundaries, scholars continue to impose the hypothesised Galilean/Judean cultural divide."[59] In other words, Jerusalem and its institutions also held a strong attachment for Galilean Jews, most of whom were descended from Hasmonean settlers; similarly, Freyne disagrees with those who assume a "deep-seated opposition between Galilee and Judea / Jerusalem."[60]

Related to the evaluation of Judaism in Galilee is the question of religious bias in the academic retrieval and assessment of Galilee.[61] It is true that some approaches to the retrieval and evaluation of the past—whether the past of Galilee or some other place—have at times served religious and theological agendas. But the possibility of bias does exist if Freyne's assertion is accurate: that the "Lenski-Kautsky model" is one in which "politics, economic, and class struggle [are] deemed more important than religion" in evaluating the dynamics of Herodian Galilee.[62] The reductionist tendencies of explanatory models drawn from the social

---

57. Freyne, *Galilee from Alexander*, 273, 275.
58. Ibid., 287, 292; cf. 275.
59. Levine, "Theory, Apologetic, History," 75.
60. Freyne, *Jewish Galilean*, 93–94; see the whole of ch. 4, "Zion Beckons."
61. The neglect or denial of a religious perspective is, of course, a widespread and deep-seated bias in Western academic circles, as tellingly illustrated by Chapman, Coffey, and Gregory, *Seeing Things Their Way*.
62. Freyne, "Archaeology," 68; he actually has "Jesus and his message" in mind.

sciences are one reason for such an attitude. Another is that often social science methods appear to be driven deductively by social science models instead of being led inductively by the data itself. However, as Freyne points out, the two major revolts that took place in first century Palestine both had strongly religious dimensions as well as social, economic, and political components.[63]

SOME CONCLUSIONS

A number of conclusions might be drawn from these recent attempts to retrieve Herodian Galilee. A fairly widespread consensus has emerged that interdisciplinary approaches—for example, a combination of archaeology and social scientific perspectives alongside the literary sources—have provided an enhanced methodology for the retrieval of Herodian and early Roman Galilee. As well as references in the Gospels, Josephus names forty-five Galilean villages and the Talmud refers to some sixty-three villages in Galilee. But subsequently, as Crossan puts it, "from Jewish literary texts, then, across almost one thousand five hundred years, nothing"[64]—meaning nothing new, that is, until the critical retrieval of Galilee from a range of material alongside literary sources seemed to offer new sources of information.

In particular, it is archaeology that has contributed substantially to a more objective reading of the cultural milieu of Galilee than has been possible on the basis of the literary sources alone. Archaeology has had an especially prominent role in the retrieval. It is strongly empirical, generally cumulative in its conclusions, and begins with questions generated by the material culture of Roman Galilee itself—rather than starting with questions that arise from textual traditions. These recent studies offer the possibility of an "intertextual" hermeneutic as archaeology enhances what literary sources disclose in order to broaden interpretative horizons concerning Herodian Galilee.

Freyne offers a good example of this methodology. Although he concedes that drawing up "a coherent and plausible account of the overall ethos of the region is a . . . difficult and tentative exercise,"[65] he is also clear that the intensive archaeological investigation of Hellenistic and

---

63. Freyne, "Galilee and Judaea," 41; Levine makes the same point, and with greater emphasis ("Theory, Apologetic, History," 59–60).

64. Crossan, *Historical Jesus*, 15.

65. Freyne, "Galilee, Jesus, and the Contribution," 581.

Roman Galilee has substantially verified and clarified understanding of the Jewish ethos of that period. Freyne writes that "[T]oo often still our historical investigations are based on ancient documents only, ignoring the alternative 'text' from below, which modern processual archaeology is able to offer us through its engagement with the social sciences." He goes on to add that "[L]istening to the alternative stories 'from below' that archaeology can tell us is one way of broadening further our interpretative horizons."[66]

Nonetheless, the provisionality of archaeological and historical findings should also be noted. Although Chancey is critical of analyses that overestimate or exaggerate the extent of Greco-Roman culture in Galilee, he also concedes that, like all studies based on archaeological data, his conclusions are provisional given "the haphazard nature of archaeological discovery, the randomness of survival, and the obliteration of earlier buildings by later construction."[67] One further reason for this provisionality is that there is still no agreement over the precise definition of a number of key terms in the discussion—terms such as "ethnicity," "Jew," "Judean/*Ioudaios*," "pagan," "Gentile," "village," "city." There is, for example, no "clear theoretical idea (beyond population) about what constitutes a village or about the relation of local assemblages to elite material culture"—and this means that debates often remain at the level of unhelpful abstraction.[68] In fact, even the term "Galilee" is somewhat problematical. A survey by Ruth Vale of "Views of Galilee in the literary sources"[69] is able to illustrate the way in which the descriptions of "Galilee" in the intertestamental literature, in Josephus, and then in the Gospels and the rabbinic literature, typically and primarily emphasize Galilee as "other." She concludes that, "in archaeological terms, it might be said then that the documents are of no great help to us, since they provide only indirect data well screened through foreign, and sometimes polemicized narrative frameworks."[70]

Regional variations within Galilee itself, and complex interactions between Galilee and its neighbors, are reasons why debates continue

66. Freyne, "Galilee as Laboratory," 149, 164.
67. Chancey, *Greco-Roman Culture*, 224.
68. Oakman, "Review," 568.
69. Section heading in Vale, "Literary sources," 211–16.
70. Ibid., 216. The problem derives, she argues, from "the manner in which the literature itself has shaped our interpretation" of the archaeological data" (209).

about understanding and integrating the research findings into an integrated and plausible picture of the Galilean ethos. Upper Galilee (the Golan), for example, had begun what were to become strong trading and other commercial links with Tyre and Syria[71]—but not to the detriment of a strongly Jewish ethos, especially in its villages. Lower Galilee, partly because of the influence of its urban areas, displayed a rather greater cultural diversity but also remained distinctively Jewish in ethos. At best, the recent and continuing attempts to retrieve Galilean identity reveal the life of the region to be dynamic and fluid, and not static; Zangenberg concludes that recent research has changed the portrait of Galilee from "a monolith to a dynamic field of variety. It becomes . . . a kaleidoscope rather than a mosaic."[72] Nonetheless, it is difficult to conceive of radical changes to the general portrait presented by Freyne, Chancey, and others. Without a substantial material change in the current pattern of archaeological finds, the picture will remain one in which the Jewish contours of Herodian Galilee are clearer than ever—even if they do remain somewhat blurred in places. The Galilee of Renan's often-cited description as "a fifth gospel, torn, but still legible"[73] might now be said to be somewhat less torn and rather more legible.

---

71. See the evidence cited in ibid., 224–26; in summary: "The numismatic evidence points to Tyre as the commercial focus for Upper Galilee, and further suggests that the nucleus of its cultural life may lie to the north and east rather than south to Lower Galilee and Jerusalem" (226).

72. Zangenberg "Region in Transition," 1.

73. Renan, *Life of Jesus*, 31.

8

The Old Testament: Friend or Foe of Palestinian Christians?

Exploring the Insights of Palestinian Theologian Naim Ateek

GORDON STEWART

INTRODUCTION

THIS CHAPTER FOCUSES ON Palestinian Christian perspectives on the Old Testament, and in particular the work of prominent theologian and former Canon of St. Georges Cathedral in Jerusalem, Rev. Dr. Naim Ateek. Ateek is the founder of Sabeel Ecumenical Liberation Theology Centre in Jerusalem, the author of several books, including *Justice and Only Justice: A Palestinian Theology of Liberation* and *A Palestinian Christian Cry for Reconciliation*. He is also coeditor of several other works.[1]

Palestinian Christians like Ateek find themselves not only in a constant battle with the physical realities of the Arab-Israeli conflict but also with competing theological arguments over the land. Here they find themselves squeezed between two opposing groups: their Muslim compatriots, and Christians and Jews who read their Scriptures from a Zionist perspective.

---

1. See the bibliography at the end of this volume for a list of Ateek's works consulted in this essay.

As Ateek points out, that Muslims also have a theology of the land is not often recognized.[2] Consequently, Arab Christians in Israel and the Palestinian territories often find themselves engaged in conflictual dialogue, especially as it relates to differing convictions concerning "sacred sites," the confusion that arises from interpretations of Western military interventions in the region, and the differing perspectives—past, present, and future—of Muslims and Christians concerning the significance of Jesus / *Isa al Masih*.

In addition, and more significantly, Arab believers experience theological conflict with Jewish people, ranging from secular Jews who nevertheless lay claim to ownership of the land on the basis of ancestral connections to Abraham and Moses, to the somewhat religious and the very religious fundamentalist right, whose theology based on readings of the Hebrew Scriptures claims justification for anything from Jewish occupation of, and settlement in, territories assigned to Palestinians by the UN Partition Plan, to the expulsion of Palestinians from the land, claiming that it was given exclusively to the people of Israel in perpetuity. Sadly, even more intense attacks come from Zionist Christians who agree with these Jewish Zionist positions.[3]

Part of the challenge facing Palestinian Christians has been the need to keep abreast of the changing underpinnings of Jewish Zionism, from its more secular and political face from the nineteenth century and into the middle of the twentieth, through to an increasingly religious one, especially since the 1967 Six-Day War.[4] Ateek states that "[t]he Zionist movement was nurtured by the spirit of its day—nationalism,

---

2 Based on interpretations of the Qur'an and Islamic traditions, Muslims consider inheritance of the land to be their right following God's rejection of Israel because of disobedience. See Ateek, *Palestinian Christian Cry*, 51–52, for his references to Dr. Mustafa Abu Sway's comments on the uniqueness for Muslims of the Holy Land and of the Al-Aqsa mosque in Jerusalem.

3. Riggans, *Israel and Zionism*, 19, states: "For many Christians today the greatest visible sign of God's faithfulness is the survival of the Jewish people ... the greatest sign of all is the State of Israel, and Jewish sovereignty over Eretz Israel." He comments further: "I would suggest that Christians as Christians must give support in principle to the State of Israel as a sign of God's mercy and faithfulness, and as a biblical mark that God is very much at work in the world" (22).

4. Ateek, "Zionism and the Land," 201. That earlier secular phase also witnessed the quite separate development of Christian Zionism in evangelical circles in the West. This would eventually merge with and reinforce Zionism's secular face. See Church, "Dispensational Christian Zionism," 376–82.

imperialism, and colonialism" and adds that although Jewish people cherished thoughts of independence, "such ideas remained anathema for the *religious* Jewish communities within Europe. Indeed, each of the three main Jewish denominations, Orthodox, Conservative and Reform, rejected Zionism and considered it an aberration. For, religiously speaking, they insisted that the return to the land could be heralded only by the Messiah."[5]

From the time of World War II until the mid 1960s, Palestinian believers have seen the waning of a simply political Zionism (though it still exists in the thinking of religiously nominal Jews) and the rising intensity of its religious dimensions, supported by Christian Zionist dispensational interpretations.[6] In essence, the conflict in the land is political, and concerns the human rights of the population. But there are increasing appeals to religious arguments. Consequently, Palestinian believers are forced to tackle the land from scriptural perspectives since they find themselves to be victims of what Ateek calls "the religious-political abuse of biblical interpretation."[7]

As has been the case in the earliest stages of development of many contextual theologies in the Majority World in the past sixty years or so, for Palestinians, both Muslim and Christian, the identity issue has been central. With the long history of Arab presence in the territory known as the "Holy Land," one can understand how they believe their very existence is put in question by such language as Lord Shaftesbury's "a country without a nation for a nation without a country," and its later adaptation by advocates of the Zionist cause, "a land of no people for a people with no land."[8] When taken to their logical conclusion, these phrases indicate to Palestinians that others consider them to be a people without rights to exist, or at least no right of identification with the land they have called home for centuries.

This denial of their identity is certainly what Palestinians understand from various expressions of Zionist thought and their accompa-

5. Ateek, "Zionism and the Land," 202. To this day, ultra-Orthodox Jewish groups such as Naturei Karta view Zionism as an aberration.

6. Significant factors in this shift are the Holocaust, the formation of the state of Israel in 1948, and the 1967 war; ibid., 202.

7. Ateek, "Biblical Perspectives," 108.

8. See Muir, "Land without a People," 55–56, for a discussion of the origins of both of these slogans. Note also Garfinkle's citation of Lord Shaftesbury's words, "On the Origin, Meaning, Use and Abuse," 543.

nying actions. Referring to the proponents of Christian Zionism, Ateek identifies their emphasis on "the restoration of the Jews to Palestine as a fulfillment of biblical prophecy" and their "insistence that this restored Jewish State must be *exclusively Jewish,* making no provision for the Arabs."[9] While Palestinian Christians may acknowledge that Zionist Jews can find support for an exclusive theology of the land in their reading of the Old Testament, they themselves are opposed to such claims since in their view the New Testament makes such a reading untenable.[10]

The Zionist agenda, whether secular or religious, Jewish or Christian, is particularly focused on Jewish claims to the territory that they identify as *their* promised land. The Palestinian Christian challenge to the Zionist claims focuses on Old Testament perspectives regarding the nature of the land promises to Israel. Were those promises unconditional and permanent, or conditional and provisional? The Zionist approach raises several other questions for Palestinian Christians: How is God's character to be understood? What is divine justice? Is God partial or impartial, exclusive or inclusive? Does God have a special plan for the Jews and another plan for his "other" chosen people? And, of particular importance in our present focus, how are Old Testament promises regarding the "promised land" to be interpreted in light of the life, death, and resurrection of Israel's Messiah, the Savior of the world?[11]

THE OLD TESTAMENT AS A CHALLENGE FOR PALESTINIAN CHRISTIANS

Fervent appeals to certain Old Testament texts are at the heart of the prevailing religious Zionist agendas regarding rights to the land, whether from the perspective of Judaism or Christianity. It is not surprising therefore that many Palestinians eschew the Old Testament, considering it to be more of a foe than a friend. In what follows we will discuss some Zionist interpretations of the Old Testament that Palestinian theologians identify as problematic, and also the resources within the same Scriptures that bring them solace and enable them to challenge these Zionist hermeneutics.

---

9. "Zionism and the Land," 203 (emphasis added).

10. Ateek, *Palestinian Christian Cry,* 52–53.

11. See Awad, *Palestinian Memories,* 244, 251–53; Ateek, "Biblical Perspectives," 108–16.

The creation of the state of Israel and the mode of its establishment and associated interpretations have significantly impacted Palestinian believers' views of the Bible, particularly the Old Testament. Ateek comments on this in his 1989 work, *Justice and only Justice*:

> The God of the Bible, hitherto the God who saves and liberates, has come to be viewed by Palestinians as partial and discriminating. Before the creation of the State, the Old Testament was considered to be an essential part of Christian Scripture, pointing and witnessing to Jesus. Since the creation of the State, some Jewish and Christian interpreters have read the Old Testament largely as a Zionist text to such an extent that it has become almost repugnant to Palestinian Christians. As a result, the Old Testament has generally fallen into disuse among both clergy and laity, and the Church has been unable to come to terms with its ambiguities, questions, and paradoxes—especially with its direct application to twentieth-century events.[12]

In another context, Ateek states: "Western Christians and many religious Jews were using the same Bible as we, but claiming to take from it a revelation from God that justified the conquest of our land and the extermination of our people."[13]

What are some of the specific uses of the Old Testament that are conflicting and afflicting for Palestinians? The limited scope of this paper enables us to glance at just a few examples, with the work of Ateek in particular focus.

Some Old Testament texts that underscore God's purposes of blessing for and through Israel are sometimes read in ways that imply exclusivity. Genesis 12:3 is an example:

> "I will bless those who bless you,
> and the one who curses you I will curse;
> and in you all the families of the earth shall be blessed."[14]

This text affirms God's blessing for those who bless Abraham, and his curse on those who curse Abraham. Yet, it is read as a "command" for Christians to bless Israel, and with the implication that those who do not do so will experience God's curse.

---

12. Ateek, *Justice and only Justice*, 77.
13. Ateek, *Faith and the Intifada*, 3.
14. All biblical quotations are from the NRSV, unless otherwise noted.

On one occasion, Ateek was accompanied by Bishop Desmond Tutu on a visit to Israeli government officials in Jerusalem. As they left they were confronted by a man who shouted out the words of the verse just quoted. The line of reasoning seemed to be that those who advocate for Palestinians and their rights, are abandoning Israel, cursing them and laying themselves open to God's curse.[15] Though this is anecdotal only, the words directed at Tutu and Ateek represent an exclusivist application of a text that also underscores the inclusivist or wider universal scope in terms of God's blessing of all peoples through Abraham's offspring. In relation to God's further promise to Abraham—that "to your offspring, I will give this land" (Gen 12:7)—the New Testament makes clear that the reference to "offspring" is, in fact, to Christ (Gal 3:16). There is both challenge and comfort for Palestinian Christians in the New Testament perspective that sees the blessing to Abraham in Genesis as demonstrating both particularity and universality—the specific calling of Israel as instrument and channel of divine blessing, as well as the wider purpose that ultimately—through Christ—brings that same favor to all peoples.

Other examples of problematic texts for Ateek are to be found in Nehemiah and Ezra. When Nehemiah returned from the exile and began to rebuild, he encountered a multiethnic society including, among others, Samaritans and Arabs. The narrative records their mockery and Nehemiah's response: "You have no share or claim or historic right in Jerusalem" (2:20). When some of these wanted to assist the Jews with temple reconstruction, they received a similar retort from Zerubbabel.[16] For Ateek, it is especially troubling that such texts are used by Zionists in the present conflict over the land. He comments: "Today the political leaders of Israel show total unwillingness to share Jerusalem. They reiterate the same words: 'No share or claim or historic right.'"[17] He comments further, "These texts exemplify a mind-set that is closed and narrow, that considers itself above others, and refuses to accept people as they are. Such a position expresses a theology that is exclusive, narrow, and xenophobic and it can never lead to peace, whether in its historic setting or in our contemporary context."[18]

---

15. Ateek, "Zionism and the Land," 206–7.

16. Ezra 4:3: "You shall have no part with us in building a house to our God; but we alone will build to the Lord, the God of Israel."

17. Ateek, *Palestinian Christian Cry*, 143.

18. Ibid. Ateek comments on Nehemiah's and Ezra's emphasis on the purity of Jewish

In more general terms, Palestinians rightly question those who make a direct identification of the inhabitants of the state of Israel today with the people of Israel in Old Testament history. Ateek's grievance is evident in his critique of the stance of Paul van Buren, who proposes *A Theology of the Jewish-Christian Reality*:[19]

> ... van Buren uses the term "Israel" so loosely that he does not distinguish between biblical Israel and the modern State of Israel. In one place he refers to God as fighting against the Arabs on the side of the Jews in 1948 as in the time of Joshua. In fact, modern Israel is, for him, the direct continuation of biblical Israel—he does not question the differences.... By implication, he not only disassociates Israel from any injustices, but also gives it God's approval and blessing ... he considers those Jews who acted in creating the State of Israel as themselves carrying out the act of God.[20]

The term "Israel" then has come to be used in quite different ways than what would have been familiar to a Palestinian Christian in the first half of the twentieth century. Ateek recalls from childhood the usual connotation of the word "Israel" as used in the Psalms, for example. It was understood to be referring neither to a modern geopolitical entity nor to the kingdom of Israel in the eighth century, but to "a religious community of devout worshippers of Israel's God."[21] He comments further,

> "Israel" signified "God's people," and we worshippers of God were living members of Israel, but members only conditionally. Our membership was conditional on our obeying God's commands and following His precepts as these had been declared by Him through the mouth of His Prophets. This traditional spiritual connotation of the name "Israel" has been supplanted today by a political and military connotation.... This picture has now effaced that one in our minds. It has effaced it, whoever we are: Jews or Christians, diaspora Jews or Israelis, believers or agnostics. The present-day political Israel has, for all of us, obliterated

---

blood and the resultant conflicts with other inhabitants of the land (ibid., 72). A further example of what Ateek identifies as an exclusivist text is Isa 61:5–6 (ibid., 55–56).

19. Van Buren, *Discerning*.
20. Ateek, *Justice and only Justice*, 63.
21. Ibid., 77.

or, at least, adumbrated, the spiritual Israel of the Judeo-Christian tradition. This is surely a tragedy.[22]

Concomitant with this, and adding to the Palestinian sense of grievance, is the Zionist tendency to identify present day Palestinians with the Canaanites who were to be eliminated in the conquest under Joshua, with the associated view that the divine sanctions in place then may be invoked today. Ateek questions the value of texts that record God's command to totally destroy Jericho and its inhabitants, concluding that such injunctions represent "a stage of development of the human understanding of God that we must regard, in light of Christ's revelation, as inadequate and incomplete."[23]

When present-day religious Jews claim that they are the rightful inheritors of the land, they frequently appeal to the Hebrew Scriptures that promise that the land is theirs as an everlasting possession.[24] For Jewish Zionist readers, it appears to be a relatively short step from seeing their present occupation of the land as the fulfillment of God's justice to the presumed role of meting out injustice to those deemed unworthy and unlawful dwellers in that same land.[25] Palestinian believers question a reading of the Old Testament that concludes that God is partial, that his justice is preferentially available for the people of Israel.

Palestinian Christians may find present-day Jewish claims to the land based on the Old Testament more understandable—though not thereby more defensible—than the claims made by Christians, especially evangelicals, regarding those "rights." Ateek writes:

> Strangely—shockingly—the Bible has been used by some Western Christians and Jews in a way that has supported *in*justice rather than justice. Liberation theologians have seen the Bible as a dynamic source for their understanding of liberation, but if some parts of it are applied literally to our situation today, the Bible

---

22. Ibid., 76.

23. Josh 6:17–21. See ibid., 83.

24. See, for example, God's words to Abraham in Gen 17:8: "The whole land of Canaan, where you now reside as a foreigner, I will give as an everlasting possession to you and your descendants after you; and I will be their God" (TNIV).

25. Chapman, *Whose Promised Land*, 245, quotes the Zionist Arthur Ruppin, writing in 1930: "On every side where we purchase land and where we settle people the present cultivators will inevitably be dispossessed. There is no alternative, but that lives should be lost. It is our destiny to be in a state of continual warfare with the Arabs." See also Ateek, *Justice and only Justice*, 75.

appears to offer to the Palestinians slavery rather than freedom, injustice rather than justice, and death to their national and political life.[26]

The Christian Zionist position is particularly hard to digest, especially those interpretations that explicitly state that God has two agendas, one for Israel and one for the church. For example, C. I. Scofield proposed that since Israel was the "earthly wife" of God and the church the "heavenly bride" of Christ, the eternal inheritance of Israel will be on earth and that of the church will be in heaven.[27] Along the same lines Chafer states, "The dispensationalist believes that throughout the ages God is pursuing two distinct purposes: one related to the earth with earthly people and earthly objectives involved, which is Judaism; while the other is related to heaven with heavenly people and heavenly objectives, which is Christianity." Chafer adds that "Israel is an eternal nation, heir to an eternal land, with an eternal kingdom, on which David rules from an eternal throne". In eternity, "never the twain, Israel and church, shall meet."[28]

Ateek struggles with such interpretations, given the overwhelming evidence of the New Testament that Christ's work transcends Jew/Gentile distinctions (Gal 3:28), that he "has made the two one, destroying the barrier.... His purpose was to create one new humanity out of the two, thus making peace ..." (Eph 2:14–15 TNIV).[29] Palestinian believers might ponder whether the apostle would view the "two distinct purposes" notion as the expression of "another gospel," verging on heresy. Ateek's critique is pertinent. Commenting on Eph 2:19–20 and 1:8b–10, he states, "viewing history from the vantage point of its fulfillment in Christ, we need to consider God's original purpose for humanity.... According to Ephesians, God's purpose for creation goes back to eternity. From the foundation of the world God's purpose for history was to create one humanity in Christ."[30] God's purpose was that in Christ "the plan of the mystery hidden for ages in God" (Eph 3:9) should now be made known, namely that "the Gentiles have become fellow-heirs,

26 Ateek, *Justice and Only Justice*, 75.

27. Cited in Sizer, *Christian Zionism*, 138.

28. Ibid.

29 See Ateek, "Putting Christ at the Centre," 55–63; Awad, *Palestinian Memories*, 265–66.

30 Ateek, *Palestinian Christian Cry*, 62.

members of the same body, and sharers in the promise in Christ Jesus through the Gospel" (Eph 3:5–6). One might say with some justification that this reflection on the Old Testament—a reflection in the light of Christ—enables us to evaluate and critique current Jewish claims and associated theologies regarding the land. The appropriateness and validity of such a reflection is emphasized by Ateek.

APPRAISAL OF OLD TESTAMENT THEOLOGIES OF THE LAND

While Ateek's main approach to the interpretation of the Old Testament is through the lens of Christ, he also rises to the challenge of finding texts within the Old Testament itself that critique Zionist arguments, texts the dominant interpretations of which have proven so problematic for Palestinians. Referring once again to Eph 2:19–22, but taking it as a starting point for another line of thought linked with Old Testament prophetic themes, he writes,

> [t]his passage is pregnant with Old Testament references to the land that become redundant in Christ. The first is the reference to "strangers and aliens," or those non-Israelites who had no right to the land, yet were supposed to be treated kindly and justly because God was their protector. After the exile, according to Ezek 47:21–23, aliens were supposed to receive the same inheritance to the land by order of God.[31]

Ateek sees in this text

> one of the rare moments in the development of Old Testament theology where a new theology breaks in, a theology that includes non-Israelites and gives strangers and aliens the same inheritance of the land. Undoubtedly, the exile had a great impact on the Israelites and stretched their concept of God. These words of Ezekiel must have seemed a great contradiction of the many injunctions in the Torah against even making peace with the indigenous people of Canaan. The Torah leaves only two options in dealing with the indigenous people of the land: expulsion or

---

31. Ibid., 63. Ezek 47:21–23 (TNIV) reads: "You are to distribute this land among yourselves according to the tribes of Israel. You are to allot it as an inheritance for yourselves and for the foreigners residing among you and who have children. You are to consider them as native-born Israelites; along with you they are to be allotted an inheritance among the tribes of Israel. In whatever tribe foreigners reside, there you are to give them their inheritance, declares the Sovereign LORD."

> annihilation. Ezekiel . . . has radically changed course by writing that God demands an equal inheritance for all the residents in the land, regardless of their ethnic or racial background.[32]

Here Ateek appears to overlook the numerous references in the Torah and elsewhere that underscore Yahweh's concern for the alien or foreigner, as well as for the widow and orphan.[33] Expulsion and annihilation may seem to be appropriate terms to describe the conquest of the land under Joshua, but again and again the Torah reveals the common ethical requirements for native-born Israelites and foreigners. Ateek, however, discerns the development of a radically different message in some of the later prophets. It is understandable that for Jewish readers the Torah will be a genuine source of theology concerning the land, but Ateek insists that the more inclusivist messages evident in the later prophets must take precedence over the earlier exclusivist emphases. For Christians, as Ateek puts it, "The Torah, as well as the rest of the Old Testament, provides a background or a history and not a binding theology."[34]

More precisely, Ateek identifies texts that are clearly exclusivist, texts that oscillate between exclusivism and inclusivism, and texts that are predominantly inclusivist, supremely Jonah. Thus he suggests that the unfolding stages of divine revelation in the Old Testament may be described as successive drafts of a theological dissertation, the earlier ones being less binding than the later. He states, "while it is quite informative and interesting to study the previous drafts, ultimately the most binding for a Christian is the final draft, verified by the witness of Jesus Christ. Unless Old Testament references correspond to a view held by

---

32. Ibid., 64.

33. Notwithstanding the understandable objection of Palestinians today to being designated "aliens" or "strangers" in the land, one cannot ignore the numerous ethical injunctions to native-born Israelites concerning their attitudes and actions vis-à-vis aliens. See, e.g., Exod 23:9; Lev 19:34; 25:23, 35; Deut 1:16; 27:19.

34. Ateek, *Palestinian Christian Cry*, 64. Ateek sees the OT as limited in usefulness for a Christian as a source for a theology of the land or indeed for any other theology, since there is the possibility of being "misled about God's purpose unless she or he looks to the New Testament for its fulfillment. Although the Old Testament indicates the development of an inclusive theology of God and the land, its evolving movement toward inclusion is incomplete and at times vacillating."

Christ, they form a rough or previous draft and cannot be considered binding."[35]

This raises questions concerning Ateek's views on the integrity and authority of the Old Testament. His strong emphasis on the ways in which the Christ event represents for the Christian the fulfillment of the unfolding divine purposes in the Old Testament is appropriate and helpful, but one wonders whether in the sieve used to evaluate the Hebrew Scriptures more is discarded than retained.

THEMES OF JUSTICE IN THE OLD TESTAMENT

Certain declarations of the Old Testament prophets are often appealed to by Zionist readers as providing the ground on which events in the twentieth and twenty-first centuries can be interpreted as the fulfillment of God's promised blessings to Israel. But the utterances of the prophets that reflect God's character and purpose in terms of mercy and justice already reflect inclusivism. This is evident in the Ezekiel passage referred to above. Other pertinent examples are prophetic injunctions such as those of Amos 5:24 and Mic 6:8. It is true that the terminology of distinctiveness and even of separation—"tribes of Israel" and "aliens and strangers"—is present in the Old Testament. But it is equally true that Israel is commanded to share with others the inheritance and enjoyment of the land entrusted to them as gift that is conditional upon covenant faithfulness. In Christ the distinctions become redundant. Referring to Eph 2, Ateek writes, "The writer of Ephesians goes a step beyond Ezekiel in revealing God's purpose when he says that in Christ there are *no longer* aliens and strangers because all have become members of the family of God. . . . The coming of Jesus Christ does not allow Christians to revert to a narrow theology of the land."[36]

At the heart of what Ateek calls narrow theologies of the land is an exclusivity arising from nationalism that justifies violence. In the introduction to the chapter "The Bible and the Land" in *A Palestinian Christian Cry*, he states, "Palestinian Christians often feel trapped between two forms of exclusivity, a Jewish form and a Muslim form."[37] Later in the same chapter he suggests that in the earlier stages of Israel's

---

35. Ibid., 58.
36. Ibid., 64 (emphasis added).
37. Ibid., 51.

history as a nation they were probably influenced by what was generally true of ancient societies, the linkage of "three important factors: the tribe/s, its god/s, and the geographical area of land where the tribe lived and moved."[38] He adds, "most people lived in henotheistic societies, in which a tribe or group of tribes believed that their god or gods were supreme.... In some societies, the land was part of a covenant between the god(s) and the tribe(s): it belonged to the god/gods, and the king or people were entrusted with it."[39]

Thus he discerns in the unfolding Old Testament story a gradual movement from exclusivity towards inclusivity, a shift from particularity towards "a more universal understanding of one God and God's relationship with all people rather than with one tribal group."[40] Nevertheless, exclusivist views did not entirely disappear.[41]

Ateek laments that this narrow-mindedness persists in present-day theologies driving the conflict over Palestine. In his pursuit of a reading of "the Old Testament through Christian eyes—or human eyes or Palestinian eyes," he does not deny that those Scriptures have a "polyphonic" character, to use Walter Brueggemann's term.[42] It is of course possible to read the Old Testament through Jewish or secular eyes, but as Ateek points out, "the text makes most sense when read primarily through the lens of Jesus Christ. In reading it with my Palestinian eyes, I see its meaning and its relevance for my social and political context. *When I read the Old Testament, it is with an eye toward those narratives that reflect the inclusive and nonviolent message of Christ.*"[43]

While Palestinian theologians see Zionist Christians using Old Testament passages selectively to support their positions, it is also fair

---

38. Ibid., 63.

39. Ibid., 63.

40. Ibid.

41. Ibid. Ateek states: "although some learned during exile that there is one creator God who is concerned about others ... many held on to a narrow theology of God and a chosen people."

42. Ibid., 54. Ateek seeks to respond to Brueggemann's critique of some Christians' supersessionism, according to which "Jewish religious claims are overridden in the triumph of Christian claims," and his view that it is misusing the Old Testament to present only "one single, and exclusivist construal, namely the New Testament Christological construal, thereby violating the quality of generative openness that marks the Old Testament text" (Brueggemann, *Theology*, 729 and 732).

43. Ibid. (Emphasis added).

to say that some proponents of Palestinian theology are not beyond a similar temptation. Ateek himself is aware of such a danger. Palestinian believers, he affirms, must look for a criterion that is "both biblically and theologically sound, lest it in turn become a mere instrument to oppose Jewish and Christian Zionists and support subjective Palestinian claims and prejudices."[44] As they find themselves face to face with the political "abuse" of the Bible, Palestinian Christians search for a hermeneutic that will enable them "to identify the authentic Word of *God* in the Bible."[45] He explains the need for discernment as to whether a particular passage of Scripture is "the Word of *God* to them . . . reflecting the nature, will, and purpose of *God* for them" or whether it is "a reflection of authentic human understanding about God at that stage of development."[46] He comments, "to put it bluntly, is it basically a statement from humans put into the mouth of God, that has become confused as an authentic message from God to people? Do the words reflect an authentic and valid message from God to us today?"[47]

The authority and integrity of the Old Testament seems to be in question in some of Ateek's interpretative approaches, with the relativizing of various texts. For the most part, the Hebrew Scriptures may only be "authentic" in the sense that they accurately record the inadequate human perceptions about God at particular times of Israel's history. It seems that, for Ateek, the Old Testament contains the authentic word of God much less frequently than it does a human word. But the criterion that forms the basis of his selective approach is Christ:

> The hermeneutic must ring true of a God we have come to know—unchanging in nature and character, dynamically constant rather than fickle and variable, responding to but not conditioned by time, space, or circumstances. The canon of this hermeneutic for the Palestinian Christian is none less than Jesus Christ himself . . . the *Word* of God incarnate in Jesus the Christ interprets for us the *word* of God in the Bible.[48]

As a Palestinian liberation theologian, therefore, Ateek tends to limit the usefulness of the Old Testament to its more obvious foreshad-

---

44. Ateek, *Justice and only Justice*, 79.
45. Ibid.
46. Ibid.
47. Ibid.
48. Ibid., 79–80.

owings of the inclusiveness evident in the ministry of Jesus. Space does not permit us to explore in depth a number of insights that Ateek offers from various other Old Testament contexts that represent a previewing of and harmonizing with God's revelation in Jesus Christ. Included in such are the fruitful discussions of the post-exilic tensions between the idealism of longings for the Davidic warrior king and the Suffering Servant,[49] or between the exclusivist and nationalist perspectives evident in prophets like Haggai over against the more progressive emphases seen in the new covenant visions of Jeremiah, Ezekiel, and Second Isaiah, or between what is seen as a militant theology anticipating a restored monarchy on the one hand and new concerns for non-violence and justice on the other.[50] The parallels between the experiences of life under occupation for post-exilic Jews and present-day Palestinians are drawn, with particular focus on new theological emphases concerning faithfulness to God, issues of morality, mercy, justice and non-violent resistance.[51] These developments are seen as anticipating Jesus' responses to life under occupation. Rather than giving in to aspirations for a Davidic kingly deliverer, Jesus "chose a different ethic—that of Daniel and the Suffering Servant."[52] Jesus' ethic of non-violence is foreshadowed in these Old Testament contexts and provides the model for Palestinians in the present reality.[53]

Jonah, one of the last books of the Old Testament to be written, is for Ateek the supreme example of this inclusive theology. He refers to the book of Jonah as "the genius and climax of Old Testament theology," and its author as "an archetypal Palestinian Liberation theologian."[54] Of course, the prophet is portrayed as an Israelite nationalist, holding contempt for the Assyrian oppressors and exhibiting anger at even the possibility of their repentance, but Ateek believes that whereas Isaiah and Jeremiah "fluctuate between an inclusive and exclusive view of God,

---

49. Ateek, *Palestinian Christian Cry*, ch. 7, "Son of David or Suffering Servant?"

50. Ibid., ch. 10, "Daniel or Judah Maccabeus."

51. Ateek sees a significant polarizing of theological perspectives in the post-exilic period. This is evident in a comparison he makes between the Maccabeans and Daniel: "While the Maccabean revolt reinforced the building of faith in a God that marches to war using violence, arms, and bloodshed, Daniel turned to building a faith with which God's followers can resist evil through non-violent resistance" (ibid., 136).

52. Ibid.

53. Ibid., 136–39.

54. Ibid., 54.

people and the land, and vacillate between a nationalist and a universal view, the author of *Jonah* is very consistent in his inclusive and universal message."[55] The author, Ateek comments, "critiques much of the theology around him and maintains that any religion that reflects a tribal and xenophobic god cannot be genuine.... In my understanding, the inclusive text of *Jonah* is a standard against which Old Testament theology must be measured."[56]

More specifically, the narrative genre is seen to be an appropriate and effective vehicle for the delivery of a revolutionary theology that challenged the people's ethnocentrism and focused their attention on three crucial themes: "a theology of God, a theology of the people of God, and a theology of the land."[57] In relation to God's character, emphasis is placed on his role as creator and Lord of history, and his impartiality, extending forgiveness and mercy beyond the boundaries of Israel.[58] In terms of those who are included in the people of God, even the brutal Assyrians respond to the call to repentance, and "fall within the care and embrace of a God who shows concern for their well-being."[59] In terms of a theology of the land, Jonah challenges the tribal perspective that sees God as confined to a certain geographic territory: God is present and active everywhere.[60] The relevance of these themes of inclusion for the realities of the present-day conflict is made clear by Ateek, who challenges the Zionist arguments:

> The message of Jonah has great relevance for those of us who live in Israel-Palestine as it addresses the core religious and theological issues underlying the conflict. Many religious Jews continue to see themselves in a special relationship with God: they are God's chosen people, God belongs to them alone, and the entire land of Israel is their eternal patrimony from God.... In essence, what the author of the book of Jonah was battling against at the end

---

55. Ibid., 54–55.
56. Ibid., 55.
57. Ibid., 73. The three theological themes are discussed further on 73–75.
58. Ibid., 74.
59. Ibid. Of the author of Jonah, Ateek comments: "In many ways his message intended to liberate God from the narrow theology of the day and liberate his people, the Israelites from a tribal mentality that produced arrogance, haughtiness, and presumptuousness. They needed to wake up to the fact that God is the God of all and that they constitute but one small part of the people of God."
60. Ibid.

of the fourth century BCE still constitutes the main theological problems we Palestinians face in the conflict today. In the name of an antiquated tribal theology that still insists on a special Jewish god, on the privileges of a special people of God, and on a unique Jewish right to the whole of the land of Palestine, the Palestinians are oppressed and dehumanized, and their claim to the land on which many families have lived for centuries is negated.[61]

Jonah is thus a text in which Ateek finds rich theological resources, providing from within the Old Testament the strongest challenge to interpretations that seek to justify exclusive and nationalistic claims, and portraying the inclusiveness of the divine purpose and its universal scope.

CONCLUSION

The way in which the Old Testament has been used to support Zionist perspectives and justify violence toward the Palestinians has led some Palestinian believers to avoid the Old Testament. Ateek explores ways to overcome this tendency. We discern in his work a thorough examination of Old Testament texts that have been interpreted problematically, and an intentional searching for resources within the Old Testament that reflect the character of God as manifest supremely in the life and work of Christ. Ateek's approach to the Old Testament is characterized by a careful selectivity. In reading the Old Testament exclusively through the "lens of Christ," looking for that which harmonizes with Jesus' inclusive and non-violent ministry, Ateek concludes that portions of Scripture discordant with the Christian vision are best understood as a human word rather that the word of God.

It is acknowledged that developing stages of God's self-revelation within Scripture can be discerned. These are explained in terms of a movement from exclusivism, embodying a nationalistic vision that is focused on Israel itself, to inclusivism, in which a more universal view is embraced. The temptation here is to conclude that earlier Old Testament texts have less or no theological value and that only the few, like Jonah, that fully foreshadow God as revealed in Christ are the true word of God. One can understand that in his motivation to provide pastoral encouragement and support for Palestinian Christians, his reading of the Old Testament is selective. As the first and most prominent Palestinian

61. Ibid., 74–75 (emphasis added).

liberation theologian, Ateek constantly seeks to encourage and strengthen Palestinian Christians. His call on behalf of the Palestinians is for a theology of liberation from oppression and dehumanization. This necessitates the liberation of theology from Zionist interpretations based on selective readings of the Old Testament that fail to recognize therein the unfolding vision of a God of mercy and justice, whose universal purposes for humankind are supremely revealed in Jesus Christ. The great strength of Ateek's work is that it provides Palestinian Christians with rich theological treasure and empowerment for life and non-violent resistance under occupation from within the very Scriptures so commonly and perversely used against them. Thanks to his interpretive work, the Hebrew Scriptures *can* be more of a friend than a foe for Palestinian believers. His writings, and his work through the ministry of Sabeel, vigorously challenge unbalanced and dehumanizing approaches to the Old Testament, and provide inspiration through his Christ-focused hermeneutic.

9

Evangelical Social Conscience and the Challenge of Christian Zionism

STEPHEN TOLLESTRUP

INTRODUCTION

THE SUBJECT OF ISRAEL and the land moved well past curious and speculative discussion some decades ago. Even before the founding of the state of Israel, the rhetoric of the debate was marked by bullets, militias, propaganda, and political activism with protagonists from both the Israeli and the Arab sides. The intense heat and obscuring smoke has been further fueled by powerful international actors with agendas that have exacerbated the conflict. Today, groups who claim the right to occupy the land rally behind both the Old and the New Testaments, the Koran, the founding papers of Zionism, United Nations minutes and resolutions, national myths, as well as political circumstances and realities, particularly in post-Holocaust Europe. Supplementing all this is the influence of the powerful Christian Zionist lobby, pushing peace and reconciliation further into the background.[1]

---

1. See, e.g., "ICEJ Response." This document by the International Christian Embassy Jerusalem (ICEJ) is a response to a letter addressed to President George W. Bush from 36 leading evangelicals, seeking a more balanced and equitable solution to the Israeli-Palestinian conflict. The letter criticizes any suggestion of "historical or moral equivalence" between the political claims of Palestine and Israel, claims that the authors of the original letter fail to grasp the biblical paradox of "free grace" versus "divine election," and also claims that the authors promote "replacement theology." An examination of the original letter shows that none of these claims is valid.

This paper is concerned with the growing influence that Christian Zionism exerts on evangelicals and evangelical congregations. I will demonstrate how this influence has monopolized much of the discussion on Zionism and the Middle East conflict within the evangelical church, and has also exerted considerable political lobbying power on behalf of Zionist goals.

I first became aware of Christian Zionism in 1997, following a visit to the West Bank. TEAR Fund New Zealand had launched a public appeal for funds to assist Palestinian refugees in building a kindergarten complex at Deheishe refugee camp near Bethlehem. It was a non-political project, formulated in conjunction with the local Christian community, seeking to provide books, art tables and craft supplies, as well as supplementary stipends and training for the teachers and parent assistants. All the children had refugee status and many had family members under detention in Israel on political charges.

Almost as soon as the appeal was publicized Christian Zionist groups in New Zealand, Australia, and the United Kingdom led a series of publicity attacks with their stated aim to have TEAR Fund suffer financial consequences should it express the view that Palestinians, young or old, were "victims" or had any valid grievance claims. When I sought advice from church and pastoral colleagues, most of whom were evangelical or charismatic Christians, I found almost unanimous support for TEAR Fund, as well as surprising exasperation with the influence of Christian Zionism in their congregations.

I dispute neither the right of the state of Israel to exist under its mandated and accepted UN borders nor the right of the Jewish people to have a homeland. Neither do I deny the biblical imperative to show kindness to and to comfort the Jewish people. As a follower of Jesus the Jew, I have a responsibility to extend the love of God to the Jewish people, not only in response to a biblical command, but also, and perhaps more pertinently, out of shame for the two millennia of persecution wrought by Christians. Indeed, anti-Semitism is uniquely European and troublingly Christian in character.[2] But I question the assumption that any of this means that I should not be concerned about the denial of human rights to the Palestinian people.

---

2. Kohl, "Holocaust," 9.

THE NATURE OF CHRISTIAN ZIONISM

Early expressions of Christian Zionism emerged with such people as Jonathan Edwards and George Whitefield.[3] It was systematized by Edward Irving and John Nelson Darby,[4] and popularized by C. I. Scofield.[5] Today, it flourishes primarily among evangelical and charismatic Christians, where Zionist Christian leaders often exercise a self-appointed status as spokespersons for the evangelical community, with the resultant unfortunate impression in the wider community that to be evangelical also entails being Christian Zionist.[6]

Increasingly Christian Zionism, especially in its more popular forms, is marked by a comprehensive restorationist position, and a narrow interpretation of Old Testament covenantalism. It also serves a naïve political perspective as it attempts to apply prophetic and apocalyptic writings to contemporary international relations.[7] To illustrate this, I quote a definition from Mikael Knighton, the founder and executive director of Christians Standing with Israel, an Israel advocacy organization seeking to promote a sound awareness and understanding of the Hebraic roots of Christianity. Knighton writes,

> Christians who see the re-gathering of the Jewish people in their land, as well as the establishment of the sovereign nation of Israel in 1948, as the literal fulfillment of biblical prophecy are known as "Christian Zionists." Christian Zionists see the Jewish people as the "apple of God's eye"—his chosen people, and hold firm that God's promises, established in the Abrahamic covenant, remain in effect today.
>
> Christian Zionists are "biblical advocates" for the Jewish people and the state of Israel. Furthermore, they stand in firm diametrical opposition to land concessions of any sort that involve the forfeiture of the holy land of Israel as it is a sacred manifestation of the promises of God to the people He calls the "apple of His eye."[8]

---

3. Sizer, *Christian Zionism*, 29–30.
4. Ibid., 42–52.
5. Ibid., 74–77.
6. McKay, "Christian Soldiers," cites Falwell as claiming to speak for seventy million evangelicals, who immediately assemble when they detect an anti-Israel bias on the part of the U.S. government.
7. See Church, "Dispensational Christian Zionism," 387–90.
8. Knighton, "Christian Zionist."

The term "biblical advocates" in the above quote highlights a further trend. Some Christian Zionists, most notably the International Christian Embassy Jerusalem (ICEJ), have begun to describe themselves as "*biblical Zionists*," using the term "biblical" in an effort to create some sense of legitimacy, and also to distance themselves from some of the more strident groups.[9] However, this is a provocative term. The modifier "biblical" should be read as an attempt to legitimize and anchor Christian Zionism in respectable orthodoxy, while designating dissenters as "unbiblical." It is a further attempt to move the discussion beyond healthy and vigorous debate between Christians, to the co-option of doctrine, a theological "land grab."

CHRISTIAN ZIONIST CLAIMS REGARDING THE LAND

The following statement from the Third International Christian Zionist Congress represents the beliefs of many Christian Zionists:

> According to God's distribution of nations, the land of Israel has been given to the Jewish People by God as an everlasting possession by an eternal covenant. The Jewish People have the absolute right to possess and dwell in the land, including Judea, Samaria, Gaza and the Golan.[10]

The resolution is amplified and more clearly nuanced in the following supporting text:

> As a faith bound to love and forgiveness we are appreciative of the attempts by the Government of Israel to work tirelessly for peace. However, the truths of God are sovereign and it is written that the land which He promised to His People is not to be partitioned . . . It would be further error for the nations to recognize a Palestinian state in any part of Eretz Israel.[11]

The statement "It would be further error for the nations to recognize a Palestinian state in any part of Eretz Israel" is important to grasp, as it challenges any expectation of a homeland for the Palestinian people. Palestinian rights, whether secular, Christian, or Muslim, are by this statement excluded from any consideration, on the basis of some text said to be "written." The solemn sounding language gives the impression

---

9. ICEJ, "Position", line 2.
10. "Proclamation," ¶ 10.
11. Ibid, "A Sense of the Resolutions," ¶ 2.

of a biblical quotation, although no reference is given. Of course, there is no such biblical text.

Compare this claim with a comment from Walter Brueggemann:

> It strikes me as enormously hazardous to cite a supernatural right in the midst of *realpolitik*, especially when the right is entwined with military ferociousness and political exclusivism. While such a right may serve self-identity, it makes sense only inside the narrative. Outside the narrative it is no more than ideology, and so offers no basis for the hard work of peace and justice.[12]

Bruggemann rightly recognizes the danger. While Scripture provides us with insight and revelation, to impose a predictive inference into the current Middle Eastern conflict is a serious and dangerous miscalculation. Two millennia of Christian history have shown the prevalence of prophetic misfires, especially of eschatological predictions based on faulty biblical interpretation and presumptions. Today these same predictive errors have the potential to lead the people of Israel and Palestine further away from peace and conflict resolution.

THE PERVASIVE INFLUENCE OF CHRISTIAN ZIONISM

If we take a generous view that three quarters of the thirteen million people worldwide identifying their ethnicity as Jewish support the claims of Zionism, even in the broadest political sense—a vision for the self-determination of the Jewish people and a sovereign Jewish national homeland—we could estimate that there are around ten million Jewish Zionists.

How does this compare with the number of Christian Zionists? Numbers are difficult to pin down. Within the United States Donald Wagner estimates a figure of around twenty to twenty-five million fundamentalist Christians who would adhere to the Christian Zionist perspective.[13] This can be corroborated by a U.S. census estimate that 10 percent of the voting public identify themselves as Christian Zionists.[14] Davidson places the estimate higher still at forty million.[15]

---

12. Brueggemann, "Three Responses," lines 21–25.

13. Wagner, "Blackstone to Bush," 42.

14. Haija, "Armageddon Lobby." See also McKay, "Christian Soldiers," where Falwell estimates around seventy million Christian Zionists.

15. Davidson, "Manifest Destiny," 158.

These numbers only reflect the movement in the U.S. The Christian Zionist movement in other countries is significant and includes the United Kingdom, Netherlands, Canada, Scandinavia, Australia, and New Zealand. The ICEJ has branches in around sixty countries.[16] In other words, and more significantly, Zionism, in numerical terms, is now a predominately Christian movement, a movement with activists and lobbyists attempting to shape the political destiny of Israel, as well as the theology of the church.

CHRISTIAN ZIONISM AND ANTI-SEMITISM

While Christian Zionists are very quick to impute anti-Semitism to those who challenge their position, that position also has some surprising anti-Jewish characteristics and overtones. As Gorshem Gorenberg, associate editor of the *Jerusalem Report* and founder of the Israeli religious peace movement Netivot Shalom, writes "Christian Zionism is not in fact a Zionist theology, but in fact a classic anti-Jewish ideology."[17] Later he explains,

> I would reject the view that these people are supporting Israel in any deep sense. They are not interested in the welfare of the Jews . . . certainly not in the most pragmatic sense. I would argue that the thing most in the interest of Israel is reaching a peace agreement, but such considerations simply do not figure in the scheme of Christian Zionists because their goal is not peace in the pragmatic, political sense. It is to bring the end . . . The Jews must cease to be actors in the Christian drama . . .[18]

CHRISTIAN ZIONISM AND THE UNDERMINING OF EVANGELICAL ORTHODOXY

I have become increasingly alarmed at the potential for Christian Zionism to undermine evangelical orthodoxy. Responding to Sizer's *Christian Zionism*, Ronald Clements, Professor Emeritus of Old Testament studies at King's College, London, comments concerning Christian Zionism, "a firm principle of Christian hope has been distorted and misapplied in a cruel and destructive manner. Until the Christian attitude to Zionism

---

16. "ICEJ Worldwide."
17. Gorenberg "Danger of Millenial Politics," 192.
18. Gorenberg, ibid, 198.

is changed, I fear that the situation will continue to deteriorate and that those evangelicals who have embraced Zionism will continue to do immense damage to the Christian Church."[19]

Christian Zionism, committed to an uncritical literalist and fundamentalist reading of Scripture, has become theologically sterile, and open to the charge of being heterodox. Increasingly it finds itself in a cul-de-sac, without any significant engagement with contemporary biblical and theological scholarship. For this reason there is no evident appreciation of recent theological thinking on justice, non-violence, structural and social analysis, or power. There is no real attempt to understand theological perspectives from the developing world or marginal theologies, and certainly no interest in engaging with Palestinian Christian thinkers such as Naim Ateek,[20] Alex Awad,[21] and Jonathan Kuttab.[22] The result is a blunting of evangelical biblically based social critique and a failure to grasp a more holistic perspective where the whole of human life—spiritual, political, and social—is challenged by and offered the opportunity of redemption.

Traditional evangelical perspectives are also at risk from the influence of the Christian Zionist movement. One perspective at risk is the doctrine of the all-sufficiency of the work of Christ in salvation and cosmic redemption, where all things are radically reconciled and every promise of the covenant finds fulfillment in Christ (2 Cor 1:18–20; Gal 3:15–18). As N. T. Wright points out,

> Paul expounds this statement of covenant renewal in relation to what God has done in Christ and by the Spirit... And the result is that now, instead of the return of ethnic Israel to the holy land, as envisaged in Deuteronomy, the message goes out to all people. As in Romans 8, the whole world has become the holy land, claimed through the gospel of Jesus the Messiah on behalf of the creator God.[23]

---

19. Clements, "Commendation."
20. For the writings of Ateek see ch. 7 of the present volume.
21. See, e.g., Awad, *Palestinian Memories.*
22. See, e.g., Kuttab, "Justice and Mercy."
23. Wright, *Fresh Perspective*, 32.

And again,

> When God fulfils the covenant through the death and resurrection of Jesus and the gift of the Spirit, thereby revealing his faithful covenant justice and his ultimate purpose of new creation, this has the effect *both* of fulfilling the original covenant purpose (thus dealing with sin and procuring forgiveness) *and* of enabling Abraham's family to be the worldwide Jew-plus-Gentile people it was always intended to be.[24]

CHRISTIAN ZIONISM AND EVANGELICAL SOCIAL CONCERN

In the second half of the twentieth century, beginning perhaps with the U.S. civil rights movement, and then with the first Lausannne Congress in 1974, evangelical Christianity has made significant gains in the areas of social concern and social justice thinking. Christian Zionism, with its pervasive influence among evangelicals, is in a position to undermine these gains. The civil rights movement challenged the evangelical church both in the United States and internationally to consider and make explicit its position on human rights and biblical justice. The impact of this was noted and addressed in the 1966 Wheaton Declaration:

> Whereas evangelicals in the eighteenth and nineteenth centuries led in social concern, in the twentieth century many have lost the biblical perspective and limited themselves only to preaching a gospel of individual salvation without sufficient involvement in their social and community responsibilities.... We urge all evangelicals to stand openly and firmly for racial equality, human freedom, and all forms of social justice throughout the world.[25]

Eight years later the same theme was endorsed internationally in the Lausanne Covenant.

> We affirm that God is both the Creator and the Judge of all people. We therefore should share his concern for justice and reconciliation throughout human society and for the liberation of men and women from every kind of oppression. Because men and women are made in the image of God, every person, regardless of race, religion, color, culture, class, sex or age, has an intrinsic dignity

---

24. Ibid., 37.
25. "Wheaton Declaration," 23–24.

because of which he or she should be respected and served, not exploited. Here too we express penitence both for our neglect and for having sometimes regarded evangelism and social concern as mutually exclusive.[26]

At their simplest, evangelical perspectives on social justice are based on three biblical assertions. First, human dignity is based on the recognition that men and women are created in the image and likeness of God. All people bear the *imago Dei* and on that basis are afforded basic human rights regardless of race, creed, gender, disability, economic or social status. Secondly, God acts to liberate the poor and the oppressed. He concretely acts in history to exalt the poor and the oppressed and to challenge all oppression. Thirdly, as a result of God's compassion and his solidarity with the poor and oppressed, it is expected that God's people will authenticate their identity by being on the side of the poor and the oppressed (Jer 22:13–17; Ezek 16:49–50).

But Christian Zionism will have none of this. The state of Israel is equated with the people of God, and the Palestinian people are treated as unimportant, second-class citizens. To take one pertinent example: while the per capita GDP in 2009 in Israel was USD $28,400, the 48th highest in the world, in the Gaza and the West Bank it was just USD $2,800, ranking 166th.[27]

While there are some moderate voices,[28] they are rare, and most of the time Christian Zionists never challenge Israel's behavior. Even Israel's most extreme actions, including home demolitions, deportations, and the extensive bombing campaign of Gaza in early 2009, fail to generate censure. In fact, it is just the opposite. The UN Goldman Report (written by a Jewish jurist), which was critical of the conduct of both Israel and Hamas during the 2009 Gaza conflict, was vehemently attacked for its criticism of the Israeli military.

Evangelical Christians need to take care not to allow the watering down of the biblical demands for justice in the Middle East. The evangelical social justice heritage is significant and important. It is theologically orthodox and distinctive, and it is a platform for witness to a watching world. Christian Zionism's tacit support for violence and power as

---

26. "Lausanne Covenant," ¶ 5, "Christian Social Responsibility."

27. CIA, *World Factbook*. In Israel 23 percent of the population are estimated to live below the poverty line, while in Gaza and the West Bank the number is 46 percent.

28. See Wilson, *Armageddon Now*, 196–98; Walvoord, *Israel in Prophecy*, 19; Yaakov, "Unexpected Alliance," 80–81.

a solution and remedy fly in the face of Christian teaching. Thus John Stott is absolutely correct in identifying Christian Zionism as "biblically untenable."[29]

It is deeply troubling that evangelicals rightly scandalized by poverty and injustice inflicted upon the poor in India or Darfur seem, influenced by Christian Zionist propaganda, to be unable to question the actions of Israel on issues such as the expansion of settlements on Palestinian land, the blockade of Gaza, the scandalous poverty of Palestinians or the daily humiliations they endure under Israeli occupation.

SOME PROPOSALS FOR A WAY FORWARD

Informed evangelical Christians need to take responsibility for this state of affairs, and begin to challenge the Zionist mindset. The following proposals are put forward as a plan of action.

First, Christian leaders should take the challenge of Christian Zionism seriously as a threat that undermines its intellectual base. A determined effort is needed to carefully research the issues, in particular the biblical requirement for justice, and the ethics of God's kingdom. Justice should be an exegetical key, for justice and compassion can authenticate the character of true ministry, as well as form an essential element of effective discipleship. After the research has been done, church leaders should be prepared to facilitate healthy discussion on Zionism, confidently and respectfully, while guiding the congregations God has entrusted to them.

Second, evangelicals should reach out on the broad popular level, countering the influence of popular Zionist writers such as Tim LaHaye,[30]

---

29. See Wagner, "Beyond Armageddon." Wagner writes, "In February 1987, I had an opportunity to meet Dr. Stott and asked 'What is your perspective now on Zionism and Christian Zionism in particular?' He paused, then answered: 'After considerable study, I have concluded that Zionism and especially Christian Zionism are biblically untenable.'" Wagner comments, "Dr. Stott's response is significant for several reasons. First, it marks a clear position by one of the world's great Evangelical thinkers, a leader of impeccable credentials. Second, it reflects the logical conclusion of a Lausanne Evangelical who may not have had cause to ponder the Palestine question until the late 1980s, but clearly had changed his thinking by 1988. Third, it is a reminder that changes among Evangelicals on an issue such as Palestine must have a clear biblical foundation, or there will be no change at all."

30. E.g., LaHaye and Ice, *Charting the End-Times*.

Hal Lindsey,[31] David Pawson,[32] and the late Derek Prince.[33] A steady stream of books has challenged Christian Zionism over the last thirty years, but not many are readily accessible, and some assume their readers already have background knowledge and agree with their position. Christian Zionism does not thrive among biblically or theologically literate people; it thrives where believers have weak foundations and poor interpretative skills, and follow a style of leadership that discourages independent thinking and the tackling of tough issues. A clear, reasoned, popular and easily accessible evangelical response is called for. Such a response would lay out the issues concisely and methodically, building a biblical, historical, and moral case.[34]

Third, the charge of anti-Semitism has a powerful censoring effect upon Christians. It arouses a sense of guilt and revulsion, anchored in the healthy recognition of historical Christian complicity in anti-Semitism. We recoil from the term as well as we are mindful of the dangers to our ministries should the accusation gain traction in others' minds. We need to take care to carefully demarcate the space between a robust resistance to the injustice of expansionist Zionism and the evils of anti-Semitism. To question Zionism, to critique its abuses, is not anti-Semitic. Indeed, to critique the state of Israel and to challenge Zionism, rather than being anti-Semitic, is an act of courage and compassion towards Israel that encourages lasting peace and prosperity for her and the region. As Nelson Mandela said of a similar struggle in South Africa,

> My hunger for the freedom of my own people became a hunger for the freedom of all people, white and black. I knew as well as I knew anything that the oppressor must be liberated just as surely as the oppressed. A [person] who takes away another [person's] freedom is a prisoner of hatred . . . is locked behind bars of prejudice and narrow-mindedness. I am not truly free if I am taking away someone else's freedom, just as surely as I am not free when my freedom is taken from me. The oppressed and the oppressor alike are robbed of their humanity.[35]

31. E.g., Lindsay, *Late Great Planet Earth.*
32. E.g., Pawson, *When Jesus Returns.*
33. E.g., Prince, *Promised Land.*
34. Web-based resources for small group and congregational use and study are available, although of varying quality. The website Challenging Christian Zionism, at http://www.christianzionism.org, is a good place to start.
35. Mandela, *Long Walk,* 624.

Fourth, we need real engagement with the Palestinian church and Christian community, listening to their perspective without the noise of Christian Zionist propaganda. Christians in Palestine are our brothers and sisters in Christ, and we need to listen to and respect their stories. We do this by reading, inviting them to visit our churches to tell their stories, and following their blogs. We need to get away from pre-scripted "Holy Land" tours and get among the Palestinian people and their hospitality. Forty-eight hours on the West Bank can totally change a person's perspective on Zionism.

Finally, evangelicals need to recover peacemaking as a central mark of Christian witness. Our congregations should be "peace churches," clearly renouncing violence and coercive power. Christian Zionism will not thrive where peace and compassion towards all exist and where each human encounter bears the possibility of seeing the face of Christ.

CONCLUSION

Ultimately our response to the challenge of Christian Zionism needs to take place and make sense at the grassroots level of each congregation. That is where serious challenges to orthodoxy take root and quietly grow. As evangelical Christians, we should note with concern the way that Christian Zionism undermines evangelical theology and worldview, especially our proud social justice heritage that stretches back to Wesley and Wilberforce. Christian Zionism's preoccupation with the interpretation of presumed predictive elements of the prophetic tradition, particularly around the land as covenant promise, has failed to address the ethical, social, or the deeper redemptive meaning of these texts. The result has been an attenuating influence on evangelical social thinking as well as on orthodox theology. While we should take seriously the scriptural imperative to bring comfort to the Jewish people, Christian Zionism is not the way to do it. Rather, Christian Zionism needs to be challenged and thoroughly critiqued, and concern for peace and justice throughout our world, and especially in Palestine, needs to be vigorously reasserted and placed back squarely in the center of personal Christian discipleship and congregational life.

10

When Land Is Layered

Jacob in Conversation with Colonizer (James Cook) and Colonized (Te Horeta Te Taniwha)

Steve Taylor

An autobiographical note might best introduce this chapter and the place it occupies within this volume. I write as a New Zealand Pakeha, my life unavoidably and powerfully shaped by the actions of my ancestors who migrated from Great Britain to settle in Aotearoa New Zealand in the nineteenth century. One response to my narrative of migration is placed as guilty Other, complicit in indigenous (in this case Maori) experiences of displacement, colonization, and marginalization. Through an act of ancient migration, I now walk on anOther's land.

Paul Ricoeur suggests a three-step process in interpreting texts. First, there is *the world behind the text*.[1] Second, there is *the world in the text*.[2] Third, there is *the world in front of the text*. "The fact is, however,

---

1. "A visit to the world behind the text is indispensable for the interpreter ... the content of the text and its message are clothed in the terms, ideas, symbols, concepts, and categories which are current in the author's world. If the interpreters do not give serious attention to that world *behind* the text, whatever they say about the world *within* the text—the literary context—will be less than it should be." Tate, *Biblical Interpretation*, 56. Tate refers to Ricoeur, *Essays*.

2. "The ability to recognize [genres] enhances a reader's appreciation for the literary artistry of literature.... The interpretation of a text is exactly that—the interpretation of the whole and not just the stringing together of the interpretations of disjoined individual units. A narrative, a poem, a gospel, an apocalypse, or an epistle is a single generic whole, and each must be approached with full knowledge of the conventions and dynamics characteristic of it." Tate, *Biblical Interpretation*, 71.

none of us are model readers . . . ; moreover, no two readers are identical; neither are we ever individually the same reader twice . . . ; each reader has an individual imagination and as such fills out a text in individualistic ways."[3] This suggests that one way to approach a biblical study of land is to begin with *the world in front of the text*, specifically by foregrounding personal narratives of migration, as a way of paying attention to biblical narratives regarding land.

Thus a few years ago, I began a process of reading the Bible, specifically looking for texts that narrated journeys of migration. The Jacob narrative of Gen 28:10–18 is one such text. The text narrates a migrant journey. Central to the narrative is the dream of every migrant—that of finding a landed place that is safe and prosperous. These are the "pull" factors of migration, and Gen 28:10–18 begins a journey that will include the migrant (Jacob) finding a new business and a new business partner (Laban). Over time, Jacob becomes en-"joined," as many migrants do, in marriage (to Leah and Rachel). Equally evident in this migrant narrative are the "push" factors, for example, the familial conflict that exists between Jacob and Esau.

Migration is never only individual; it is always communal. So Gen 28:10–18 is essential, both physically and as narrative, in the shift in identity that Jacob experiences (being renamed "Israel"), in which identity is located between a people and a "promised land." In naming this migrant reality, a "missing voice" must also be heard; for in the claim of "promised land" the migrant's descendants have become occupier and displacer, bringing about a contested legacy that haunts our planet to this day.

Thus the act of reading *the world in front of the text*, specifically with regard to migration, brings into focus a complex relationship between migration and land. A resonance emerges between my location as Pakeha and the post-colonial awareness of anOther's land, and the Jacob narrative.

As a next step in the research process, and in order to deliberately accentuate *the world in front of the text,* I examined a set of literary texts. *The Writing of New Zealand: Inventions and Identities* is a collection of writings chosen because of the way "various New Zealands have been invented and reinvented in writing . . . [as] an ongoing exploration of

---

3. Ibid., 162.

what it can mean to be from this place."[4] The collection includes a pair of texts grouped under the "Discoveries." These are "James Cook: The Voyage of the *Endeavour*"; and "Te Horeta Te Taniwha: An Account of Cook's Visit."[5]

In reading these two texts, migrant journeys and the colliding of worlds are brought into focus. The voices of colonizer (James Cook) and colonized (Te Horeta Te Taniwha) lie alongside each other. They undermine a "European preoccupation with discovery," revealing themselves as "transparently fallible and timebound interpreters."[6] To use these readings helps to foreground *the world in front of the text* as one with multiple narrations of the Other. Land is layered, replete with narratives of colonized and colonizing. This then opens up new angles on the Jacob narrative and, in turn, biblical theologies of land. Application can also be made with regard to contemporary issues surrounding Israel and Palestine.

In sum, in foregrounding the world in front of the text by conducting a migrant's reading of Gen 28:10–18, fresh contours for a theology of land are suggested.

A PRE-PEOPLED READING OF GENESIS 28:10–18

We begin with a pre-peopled reading. It is always tempting to conceive a migrant's journey as proceeding from one peopled place to another peopled place. In doing so land can become viewed as a category that exists only in relation to people.

Land

But what about the land—any land—pre-people? What does it mean to conduct a pre-peopled reading, to engage migratory texts respectful of the whole of the natural environment that precedes people? Such a reading is in fact suggested when one considers the narratives of Gen 1 and 2 in a linear fashion. They start with the forming and shaping of land and wildlife. Only subsequently are humans birthed by the *ruach*, or breath, of God.

---

4. Calder, *Writing of New Zealand*, 9.

5. Ibid., 19–22, 26–30. The other two texts are "Te Rangi Hiroa: The Discovery of New Zealand," 15–18; and "Joseph Banks: *Endeavour* Journal," 23–26.

6. Calder, *Writing of New Zealand*, 11.

To conduct such a reading with specific reference to Gen 28, one might employ *Nga Uruora* by Geoff Park.[7] The book uses multiple readings (ecological, historical, personal narrative) to offer fresh perspectives on the landscapes of Aotearoa New Zealand and human relationships with the land. In doing so, it offers a pre-peopled reading of the land. We learn of a land of giant trees and abundant birdlife. We are reminded that Aotearoa New Zealand is a land of fertile flatlands, richly silted with pliant humus, "ancient, stored soil carbon [that will] be exported out of the ecosystem with the butter, milk and meat."[8] Park notes the presence of pre-existent highways—in the form not of roads, but of rivers that will become the conduits by which Maori convey fish and pipi. *Nga Uruora* suggests a pre-peopled reading in which land might be seen as gift; or in the words of Wakefield, land as "immense surplus of native productions," "level ground . . . deep and navigable rivers," "one of the fittest places in the world for an industrious and enterprising colony."[9]

Walter Brueggemann suggests four categories by which the Israelites framed their relationship with the land.[10]

- *Land is gift*; not to be taken and occupied, but enjoyed in gratitude, in relationship with the Gift-Giver.
- *Land is temptation*; for land comes with the possibility of forgetting the work of the Gift-giver—God active in creation of land and of the nation of Israel, redeeming from slavery in Egypt and through desert migration.
- *Land is task*; and so the Torah provided guidance by which land might be managed responsibly.
- *Land is threat*; for to cross the watery boundary that is the Jordan River takes courage.

Using a text like *Nga Uruora* to conduct a pre-peopled reading offers similar resonances. The "immense surplus" of "ancient, stored soil carbon" suggests New Zea/*land* is *gift*.[11] Simultaneously, this *gift* of "immense surplus" becomes a *task* for every migrant people. Whether

---

7. Park, *Nga Uruora*.
8. Ibid., 24.
9. Ibid., 25, citing Wakefield, *British Colonization*, 296.
10. Brueggemann, *Land*, 43–65.
11. Park, *Nga Uruora*, 24-25, citing Wakefield, *British Colonization*, 71.

Maori, Pakeha, or Asian, all people are faced with the task of making a living in and from the gift of New Zea/*land*. Such a *task* opens the migrant to *temptation*, for "[h]ow we inhabit a place can be the most telling expression of how we sense its worth, our intention for it and our connection with it."[12] Land is *threat*, for New Zea/*land* will become a mirror, reflecting "the tremendous violence and waste that attended the furious, meticulous work of Britain's mission in New Zealand."[13] Our actions become a demonstration of our theological understandings. Will we respect gift and go about our tasks justly? Or will we give in to the temptation to exploit both the gift of land and all others who live in the land?

Thus employing *Nga Uruora* offers us a pre-peopled reading. It suggests that all theologies of land—whether biblical, contemporary Middle Eastern, or in New Zea/*land*—must start with an appreciation of land as gift, task, temptation, and threat. This is the first layer of a "landed" reading.

What might such a reading allow us to hear with specific regard to Gen 28:10–18? First, before Jacob, there was land. Jacob is walking across what were then the prodigiously fertile alluvial plains of the Middle East. Jacob is offered these fertile lands as gift: "I will give you and your descendants the land on which you are lying" (28:13). He appreciates this gift: "How awesome is this place!" (28:17). How similar, perhaps to those who first see New Zea/*land* (whether Pacific explorer or Pakeha settler). We see this in Edward Gibbon's response to the gift of New Zea/*land*, in which he enthuses over this "immense surplus."[14] Such is the human response to gift. And is not land as task and temptation suggested by the pun in Gen 28:14? "Your descendants will be like dust." Will Jacob's descendants turn the prodigiously fertile alluvial plains that were the Middle East into a dustbowl? Thus a pre-peopled reading brings to the foreground the fact that theologically and biblically, land is gift, and with the gift comes task. Such is the challenge for all migrants.

---

12. Park, *Nga Uruora*, 21.
13. Ibid., 20–21.
14. Ibid., 25, citing Wakefield, *British Colonization*, 71.

Indigenous Species

One final note on this pre-peopled reading. This comes by reading a very different pre-peopled reading, the poem "Tuatara" by Nola Borrell.[15] The poem is written from the perspective of a tuatara (indigenous lizard). Again, as with *Nga Uruora*, it allows us to consider a pre-peopled reading. The poem commences with the tuatara advising the migrant

> Keep your distance
> you're new here
> rough-edged and arrogant

Such words apply to all migrants, whether recent or not, whether Maori or Pakeha or Asian; for all migrants step onto land as gift. Surely the Middle Eastern equivalent of a tuatara would have gazed on Jacob as he slept the night at Haran. "Tuatara" reminds us that any pre-peopled reading of land as gift includes wildlife. With the *gift* of land comes the *task* of caring for indigenous species.

Such a reminder is consistent with the narratives of Gen 1 and 2. Days five and six affirm that pre-people the land will "teem with living creatures" "according to their kinds" (1:20, 24). And with that gift comes the responsibility. Will the dust of the descendants cause the destruction of indigenous species? Or will the land, pre-peopled with wildlife, have the last word? Hence the salutary reminder which concludes "Tuatara."

> Not that I'm worried
> I've outlived the dinosaur
> I may outlive you
> How many years did you say you'd been here?

Thus far, we have seen how several literary texts aid us in conducting a first, pre-peopled reading of the Jacob narrative. Reading *the world in front of the text* has suggested elements essential to a migrant theology: that before the migrant (whether Jacob, Maori or Pakeha), was land—"peopled" with indigenous species, offered as both gift and responsibility.

---

15. Borrell, "Tuatara," 216.

A SECOND READING: TE HORETA TE TANIWHA

In the days long past, when I was a very little boy, a vessel came to Whitianga.[16]

So begins the narrative of Te Horeta Te Taniwha, his account of encountering the *Endeavour*. Colonizers tend to imagine an empty land. Reading the account by Te Horeta reminds us that New Zealand was already peopled. The text of Gen 28 hints at a similar narrative. A textual note in the Good News Bible suggests that 28:11 be translated "When [Jacob] reached a 'holy place.'" If Jacob is migrant and visitor, then this place can only be holy because a people have already named it "holy." Sensitized by reading Te Horeta, we wonder if Jacob is in fact not alone. Surely he is crossing a land already peopled.

This has immediate implications. Does this mean that Yawheh has not offered Jacob a vacant land, but rather a partnership in a land already peopled? What might this suggest about the way a migrant might view ownership in relation to land?

Ownership of Land

In fact, different understandings of ownership are immediately apparent when reading the narrative provided by Te Horeta:

> Our tribe was living there at that time. We did not live there as our permanent home, but were there according to our custom of living for some time on each of our blocks of land, to keep our claim to each and that our fire might be kept alight on each block, so that it might not be taken from us by some other tribe.[17]

For Te Horeta, this New Zea/*land* is not a vacant lot for a European colonizer, like Cook, to own. Neither is his understanding of ownership consistent with European views of land. For Te Horeta, ownership does not require constant occupation. Rather, people move around their land, given the "custom of living for some time on each of our blocks of land." For Te Horeta, empty land can still be owned land.

Contrast this with Captain Cook's English eye. He comes from a culture in which ownership is evident because land is fenced and hedged "so that not for a moment would the ownership of a single square inch

16. "Te Horeta Te Taniwha," 26.
17. Ibid.

… be open to doubt or dispute."[18] Thus culturally, while for Maori "our tribe was living there," to a European eye this fertile New Zealand was vacant and untouched.

> "The impression given in the *Endeavour* journals was of a fertile land left wild and barely entered … a few meager cultivations, fishing nets and canoes in the muddy river, and beyond, an emptiness never used, where all had yet to be created."[19]

Given this cultural perspective, if land was empty, it deserved to be forfeited. Note the cultural clash evident in the 1843 New Zealand Company newsletter.

> All this chatter about the rights of the natives to land which they have let idle and unused for so many centuries cannot do away with the fact that, according to God's law they have established their right to a very small portion of these islands.[20]

Yet for Te Horeta, empty land can be owned land. Further, empty land can actually be managed land. Te Horeta hints at a strategy of land management as he notes that "our fire might be kept alight on each block." In *Nga Ururoa*, Park makes this clear, describing the use of fire as essential to Maori land management. Park argues that Maori had a highly developed "give-and-take" relationship with their land, a "landscape manipulation" based on observation of the land and its fragility, and on an intentional cultivation of indigenous plants, including lowland forests.[21]

The understandings of land ownership evident in Te Horeta's account suggest another way of understanding God's gift of land to Jacob (Gen 28:13). Perhaps God was not giving Jacob land to own and fence? Instead, if Jacob was being watched by not only wildlife, but also humans, then was God not giving Jacob land to use in harmony and sustainable partnership with those who are already present?

This suggests a theology of land in which gift is framed in terms of partnership. Could the Maori understanding of land offer a different hermeneutical lens by which to read Gen 28 in the Middle East today?

---

18. Park, *Nga Uruora*, 26.
19. Ibid., 50.
20. Ibid., citing a 1843 New Zealand Company newspaper.
21. Ibid., 46.

The Supernatural

> *One of our aged men said to our people, "He [Cook] is asking for an outline of this land"; and that old man stood up, took the charcoal, and marked the outline of Te Ika a Maui. . . . After some time the chief goblin [Cook] took some white stuff, on which he made a copy of what the old chief had made on the deck, and then spoke to the old chief. The old chief explained the situation of the Reinga at the North Cape . . . but the goblins did not appear to understand anything about the world of spirits spoken of by the old chief.*[22]

The narrative of Te Horeta is marked by an awareness of the supernatural world. Asked to draw their land, Maori name a spirit world that is integrated with how they map, or narrate, their land. The place of supernatural is evident at other places in Te Horeta's narrative. The *Endeavour* is a "tupua, a god," and the ships crew is made up of "goblins."[23]

Such a reading warns us not to walk past the supernatural spirituality that might be present in the Jacob narrative. What types of supernatural deities were worshipped at the "holy place" of Gen 28:11? The stairway to heaven (28:12) has linguistic links to Mesopotamian mythology in which a stairway is used by messengers and the deity descended to their earthly temple.[24]

Yet it was precisely at this stairway, in the holy place of anOther, that Jacob experiences the "I Am" that is the God of Abraham and Isaac (28:13). This suggests another approach to religious pluralism. What does it mean for Christian readers of the Jacob story to be comfortable enough to be able to find "I Am" in anOther's holy place—whether mosque, temple, or dance party? With specific reference to New Zealand, could the missionaries that follow Cook be as comfortable in Maori "holy places" as Jacob?

The Hospitality of Cross-Cultural Exchange

> *When these goblins came on shore we (the children and women) took notice of them, but we ran away from them into the forest . . . These goblins [Cook's sailors] began to gather oysters, and we gave*

---

22. "Te Horeta Te Taniwha," 28.
23. Park, *Nga Uruora*, 26.
24. Walton and Matthews, *Genesis–Deuteronomy*, 59.

> *some kumara, fish, and fern-root to them. These they accepted, and we (the woman and children) began to roast cockles for them.*[25]

There is a generous hospitality that runs through Te Horeta's narrative. Perhaps the hospitality is simply the idealism of initial contact, pre-fatal impact. Nevertheless, they serve to renegotiate relationships between people.

First, the sharing of cockles as acts of hospitality with Cook's sailors leads to a different level of understanding. For "we saw that these goblins were eating kumara, fish, and cockles, we were startled, and said, 'Perhaps they are not goblins like the Maori goblins.'"[26] In other words, perspectives are being changed. While the fear of the other is a marker of much cross-cultural encounter, the narrative of Te Horeta affirms the power of food to humanize relationships, break prejudice, and enhance cross-cultural engagement.

Hospitality as a theme reoccurs in Te Horeta's account. He describes being given (what they later came to know as) seed potatoes. What is significant is that when planted, they are not to be kept, but to be gifted again.

> After these parareka [seed potatoes] had been planted for three years, and there was a good quantity of them, a feast was given, at which some of the potatoes were eaten, and then a general distribution of seed parareka was made amongst the tribes of Waikato and Hauraki.[27]

New technologies are often at the forefront of cross-cultural exchange. Here seed potatoes are gifted to Maori, and then gifted again among Maori. Awareness of new technologies in relation to migrant journeys provides yet another angle of appreciation with regard to the Jacob narrative. Is it too much to consider that while with Laban Jacob will discover "new technologies" in the form of techniques to increase fertility rates among stock (Gen 30:37–43)?[28] For Walton, "Jacob applies the science of his day to compensate for Laban's shrewd strategy . . . Jacob therefore engages in common sense selective breeding as a means to produce strong, healthy offspring (30:41)." And the use of seed potatoes

---

25. "Te Horeta Te Taniwha," 26–27.
26. Ibid., 27.
27. Ibid., 29.
28. Walton, *Genesis*, 590. See also Wenham, *Genesis 16–50*, 256.

as gift among Maori invites us to consider how might Jacob offer such "new technologies" when he returns from Haran to Israel?

In sum, the narrative of Te Horeta has been employed as a way of reading the Jacob narrative. Three themes have been outlined: those of land ownership, the supernatural, and the hospitality of cross-cultural gift exchange. Each of them has been in turn helped to spotlight elements that might be important in the Jacob story, and more generally in cross-cultural settings.

Some tentative possibilities have begun to emerge that might assist in a more post-colonial theology of land. Before turning to that we would do well to read the narrative of James Cook.

A THIRD READING: COOK'S DIARY

The diary entries of James Cook's moment of encounter with the coastline that is Te Horeta's spans four days. Two themes dominate: firstly that of weather, and secondly that of mapping.

Weather

Each day begins with a description of the weather.

> Thursday 9. Variable light breezes and cool weather. Friday 10th. Gentle breezes and Varble [sic], the remainder a Strong breeze at ENE and Hazey [sic] weather. Saturday 11th. Fresh gales at ENE and Clowdy hazey [sic] weather with rain. Sunday 12th. PM had strong gales at NE and hazey [sic] rainy weather, AM a fresh breeze at NW and Clear weather.[29]

The weather is a feature entirely absent from Te Horeta's narrative. Yet for Cook, the weather is essential. This serves to remind us that while Cook is colonizer, he is also, as sailor, at nature's mercy. This vulnerability, of being at the mercy of the elements, invites us to consider afresh the encounter between colonizer and colonized.

The Spirit of God is often portrayed within the biblical text as like the wind. For Cook, it is literally the wind that guides his journey. How might we consider the Wind of God as somehow blowing Cook and Te Horeta together and shaping a history that will never again be the same? What might be the role of providence in bringing peoples together?

---

29. "James Cook: The Voyage of the Endeavour," 19–22, specifically 19, 20.

The weather also reminds us that all people coming to Aotearoa New Zealand migrate by way of the sea. Crossing water is essential to the act of Pacific migration. But this experience of migration is alien to Jacob, whose journey occurs over land. Indeed, for Israel, to migrate across the sea required meeting Leviathan—in ancient Near Eastern symbolism, a "common symbol to represent a watery chaos that threatens life in the world."[30] This is a "missing" element in the Jacob narrative. We pause and honor the courage of all those who migrate to New Zealand, facing the chaos of the unknown, whether in a canoe, sailing ship, or Boeing 747.

Mapping

> *I went with two Boats accompanied [sic] by Mr Banks and the other gentlemen into the River which empties it self [sic] into the head of this Bay in order to examine it.*[31]

Essential to Cook's mission is the task of mapping. Land is new and definition is required. It is tempting to view Cook's migrant practice of naming as a form of colonization. Yet it is a persistent and recurring theme. Jacob defines land and place in Gen 28:19: "He called that place Bethel, though the city used to be called Luz." Further, Maori songs describe the acts of naming undertaken by their migrant ancestors.

> I will sing, I will sing of my ancestor Kupe!
> He it was who severed the land.
> So that Kapiti, Mana and Aropawa
> Were divided off and stood apart[32]

Might it be that mapping is a persistent theme in all human migration?

Indeed, in Gen 2:19, "naming" is the first task of the first *adam*. This invites us to consider the notion that to name is a very ancient way to begin participating in a place. Is it even a theological task, essential to being human? As migrants, past and present, map and name, are they participating in God's design for humans (as narrated in the Genesis creation account)?

If so, such a theology of land must consider the entirety of the Gen 2 narrative, which describes how, after naming, "not one of them was

---

30. "Monsters." *DBI*, 562.
31. "James Cook: The Voyage of the Endeavour," 19.
32. "Te Rangi Hiroa: The Discovery of New Zealand," 18.

a suitable companion to help" (2:20). Such naming is in itself a type of mapping. It suggests that in naming (or mapping), the *adam*, the first migrant, discovers they are in fact incomplete. It begins the search for a "helper suitable" (2:18). This opens up a fascinating interplay between mapping and migration. The act of naming should initiate a fresh sense of one's dependency, one's need for another, and the willingness to make space for new partnerships.

Might there be some clue here for a theology in relation to the land? Might in fact the very act of naming become the vehicle by which the voice of anOther might be heard, and by which space is opened to find a fresh configuration of being human? If so, this gives shape to a theology of providence, in which the Wind of the Spirit blows cultures together—not to colonize, but to discover their incompleteness and to be offered new possibilities in the task of being human.

Such a reading is well beyond that intended by Cook. But this reading the *world in front of the text* invites us to ponder afresh theology at the intersection of land, providence and human acts of mapping.

A POST-COLONIAL READING?

I have used four readings—*Nga Uruoa*, a poem by Nola Burrell, Te Horeta, and Cook's diary—to read the world in front of the biblical text. Themes of land, indigenous species, ownership, supernatural, hospitality, weather, and mapping have opened up some fresh angles with regard to the migrant journey of Jacob in Gen 28:10–18. Many resonate with post-colonial themes. These include the following:

- Land has been reframed to include indigenous species, and to be considered as both gift and responsibility to all migrants.

- Pluralism has been considered in light of Jacob's ability to discern "I Am" in the "holy place" of anOther.

- Awareness of Eurocentric narratives of power and control has been raised by hearing Maori understandings of land ownership, and subverted by considering a theology of providence that opens up space for the discovery of new configurations of being human.

- Reaction against Western ways of thinking and producing has been unearthed in relation to the presence of the supernatural.

- The prominence of diaspora and indigenous issues has been heard in terms of all peoples as migrants. Indeed, all people who live in Aotearoa New Zealand have, by the very fact of New Zealand being an island, had ancestors who have had to cross "watery chaos." Further, we have been exposed to hospitality as a potential mark of cross-cultural exchange, along with the potential of food to renegotiate human relationships.

This reading strategy presents itself as post-colonial in relation to a theology of land. It has used a variety of texts to deliberately read the *world in front of the text*. In so doing, it has approached what might be a familiar story in a way that has opened up new angles.

It also suggests some questions with regard the theme of the gospel and the land of promise.

- What practices are needed in order for indigenous species to be viewed as an essential part of God's gift?
- Was the promised land given as a vacant lot? Or is Israel expected to work in partnership with existing peoples?
- How might the holy place of anOther be approached as a vehicle for divine encounter?
- What place might food and acts of hospitality play in enhancing cross-culture exchange?
- Might the work of God in bringing peoples together in the Middle East be for the purpose of increasing a sense of incompleteness and need for anOther?

These questions can only be tentative and are based simply on a method of reading *the world in front of the text*. Nevertheless, we have seen that employing a variety of literary texts to deliberately read *the world in front of the text* can produce some unexpected riches and create fresh possibilities for faith and human identity in colonized spaces.

11

"God Has by No Means Rejected His People" (Rom 11:1)
A Response to the Accusation of "Replacement Theology."

Philip Church

INTRODUCTION

Some people will no doubt respond to this book with the charge of "replacement theology." An earlier version of chapter 4 was published in 2009 as part of a book giving five views on the land of Israel,[1] in which each of the five authors had the opportunity to respond to the others. Of my contribution one said, "This is replacement theology."[2] Soon after the book was published, a fellow parishioner took me aside and expressed surprise that my support for replacement theology had been so strong, and about the same time a New Zealander living in Italy sent me a copy of a book he had written on the subject.[3] Not only was I suspected of holding to replacement theology, but this was (quite rightly) seen to be a bad thing. I determined that the charge warranted some response. In this chapter I hope to show that it is groundless, and indeed, that those who make such charges are open to the suspicion of replacement theology themselves, albeit of a different type.

---

1. Church, "Promised Land," 15–25.
2. McDowell, "Response," 71.
3. Diprose, *Israel*. This book is a published version of the author's PhD thesis.

SUPERSESSIONISM

Replacement theology is a popular and somewhat emotive term for "supersessionism," that is, the notion that the church has "replaced Israel in the drama of redemption," and that the chosen people have "been superseded with the coming of Christ."[4] Gabriel Fackre identifies five types of supersessionism: "retributive replacement," which suggests that God turned from faithless Israel and abrogated the covenant after they turned from him and rejected Christ;[5] "nonretributive replacement," which focuses on the saving act of God in Christ, bringing the former age to an end and inaugurating the new age;[6] "modified replacement," which gives Jewish identity an ongoing place, but denies that "contemporary Judaism is a continuation of the Abrahamic faith of ancient Israel," pointing rather to the "sole-sufficiency of Christ as the way to God";[7] "messianic replacement," which stresses Jewish evangelism along with the necessity for Jews who have come to faith in Christ to retain their Jewish identity, thus replacing traditional Judaism with messianic Judaism;[8] and "Christological election," which proposes that Israel has a continuing place in the purposes of God in spite of her rejection of Christ and present alienation from God. This alienation is only temporary and ultimately "all Israel will be saved."[9] Thus the church has replaced Israel, but only for a time.[10] There is an element of truth in Fackre's categories of nonretributive replacement (for the coming of Christ has indeed in-

---

4. Fackre, *Ecumenical Faith*, 147. Kim, *Polemic*, 6–7, works with a definition provided by Littell, *Crucifixion*, 30, that supersessionism "is composed of two essential ideas: that God has abandoned the Jews, and that the church replaces the Jewish people as the New Israel." Diprose defines replacement theology as the view that "the Church completely and permanently replaced ethnic Israel in the working out of God's plan as the recipient of Old Testament promises originally addressed to Israel (*Israel*, 2).

5. Fackre, *Ecumenical Faith*, 148–49.

6. Ibid., 149–50.

7. Ibid., 150–51.

8. Ibid., 151–52.

9. Ibid., 152–53

10. Fackre places these views on a continuum from the most extreme supersessionism manifested in the retributive replacement view to the least extreme in the christological election view. The last named view is taken from Barth's exegesis of Rom 9–11, which he explains is both complex and profound, and seems to be supersessionist to the extent that while Judaism continues to exist, it does so in order to reflect God's judgment on Israel. Fackre then lists eight "antisupersessionist" views (pp. 153–62), before giving his own take on "evangelical antisupersessionism" (pp. 162–67).

Church—*"God Has by No Means Rejected His People" (Rom 11:1)* 149

augurated the new age); and modified replacement (for Christ is indeed the only way to God for both Jew and Gentile), but even here, the word "replacement" is out of place.

Diprose's book traces supersessionism from the New Testament era until the present day. It is a useful survey, although like all historical surveys, presented from a particular point of view. He detects supersessionist views in the writings of a number of authors from the post-apostolic era, starting with the Epistle of Barnabas in the second century and extending to Gregory I in the sixth.[11] Much of what he describes here probably falls into Fackre's category of retributive replacement. Diprose then discusses canon law where he finds supersessionism enshrined in ecclesiastical documents from Nicea in 325 to the fourth Lateran Council in 1215.[12] He detects a turning point in attitudes to Israel with the German author Alsted (1599–1638) and the English Puritans, Finch and Goodwin,[13] and he notes the important place of Israel in dispensationalism. Diprose, however, argues that his own work considers Israel for its own sake, rather than part of any particular theological system.[14] Nevertheless, he looks forward to Christ's reign and the fulfillment of unfulfilled Old and New Testament prophecies, which will involve Israel entering a time of national repentance leading to the inauguration of God's new covenant with this ethnic group beginning the millennium.[15]

ISRAEL AND THE CHURCH IN THE NEW TESTAMENT

Diprose's work is based on the assumption that the contemporary State of Israel can be equated with the Old Testament people of God. He opens his first chapter with the statement "[t]he term "Israel" appears over two thousand times in the Old Testament and seventy times in the New

---

11. Diprose, *Israel*, 69–93
12. Ibid., 93–96.
13. Ibid., 2, see also pp. 194 n. 9.
14. Ibid., 2–3.
15. On pp. 14–48 Diprose discusses New Testament eschatology, and it is clear that he expects a restoration of Israel to the land in a future millennium, concomitant with the restoration of the nation. Elsewhere he claims that Jer 31:31–34 refers to a new covenant "which God intends to make with Israel and Judah following a period of national repentance" (p. 11) and later (p. 13) claims that "Israel will continue to exist as a nation until they enter the new covenant relationship described [in Jer 31:31–34]."

Testament ... [to refer] to a specific ethnic group,"[16] and in a footnote adds "the nation of Israel, to which the biblical uses of the name usually refer, still exists."[17] Moreover, he calls contemporary Israel, "this elect people."[18] Thus he sees a direct line between the Old Testament nation of Israel, the ethnic descendants of these people in New Testament times, and the contemporary state of Israel.

He understands the term "the church" to refer to the people of God from apostolic times until the present, an entity quite distinct from Israel. He examines the term "the Israel of God" in Gal 6:16, and after surveying the evidence allows the possibility that it might apply to the whole people of God, including both Jew and Gentile,[19] but argues that this single text "is insufficient grounds on which to base an innovative theological concept such as understanding the church to be the new/true Israel."[20]

THE PEOPLE OF GOD IN THE NEW TESTAMENT

Nevertheless, while it might be true that the term "Israel" is not applied to the church in the New Testament, there are other considerations. A more fruitful field of enquiry is the identity of the people of God. The word *laos* appears around 140 times in the New Testament, frequently

---

16. Diprose, *Israel*, 5.

17. Ibid., 195.

18. Ibid., 25.

19. This is the view of Harvey, *True Israel*, 226, who demonstrates that Galatians argues the case that the people of God are the descendants of Abraham who believe, and that the term Israel is synonymous with this term. He concludes, "It is no longer a question of 'Jews' on one side and 'Gentiles' on the other, because the faith of Abraham ... is now displayed among the Gentiles ... Since 'Israel' has always been associated with 'the people of God' [the term] will now serve to demonstrate that ... God has one people regardless of their origin." Along similar lines, both Chrysostom and Justin Martyr concluded that the reference was to the Christian church as "the true, spiritual Israel" (Justin, "Dialogue with Trypho," 11:5), a reading followed by Nils Dahl and Ulrich Luz (cited in Bruce, *Galatians*, 274). Davies ("Paul," 10), disputes this and applies it to "the Jewish people as a whole," as also Bruce (*Galatians*, 274). Burton, *Galatians*, 358 believes it applies to a believing remnant with Israel, as does Richardson, *Israel*, 80–83, who considers that the expression refers to a remnant within Israel who "are going to come to their senses and receive the good news of Christ." Longenecker, *Galatians*, 297, suggests that this expression is a reference to Paul's opponents at Galatia, who may have referred to themselves in these terms.

20. Diprose, *Israel*, 43–44.

referring to the nation of Israel, although in several texts there is a different referent.

In Acts 15:14 James addresses the Jerusalem council, responding to Peter's speech about the spread of the gospel to the Gentiles: "Simeon has related how God first looked favorably on the Gentiles, to take from among them a people for his name."[21] In line with normal usage James uses the word *ethnos* to refer to the Gentiles, but then makes the outrageous statement that God had taken from these Gentiles (*ethnoi*) a "people (*laos*) for his name." Moreover, he finds support for this from the prophetic scriptures. James cites Amos 9:11–12, a text that refers to the rebuilding of the fallen tent of David, and claims that it is fulfilled in the inclusion of Gentiles in the people of God.[22]

Paul does something similar when he cites Hos 2:25 in Rom 9:25–26: "those who were not my people I will call 'my people.'" Like James, Paul finds support from the prophetic scriptures for his contention that "the objects of mercy that God has before prepared for glory" (Rom 9:23) include Gentiles as well as Jews.

These ideas come to full expression in Eph 2:11–12, where Gentiles, previously "without Christ ... aliens from the commonwealth of Israel, and strangers to the covenants of promise," are said to have been brought near by the blood of Christ. But this is not all. The text also claims that God has now made "one new humanity" (v. 15, those who are in Christ) out of the two (Jew and Gentile). Gentiles are "no longer strangers and aliens, but ... citizens with the saints and also members of the household of God" (v. 19). There is no suggestion that Israel has been replaced or superseded. Significantly, it is Israel who are the saints (*hagioi*) and the household of God, to whom Gentile followers of Jesus have been joined. The notion of "replacement" does not even feature. Nor is it a "Gentile" church that believing Jews become part of. It is entirely the other way around. We Gentiles are joined with the "saints" of Israel.

Peter has a similar view. Exodus 19:4–6 records God's address to the Israelites camped at the foot of Sinai,

> You have seen what I did to the Egyptians, and how I bore you on eagles' wings and brought you to myself. Now therefore, if you obey my voice and keep my covenant, you shall be my treasured

---

21. Unless otherwise noted Bible quotations are from the NRSV.

22. James has nothing to say about the suggestion that the fallen tent of David might be rebuilt again in the last days to usher in the second coming of Christ.

possession out of all the peoples. Indeed, the whole earth is mine, but you shall be for me a priestly kingdom and a holy nation.

In 1 Pet 2:9–10 Peter addresses these very words to believers in Jesus scattered throughout Asia Minor (1 Pet 1:1–2),

> but you are a chosen race, a royal priesthood, a holy nation, God's own people, in order that you may proclaim the mighty acts of him who called you out of darkness into his marvelous light. Once you were not a people, but now you are God's people; once you had not received mercy, but now you have received mercy.

These believers in Jesus, probably Gentiles,[23] are the people of God, described with words taken from Exod 19:6. Here the Exodus generation and their descendants, as well as Gentile believers in Jesus addressed by Peter are described in the same terms, intimating that there is only one people of God. Whether or not the church is the new/renewed Israel is never raised in the New Testament. What is clear, however, is that followers of Jesus, whatever their ethnic background, constitute God's people.

DEFINING THE PEOPLE OF GOD MORE CLOSELY

Had Diprose considered the identity of the people of God in the New Testament, rather than the distinction between Israel and the church he might have come up with different conclusions, for the New Testament does not restrict to Israel alone the promises of blessing announced to Abraham, but widens them so that Gentiles are included. Diprose begins with the promises to Abraham in Gen 12:1–3,[24] but overlooks the fact that this text, which refers to God's blessing of the nations through Abraham, is consistently read in the New Testament with reference to the inclusion of Gentiles in the people of God. "Those who believe," says Gal 3:7 "are descendants of Abraham." As Longenecker notes "Paul found Gentiles at the very heart of the Abrahamic covenant."[25] On the string of Old Testament texts cited in Rom 15:9–12,[26] Longenecker comments, "Paul found God's saving purpose toward Gentiles everywhere in the Old Testament . . . He wants his Gentile converts to know that they were in the mind and purpose of God when God gave his covenant to

---

23. 1 Peter 1:14, 18; 4:3 could hardly apply to ethnic Jews, see Best, *1 Peter*, 19–20.
24. Diprose, *Israel*, 5.
25. Longenecker, *Galatians*, 115.
26. Ps 18:49; 2 Sam 22:50; Deut 32:43; Ps 117:10; Isa 11:10.

Abraham."[27] Since the coming of Jesus the identity of the people of God is defined not by physical ancestry nor by ethnic descent, but by faith in Jesus.

It is clear that the New Testament authors considered Christ to inherit the promises made to the Old Testament people of God, and that the church inherits the blessings of Israel through Christ, and that in Christ, Gentiles become part of the one people of God.[28] This people began with God's election of Abraham. The Abrahamic promises of numerous descendants and of the blessing of the nations came to fruition first in the Old Testament Israelites and ultimately in Christ and his church, which has always included believing Jews.

Replacement theology is a confused category that only makes sense when a false distinction is posited between the Old Testament people of God and the New Testament people of God, and when the secular state of Israel is equated with the Old Testament people of God. A more precise term might be "extension theology." Christopher Wright writes

> the realities of Israel and the Old Testament ... [are taken] up into a greater reality in the Messiah. Christ does not *deprive* the believing Jew of anything that belonged to Israel as God's people; nor does he give the believing Gentile anything *less* than the full covenantal blessing and promise that was Israel's.[29]

REPLACING THE PEOPLE OF GOD WITH A SECULAR STATE

Nevertheless, there is another kind of replacement theology. As part of the continuing debate over my contribution to the *5 Views* book, one W. Millward wrote to the editor of the NZ Christian newspaper, *Challenge Weekly*. In a letter published in the 8 June 2009 issue, he writes, "I value the teaching that the Abrahamic covenant is God's decision to save the

---

27. Longenecker, *Galatians*, 115.

28. The suggestion that the church and Israel are to be sharply distinguished is relatively recent, stemming from the speculations of John Nelson Darby in the nineteenth century. Murray cites Darby as saying "I deny that the saints before Christ's first coming, or after his second, are part of the church [and Murray adds], [w]ith breath-taking dogmatism ... [Darby] swept away what had previously been axiomatic in Christian theology" (Murray, *Puritan Hope*, 200). For a recent treatment claiming a distinction between Israel and the Church see Wilkinson, *Zion's Sake*, 17–19. However, Wilkinson makes no attempt to justify this notion. He simply attributes it to Darby (pp. 101–2), with no critique.

29. Wright, "Christian Approach," 19.

world and it brings into being the vehicle (a people and a land) God is going to use the save the world."

While it is true that God chose Israel to be his unique vehicle to bring redemption to the world, Millward applies this to the contemporary state of Israel, as also does Rob Yule when he assigns to Israel "the responsibility to bring reconciliation in the Middle East, and administer peace and justice on earth."[30] Yet, in the one true Israelite, Jesus Christ, God has fulfilled his purposes to redeem the world and bring in his kingly reign. God's choice of Abraham was so that Abraham's offspring would be the vehicle by which he would redeem the world. That offspring was Jesus Christ, not the contemporary state of Israel. Paul's argument in Gal 3:15–18 sounds odd to twenty-first century ears, but makes the same point. The word for "offspring" is singular, not plural, and refers to Christ. To propose that God will redeem the world through the state of Israel effectively renders the suffering, death and resurrection of Christ to no effect, and is tantamount to a theology of empire, suggesting that God will bring about his kingdom through the military might of this modern secular state. In this brand of theology Christ and his church are replaced with a secular nation-state.[31]

HAS GOD AFTER ALL REJECTED HIS PEOPLE?

But, if the people of God are now the followers of Jesus, is it then true after all that God has rejected his people?

In his study of the name "Israel" in ancient Jewish and early Christian literature, Harvey suggests that the community referred to as Israel was always a mixed community of both faithful and unfaithful people.[32] This is no clearer in the New Testament than in Rom 9–11 where Paul deals with the problem of Israel's unbelief.

Paul sets the agenda for his treatment of this perplexing issue by observing this precise phenomenon. "For not all Israelites truly belong to Israel, and not all of Abraham's children are his true descendants" (Rom 9:6–7). Paul recognizes that within ethnic Israel there is a smaller group, "spiritual" or "believing" Israel, and he denies that unbelieving Jews, outside this smaller group, can be counted among the descendants

30. Yule, "Christians and Israel," 68.

31. For further development of these ideas see Church, "Dispensational Christian Zionism," 375–98.

32. Harvey, *True Israel*, 188.

CHURCH—*"God Has by No Means Rejected His People" (Rom 11:1)* 155

of Abraham. Since the descendants of Abraham are the people of God, Paul in effect excludes unbelieving Israel from God's people.

In Rom 11:1 he asks the rhetorical question. "Has God rejected his people"? He replies in the strongest possible terms, *mē genoito* (by no means)! Significantly, however, Paul's denial of supersessionism is not in terms of national Israel (whether present or future),[33] but in terms of his own Jewishness, "I myself am an Israelite, a descendant of Abraham, a member of the tribe of Benjamin. God has not rejected his people whom he foreknew" (vv. 1–2). That God has not rejected his people is seen not in the latter day restoration of Israel to the land of promise, but in God's call to Paul the Jew to follow Jesus Christ, becoming "apostle to the Gentiles," taking the good news of Jesus Christ to the heart of the Roman Empire, and ultimately dying for his faith.[34]

At the end of Rom 11 Paul summarizes his argument:

> I want you to understand this mystery: a hardening has come upon part of Israel, until the full number of the Gentiles has come in. And so all Israel will be saved; as it is written, "Out of Zion will come the deliverer; he will banish ungodliness from Jacob." (Rom 11:25–27).[35]

Given the clear distinction between Israel and the Gentiles in the first part of this quotation, it is difficult to see anything but a reference to ethnic Israel in the expression "all Israel" in 11:26.[36] In these two verses "all Israel" is compared with "part of Israel," a similar distinction with which Paul began his discussion in Rom 9:6–7 ("not all Israelites truly belong to Israel, and not all of Abraham's children are his true descendants").

These verses reflect the phenomenon present throughout Rom 9–11, that Israel is always a mixed community of faithful and unfaith-

---

33. Robertson, *Israel of God*, 179, notes that Paul's question is not "[h]as God rejected ethnic Israel with respect to his special plan for the future?" but "[h]as God rejected ethnic Israel altogether . . . ?"

34. Ibid., 210–14; Dunn, *Romans 9–16*, 644; Cranfield, *Romans*, 2: 544.

35. In this quotation Paul has changed the preposition "to" in Isa 59:20 (the deliverer will come to Zion) to "from" in Rom 11:26 (the deliverer will come out of Zion). The significance of this change will be discussed below (footnote 41).

36. Cranfield, *Romans*, 2: 576, proposes that "all Israel" could refer to (1) God's people, both Jew and Gentile, (2) the elect of the nation of Israel, (3) every individual member of ethnic Israel, and (4) ethnic Israel as a whole, but not necessarily every single member. He concludes that it is "virtually certain" that Gentiles are not included in "all Israel," and argues for his option 4 (pp. 576–77).

ful people.[37] Part of this mixed community has been hardened, and this hardening can be expected to continue, but alongside these God is calling the elect (11:13–14), and "some" are coming to faith. The conclusion to the argument in 11:25–26 is that ultimately all the elect (as in 9:6) will come to faith, and in this way (*kai houtōs*)[38] "all Israel" will be saved.[39] As Roberston argues, "all Israel" refers to "all of the elect within the community of Israel."[40] Just as only the faithful remnant is counted among Israel in Rom 9:6, so also in Rom 11:25.[41]

Consequently, "all Israel" has nothing to do with the state of Israel. It signifies all the elect among the Israelites, responding to the call of God, and coming to faith in Christ. The number of the elect grows as "some" (11:14) come to faith as Paul himself had done (Rom 11:1–2), and can be expected to continue to grow (11:15) as Israelites in greater numbers

---

37. See footnote 32 (above). In 11:5–7 Paul refers to "a remnant chosen by grace" and distinguishes between the elect (*hē eklogē*) and the rest (*hoi loipoi*) who were hardened; and in 11:14 he works as an apostle so that "some" of his own people will be saved. As Robertson, *Israel of God*, 184, notes, "God never has obligated himself to save every single individual of a particular group of people."

38. This is a logical, not a temporal expression, see ibid., 180–82.

39. Paul's thought is complex, and indeed according to this reading "all Israel" seems to refer to "the elect of Israel." It must not be forgotten that in 9:6–7 Paul has excluded unbelieving Israelites from the true Israel.

40. Ibid., 186–87. Robertson goes on, however, to suggest that a more likely reading is that "all Israel" includes all the elect, both Jew and Gentile (187–98). This seems to me to be [unlikely], in the light of the reference to "part of Israel" and "Gentiles" in the previous verse.

41. Scott, "'All Israel,'" 318–19, concludes that "all Israel" includes "the previously saved minority (the remnant) and the presently hardened majority of Israel," who will be saved at the Parousia when the deliverer comes from Zion (pp. 521–24), a reading that does not take enough account of the change in the preposition in Paul's quotation of Isa 59:20 in Rom 11:26. Scott also considers that Paul had a "Jerusalem-centred hope" (p. 493), relying on Horbury, "Land, Sanctuary and Worship," 207–24, however, Horbury's arguments are largely unconvincing. Diprose, *Israel*, 145–48, likewise argues that the reference to Zion in Rom 11:26 is an allusion to the land as part of the restoration of Israel at the Parousia. He notes the change in the preposition, but proposes that the implication is that "the deliverer will turn away the 'wickedness' . . . of "all Israel, beginning from Jerusalem" (p. 147–48). However, the implications of the changed preposition go much deeper than that. Dunn argues that it indicates that Paul "does not wish to rekindle the idea of Israel's national primacy in the last days" (Dunn, *Romans 9–16*, 682), and Walker, *Holy City*, 140–41, proposes, correctly, that the reference to Zion in this verse is connected, "not with some future event, but chiefly with Jesus' recent work accomplished in Zion/Jerusalem." This deliverance accomplished by Christ led to "the consequent going out of the gospel ('from Zion')." I am persuaded by his arguments.

come to faith. Paul is still responding to the question with which he began the chapter where he claimed that his own inclusion in the elect demonstrated that God had not rejected his people. Here he brings the argument to its logical end: ultimately all the elect (11:26, cf. 9:6) within the mixed community that is Israel will be saved (in the same way—*kai houtōs*) as they are called by God.

CONCLUSION

I do not subscribe to replacement theology; I do not believe God has rejected his people. But I do believe that there is one people of God, made up of followers of Jesus Christ, both Jew and Gentile alike, all descendants of Abraham. God stills calls individuals, both Jew (like Paul) and Gentile (like me) into this one people, and if I read Rom 11:25–26 correctly, he may yet call Jews in greater numbers. But this has no implications for the contemporary state of Israel, and indeed the New Testament says not one word about any role that this state might have in the salvation of the world. Nor does the New Testament imply that God will yet literally fulfill the Old Testament prophetic oracles of salvation with this nation in a millennium. On that topic the New Testament is silent.[42]

God has done in Christ what he purposed to do when he chose Abraham. The Old Testament prophetic oracles of salvation are fulfilled in Christ and in his church, albeit in surprising and unexpected ways. And it is the worldwide expansion of Christianity rather than the rise of Zionist nationalism that continues to fulfill the purposes of God. God has no more to offer the world or Israel in terms of redemption and salvation than what he did once and for all in Christ and in his death.

---

42. Luke 21:24 is often quoted: "Jerusalem will be trampled on by the Gentiles until the times of the Gentiles are fulfilled," usually with the implication that this period will be followed by the "times of the Jews." But that is not the only, nor indeed the most logical implication. Rather, Jesus may be simply stating that the duration of the judgment of Jerusalem was limited by God, as suggested by the parallel text in Mark 13:20 (see Walker, *Holy City*, 100–101.

12

The Gospel and the Land of Promise
A Response

TIM MEADOWCROFT

THIS ENTIRE VOLUME OF essays oscillates, sometimes untidily, between "the land of promise" as the land of the Bible and "the land of promise" as the land of Israel/Palestine[1] today. In doing so, it reflects the nature of much encounter with that piece of land. Any consideration of the gospel and the "land of promise" or the land known today as Israel/Palestine must take account of that oscillation. In this response, I shall attempt to do so around four themes that seem to me to have been raised by our various authors: the land and pilgrimage, the land and politics, the land and her people, and the land and its scriptures.

If there is a common thread running through my treatment of these themes it could be a kind of "yes, but . . ." I think it would be fair to say that the matter of the gospel and the land has been explored from a range of angles, but mostly from one side of the mountain. While I disagree with very little that I have read, because I too am at home on that side of the mountain, I found myself constantly wanting a different perspective.

---

1. Any naming of the land in question is fraught. I am using "Israel/Palestine" as a neutral term although I recognize that there is no such thing.

THE LAND AND PILGRIMAGE

Evangelicals tend not to think very much about pilgrimage and the relationship of the Christian to place. Several essays in this volume reflect that. Mark Strom reminds us of the fact that the Christian faith is one constantly translated. That is, it is lived out in different ways in different places; place is not of the essence of such a faith. Mark Keown, also working from the apostle Paul, highlights the call to a cruciform life. This is a life lived out under the reign of Christ not in Jerusalem nor in Rome but "in heaven." Philip Church then explores the notion of rest in the Christian life. Once again it is a rest "not in the promised land, Jerusalem or the temple." All of these analyses diminish the importance of the land. In his exposition of the prophet Amos, Tim Bulkeley also makes the point that loss of God's favor is more significant than the loss of land.

If all of this is true (and it is), then why was I ambushed by tears as I stood and looked for the first time at the land around Beit Sahour adjoining Bethlehem, a locale once trodden by Boaz and Ruth and their even more famous ancestors? Why was I so moved when I shifted my gaze to the hills of Moab in the distance and thought of Ruth and Naomi making their long journey home, not quite sure that it was in fact going to be home when they got there? Why am I compelled to sit on the remains of the great steps up to the Herodian temple in Jerusalem and wonder if Jesus himself trod them? It is not because the land is unimportant, surely.

Somehow the ancient Christian/human tradition of pilgrimage needs to be taken account of in any consideration of the land and the gospel. Heidegger spoke of "place" as the "house of being."[2] In so doing he recognized that connection to place is a fundamental component of our God-given humanity, although he would not have expressed it like that. And of the particular "place" under consideration in this volume, Pope John Paul II reflected thus of his own trip to the "Holy Land" in 2000:

> Just as time can be marked by *kairoi*, by special moments of grace, space too may by analogy bear the stamp of particular saving actions of God. Moreover, this is an intuition present in all religions, which not only have sacred times but also sacred spaces, where the encounter with the divine may be experienced

---

2. Cited by Sheldrake, *Spaces for the Sacred*, 7.

more intensely than it would normally be in the vastness of the cosmos.[3]

As much as for Jews and Muslims, the land of Israel/Palestine connects Christians to their very being. In pondering why my evangelical soul stubbornly continues to be moved by the land of the Bible, I have to recognise that the place connects me to the events that are foundational to my faith and hence my personhood. They are as essential to my own story as the place of my birth and the country of my patrimony. This was borne home to me one day when I entered the grotto underneath the Church of the Nativity where a star marks the alleged place of Jesus' birth. To my surprise, the Catholic academic theologian accompanying me knelt and revered that spot. For all her learning, she understood better than I the importance of place in the tapestry of faith, and in doing so taught me.

It is true that faith transcends time and culture and place. In the same vein, it is also mysteriously true, as Brevard Childs so succinctly put it, that it was possible for the people of Israel to find God while in exile from their land and to lose touch with God in the land to which he had assigned them.[4] But it is also true that God is encountered in space and time, and the places and times of that encounter carry an ongoing importance. This is inherent in the concept of incarnation, of God with us. Strom, Keown, and Church are right to remind us that the gospel cannot be merely focused on the land; there is a much larger story being told than one about a small but important land bridge at the eastern end of the Mediterranean. But in saying that, it is necessary also to wrestle with the realities of place and the legitimate urge to pilgrimage. After all, the metaphor of pilgrim discussed by Church depends for its richness on the complex relationship with place and space that is the lot of humanity.

In that respect Alistair Donaldson's essay is an important pointer to an eschatological vision that includes the land. If I were to critique that perspective, though, it would be on the basis that it too easily speaks

---

3. John Paul II, "Letter Concerning Pilgrimage."

4. Childs, *Old Testament Theology*, 244–45: "... in a real sense the theological problem of the Old Testament's understanding of the land consists in a dialectic tension which both refuses to spiritualize the commitment to the land, and yet senses that the land functions as a cipher for divine blessing which could be lost even by those living within its spatial boundaries."

with Tom Wright of the whole world as "now God's holy land, and God will reclaim it and renew it as the ultimate goal of all our wanderings."[5] While such a relativizing of land is a useful counter to the excesses of political eschatology, it does seem to leave the present-day inhabitants of one particular piece of land in something of a no man's land. And that brings us to . . .

THE LAND AND POLITICS

For land is not merely a venue for pilgrimage. It is also the canvas on which the life of peoples is drawn. Just as it is not possible to live a disembodied life, so it is not possible to live a life detached from land. And the attachment to land is particular for all peoples and not merely theoretical. And so, with respect to the particular piece of real estate under discussion, if this land is important to pilgrims, who have like Ruth adopted it into their story, it is doubly significant to the millions for whom, like their ancestor Naomi, Israel/Palestine is home in every sense of the word.[6] For those people it is both the place of their birth and their patrimony as well as the place in which the story of their faiths was written. For this reason, it is not enough simply to treat the land as a metaphor or *Vorlage*[7] or place of pilgrimage or treasured museum piece, albeit an intensely disputed one. It is also a place of political endeavor.

Whether we like it or not, the politics must be entered into; not to do so is irresponsible. I was memorably reminded of this at a Jewish-Catholic interchange in Jerusalem, during which one of the Catholic participants, a Palestinian church leader, noted the commonplace that political dialogue about the land cannot be discussed without paying attention to religious dynamics. He then wryly observed that it seems much more difficult to acknowledge that religious dialogue cannot be successful unless the political context is also confronted by the dialogue partners. If one cannot talk about land without talking about religion,

---

5. Quoting Wright, *Simply Christian*, 222.

6. In naming Naomi as "ancestor," I do not differentiate between present-day peoples of the land. I believe she may legitimately be so named by all who claim a stake in the land.

7. This is a German term referring to what "lies before" the translation, hence the original from which a translation has been made. In this context I am referring back to Strom's image of translation as the means by which the Christian faith transcends the particularities of its origins.

equally one ought not to talk about religion without talking about land. That is why a contribution such as Stephen Tollestrup's survey of the justice issues raised by the land of promise and those who live on her today is crucial to the sort of enterprise represented by this volume.

Bob Robinson's essay on Herodian Galilee is a reminder that this is not a new phenomenon. Even as the Gospels were being written, the land was a venue of contest, and things were not always as they seemed; they were "dynamic and fluid, and not static." Furthermore, Robinson's account of scholarly approaches to this phenomenon indicates that the interpretation of the land and her inhabitants is subject to vested interests. In that respect, Robinson's summary of the issues has a kind of deconstructive effect in this volume, for it leads me to ask in whose interests this book of essays has been written, or who is writing their own story into the land of promise. It seems to me that a non-Zionist interpretation of the New Testament (primarily) prevails.

THE LAND AND HER PEOPLE

This has its place. As indicated above, it does enable Christians to take a less ideologically driven approach to contemporary justice issues with respect to Israel/Palestine. But it can lead to a kind of indifference to the actual people of the land in all their complexity and ambiguity. Steve Taylor sets up a conversation between the patriarch Jacob and James Cook, the English "discoverer" of Aotearoa/New Zealand. In so doing he illustrates the "interested" nature of readings of the land. Cook thought he was discovering something. Te Horeta Te Taniwha was not aware of being undiscovered; he was merely encountering a stranger. The land of Aotearoa has suffered under what Taylor calls the "collision" of those two worlds ever since.

Any consideration of the "land of promise" must take account of the peoples who live in her and the different perspectives that they represent, and the collision of worlds that occurs when they occupy the same space. It is important that they and their perspectives are not lost in the interests of the pilgrims and other outsiders who lay some kind of religious or ideological claim to the land. In his final essay rebutting the charge of "replacement theology," Church describes the vested interests of Christian Zionists in the land, including making the point that Christian Zionism is driven much more by its own theological agenda than by any interest in an outcome for the Jewish people presently living in the land. This volume of essays has tended to privilege a Palestinian perspective, and within that a Christian Palestinian perspective, on the land. It has partly done so out of a particular understanding of the person and work of Christ. It is worth asking whether that approach is also in danger at points of neglecting the interests of those who actually live on the land.

If there is a neglected interest here it would be that of the contemporary Jew with respect to Israel/Palestine. However much we argue that the gospel is bigger than the land, however well we demonstrate from the biblical witness that relationship with the land even for Jewish people is a contingent matter, it remains difficult to avoid some entitlement for the descendants of Judah to live in that place. This must be confronted. But to do so entails an encounter with the modern-day phenomenon of the state of Israel, an occupying power with a nuclear arsenal. The best approach to this that I have encountered is that of Jeff Halper, the Israeli peace activist. He argues the case for a cultural Zionism that has been disentangled from the nationalist ideology that became an inextricable part of late nineteenth century Zionist aspirations.[8] Such an approach affirms the entitlement of Jewish people to live on the land while questioning whether the best vehicle for enabling this to happen is a Jewish democracy. Indeed, he would argue, as his subtitle indicates, that to eschew a militarist nationalist agenda is the path to "redeeming Israel." In that respect his approach contrasts with an ideologically driven support of the state of Israel by Christian Zionism.

Of other occupants of the land the two most significant are Christian Palestinians and Muslim Palestinians. The perspective of Christian Palestinians is explicitly addressed by Gordon Stewart's encounter with the work of Palestinian theologian Naim Ateek. Neither group is homogeneous and much more could be said of each that is beyond the scope of this response.[9]

THE LAND AND SCRIPTURE

Stewart's work on Ateek highlights what is implicit in each of the essays herein, that the "land of promise" has to do with the nature of Scripture

---

8. Halper, *Israeli in Palestine*; see especially 63–96.

9. On the diversity of the various groupings, see a journalist's perspective in Rees, *Cain's Field*.

and its interpretation. In particular Stewart observes Ateek wrestling with the conquest narrative in the Old Testament and the manner in which it is appropriated to justify oppression of Palestinians. Ateek's response is to interpret the Old Testament through the lens of Christ. In the process he finds that there is much that can be "friend" rather than "foe" of the Palestinian people in the Old Testament. However I, with Stewart, do worry, to employ another metaphor, that "in the sieve used to evaluate the Hebrew Scriptures more is discarded than retained" by Ateek. The Palestinian experience brings into sharp relief the problematic nature of the conquest strand in the Old Testament, but one does not have to be Palestinian to be troubled by it. Walter Brueggemann's short book on violence in the Joshua narrative is helpful in this respect, but at the end I am left with the sense that he has ameliorated the problems posed by texts of violence rather than solved them.[10]

The Old Testament remains problematic, partly in its own right and partly in the way it relates to the New Testament. In that respect Peter Walker in his introduction foreshadows a number of aspects of this with respect to the significance of Israel/Palestine and her inhabitants today. One in particular that has not been addressed by other contributors concerns the role of Jesus with respect to the covenants with the children of Abraham and what that says about the Jewish people and the return to the land. It would have been good to see some of our contributors tackle other approaches to this subject than the inclusive fulfillment approach that has by and large prevailed here. For example, a fertile field of enquiry remains around the 1965 declaration by Pope Paul VI entitled *Nostra Aetate*, which emerged from the spring that was tapped by Vatican II. Consonant with an openness to "that which is true and holy" (clause 2) in other religions, the declaration includes a long clause 4 on the relation of the church and those of the Jewish faith. With its emphasis on a "common spiritual patrimony," the declaration calls the church to an appreciation of a common heritage and "fraternal dialogue." How that is worked out has been the subject of debate and is worthy of more attention. The respect that it implies for the Jewish people now resident in the "land of promise" is, however, a challenge to readers and writers of this volume. And this relates to how the message of the Old Testament is incorporated into the New Testament and the gospel of Jesus Christ.

---

10. See Meadowcroft, "Review," 102–3.

The debate also echoes within the theme with which I began this response, pilgrimage. Because they discover the present-day realities imposing themselves on the pilgrimage experience, those who go to the land as pilgrims often leave with a profound sense of displacement. For Christian and Jew the iconic image of the Dome of the Rock dominating Jerusalem disrupts the biblical experience of Mount Zion. For the Jewish pilgrim to Masada, the heroism of the last stand against the Romans is also a disturbing reminder that those same heroes had earlier massacred fellow Jews at nearby Ein Gedi who did not share their radicalism. It draws attention to the conflicted nature of contemporary Jewish society.

This sense of displacement is partly explicable as the outcome of an unexamined assumption on the part of the pilgrim that the land of today is somehow an unmediated continuation of the land of Scripture. A further related assumption is that the new covenant and the person of Jesus do not create a discontinuity between the Old Testament land and twenty-first-century land. And that is the conundrum that has fuelled this book.

Bibliography

Alexander, T. Desmond. *From Eden to the New Jerusalem: Exploring God's Plan for Life on Earth*. Nottingham: InterVarsity, 2008.

Arnal, William E. "Galilee, Galileans." In *NIDB* 2:514–18.

Ateek, Naim Stifan. "Biblical Perspectives on the Land." In *Faith and the Intifada: Palestinian Christian Voices*, edited by Naim S. Ateek, Marc H. Elis, and Rosemary Radford Ruether, 108–16. Maryknoll, NY: Orbis, 1992.

———. "The Emergence of a Palestinian Christian Theology." In *Faith and the Intifada: Palestinian Christian Voices*, edited by Ateek, Elis, and Radford Ruether, 1–6. Maryknoll, NY: Orbis, 1992.

———. *Justice and Only Justice: A Palestinian Theology of Liberation*. Maryknoll, NY: Orbis, 2003.

———. *A Palestinian Christian Cry for Reconciliation*. Maryknoll, NY: Orbis, 2008.

———. "Putting Christ at the Centre: The Land from a Palestinian Perspective." In *The Bible and the Land: An Encounter*, edited by Lisa Loden, Peter Walker, and Michael Wood, 55–63. Jerusalem: Musalaha, 2000.

———. "Zionism and the Land: A Palestinian Christian Perspective." In *The Land of Promise: Biblical, Theological, and Contemporary Perspectives*, edited by Peter W. L. Walker and Philip Johnston, 201–14. Downers Grove, IL: InterVarsity, 2000.

Ateek, Naim Stifan, Cedar Dubayis, and Maurin Tobin, editors. *Challenging Christian Zionism: Theology, Politics and the Israel-Palestine Conflict*. London: Melisende, 2005.

Ateek, Naim Stifan, Cedar Dubayis, and Marla Schrader, editors. *Jerusalem—What Makes for Peace!: A Palestinian Christian Contribution to Peacemaking*. London: Melisende, 1997.

Ateek, Naim Stifan, Marc H. Elis, and Rosemary Radford Ruether, editors. *Faith and the Intifada: Palestinian Christian Voices*. Maryknoll, NY: Orbis, 1992.

Ateek, Naim Stifan, and Michael Prior, editors. *Holy Land, Hollow Jubilee: God, Justice, and the Palestinians*. London: Melisende, 1999.

Ateek, Naim Stifan, Hilary Rantisi, and Kent Wilkens, editors. "*Our Story*": *The Palestinians*. Jerusalem: Sabeel Ecumenical Liberation Theology Center; Ann Arbor, MI: Friends of Sabeel–North America, 1999.

Attridge, H. W. *The Epistle to the Hebrews*. Hermeneia. Minneapolis: Fortress, 1989.

Awad, Alex. *Palestinian Memories: The Story of a Palestinian Mother and Her People*. Jerusalem: Bethlehem Bible College, 2008.

Baker, David L. *Two Testaments, One Bible: The Theological Relationship between the Old and New Testaments*. 3rd ed. Downers Grove, IL: InterVarsity, 2010.

Barth, Karl. *Epistle to the Philippians*. Translated by J. W. Leitch. London: SCM, 2002.

Batey, Richard A. "Sepphoris and the Jesus Movement." *NTS* 46 (2001) 402–9.

Bauckham, Richard. "The Parting of the Ways: What Happened and Why." *ST* 47 (1993) 135–51.

Beale, G. K. *The Book of Revelation: A Commentary on the Greek Text*. NIGTC. Grand Rapids: Eerdmans, 1999.

———. *The Temple and the Church's Mission: A Biblical Theology of the Dwelling Place of God*. NSBT 17. Downers Grove, IL: InterVarsity, 2004.

Beare, F. W. *A Commentary on the Epistle to the Philippians*. BNTC. London: A. & C. Black, 1959.

Beasley-Murray, George R. *Jesus and the Kingdom of God*. Grand Rapids: Eerdmans, 1986.

———. *John*. WBC 36. Waco, TX: Word, 1987.

Belt, Don. "The Forgotten Faithful: Arab Christians Feel Outnumbered and Alone." *National Geographic* 215.6 (June 2009) n.p. Online: http://ngm.nationalgeographic.com/2009/06/arab-christians/belt-text.

Best, Ernest. *1 Peter*. NCB. Grand Rapids: Eerdmans, 1971.

Black, David Alan. "On the Pauline Authorship of Hebrews (Part 1): Overlooked Affinities between Hebrews and Paul." *FM* 16.2 (1999) 32–51.

———. "On the Pauline Authorship of Hebrews (Part 2): The External Evidence Reconsidered." *FM* 16.3 (1999) 78–86.

Bockmuehl, Markus N. A. *The Epistle to the Philippians*. BNTC. London: A. & C. Black, 1998.

Borrell, Nola. "Tuatara." In *Spirit Abroad: A Second Selection of New Zealand Spiritual Verse*, edited by Paul Morris, Harry Ricketts, and Mike Grimshaw, 216. Auckland, NZ: Random House, 2004.

Brog, David. "CUFI and the Current Crisis." Brog's Blog, March 22, 2010. Christians United for Israel. Online: http://www.cufi.org/site/PageServer?pagename=Brogs_blog.

Bruce, F. F. *The Epistle to the Galatians: A Commentary on the Greek Text*. NIGTC. Grand Rapids: Eerdmans, 1982.

———. *The Epistle to the Hebrews*. Rev. ed. NICNT. Grand Rapids: Eerdmans, 1990.

———. "Eschatology." In *EDT*, 362–65.

Brueggemann, Walter. *Divine Presence amid Violence: Contextualizing the Book of Joshua*. Eugene, OR: Cascade; Milton Keynes: Paternoster, 2009.

———. *The Land: Place as Gift, Promise, and Challenge in Biblical Faith*. 2nd ed. OBT. Minneapolis: Fortress, 2002.

———. *Theology of the Old Testament: Testimony, Dispute, Advocacy*. Minneapolis: Fortress, 1997.

———. "Does the Promise Still Hold? Israel and the Land: A Response to Gary Anderson." *Christian Century* (January 13, 2009) n.p. Online: http://christiancentury.org/article/2009-01/does-promise-still-hold-israel-and-land-0.

Bulkeley, Tim. "Amos 7,1—8,3: Cohesion and Generic Dissonance." *ZAW* 121 (2009) 515–28.

———. *Amos: Hypertext Bible Commentary*. Auckland, NZ: Hypertext Bible Project, 2005. Online: http://www.bible.gen.nz/buyamos.htm.

———. "Worship and Amos: An Expository Approach." *SABJT* 18 (2009) 14–20.

Burge, Gary M. *Jesus and the Land: The New Testament Challenge to "Holy Land" Theology*. Grand Rapids: Baker Academic, 2010.

———. *Whose Land? Whose Promise? What Christians Are Not Being Told about Israel and the Palestinians.* Cleveland: Pilgrim, 2003.
Burton, Ernest DeWitt. *A Critical and Exegetical Commentary on the Epistle to the Galatians.* ICC. Edinburgh: T. & T. Clark, 1921.
Calder, Alex, editor. *The Writing of New Zealand: Inventions and Identities.* Auckland, NZ: Reed, 1993.
Central Intelligence Agency. *The World Factbook 2009.* Washington, DC: CIA, 2009. Online: https://www.cia.gov/library/publications/ the-world-factbook/index.html.
Certeau, Michel de. *Culture in the Plural.* Edited by Luce Giard, translated by Tom Conley. Minneapolis: University of Minnesota Press, 1997.
Chancey, Mark A. *The Myth of a Gentile Galilee.* SNTSMS 118. New York: Cambridge University Press, 2002.
———. *Greco-Roman Culture and the Galilee of Jesus.* SNTSMS 134. New York: Cambridge University Press, 2005.
Chapman, Alister, John Coffey, and Brad S. Gregory, editors. *Seeing Things Their Way: Intellectual History and the Return of Religion.* Notre Dame, ID: University of Notre Dame Press, 2009.
Chapman, Colin Gilbert. *Whose Promised Land?: The Continuing Crisis over Israel and Palestine.* 4th ed. Grand Rapids: Baker, 2002.
Charlesworth, James H., editor. *Jesus and Archaeology.* Grand Rapids: Eerdmans, 2006.
Childs, Brevard S. *Old Testament Theology in a Canonical Context.* London: SCM, 1985.
Church, Philip. A. F. "Dispensational Christian Zionism: A Strange but Acceptable Aberration or a Deviant Heresy?" *WTJ* 71 (2009) 375–98.
———. "The Promised Land in the New Testament and in Particular in Hebrews." In *Israel: 5 Views on People, Land and State,* edited by Glyn Carpenter, 15–25. Auckland: Vision Network of New Zealand, 2009.
Clements, Ronald. Commendation for Stephen Sizer, *Christian Zionism: Road Map to Armageddon?* Online: http://www.cc-vw.org/articles/ivp.html.
Clines, David J. A. *The Theme of the Pentateuch.* JSOTSS 10. 2nd ed. Sheffield: Sheffield Academic, 1997.
Cochrane, Charles Norris. *Christianity and Classical Culture: A Study of Thought and Action from Augustus to Augustine.* Indianapolis: Amagi, 2003.
Congress on the Church's Worldwide Mission. *Wheaton Declaration.* April 9–16, 1966. Online: http://www.wheaton.edu/bgc/archives/docs/wd66/bcov.html.
Craddock, Fred B. *Philippians.* Interpretation. Atlanta: John Knox, 1985.
Cranfield, C. E. B. *A Critical and Exegetical Commentary on the Epistle to the Romans.* Vol. 2. 6th ed. ICC. Edinburgh: T. & T. Clark, 1979.
Crossan, John Dominic. *The Historical Jesus: The Life of a Mediterranean Jewish Peasant.* San Francisco: Harper, 1991.
Crossley, James G. *Why Christianity Happened: A Sociohistorical Account of Christian Origins (26–50 CE).* Louisville: Westminster John Knox, 2006.
Davidson, Lawrence. "Christian Zionism as a Representation of American Manifest Destiny." *CMES* 14 (2005) 157–69.
Davies, W. D. *The Gospel and the Land: Early Christianity and Jewish Territorial Doctrine.* Berkeley: University of California Press, 1974.
———. "Paul and the People of Israel." *NTS* 24 (1977) 4–39.

De Vos, Craig Steven. *Church and Community Conflicts: The Relationships of the Thessalonian, Corinthian, and Philippian Churches with Their Wider Civic Communities*. SBLDS 168. Atlanta: Scholars, 1999.
Diprose, Ronald E. *Israel and the Church: The Origin and Effects of Replacement Theology*. Waynesboro, GA: Authentic Media, 2004.
Dorsey, Davi A. "Literary Architecture and Aural Structuring Techniques in Amos." *Bib* 73 (1992) 305–30.
———. *The Literary Structure of the Old Testament: A Commentary on Genesis-Malachi*. Grand Rapids: Baker, 1999.
Downing, F. Gerald. "In Quest of First-Century C.E. Galilee." *CBQ* 66 (2004) 78–97.
Draper, Jonathan. "Jesus and the Renewal of Local Community in Galilee." *JTSA* 87 (1994) 29–42.
Dumbrell, William J. *The Search for Order: Biblical Eschatology in Focus*. Eugene, OR: Wipf and Stock, 2001.
Dunn, James D. G. *Romans 9–16*. WBC 38b. Dallas: Word, 1988.
———. "The New Perspective on Paul." In *Jesus, Paul, and the Law: Studies in Mark and Galatians*, 183–206. Louisville: Westminster John Knox; London: SPCK, 1990.
Earth Bible Team. "The Voice of the Earth More than a Metaphor." In *The Earth story in the Psalms and the Prophets*, edited by Norman C. Habel, 23–28. EB 4. Cleveland: Pilgrim; Sheffield: Sheffield Academic, 2001.
Fackre, Gabriel J. *Ecumenical Faith in Evangelical Perspective*. Grand Rapids: Eerdmans, 1993.
Freyne, Seán. *Galilee from Alexander the Great to Hadrian, 323 B.C.E. to 135 C.E: A Study of Second Temple Judaism*. Wilmington, DE: M. Glazier, 1980.
———. *Jesus, A Jewish Galilean: A New Reading of the Jesus-Story*. London: T. & T. Clark, 2004.
———. "Archaeology and the Historical Jesus." In *Jesus and Archaeology*, edited by James H. Charlesworth, 64–83. Grand Rapids: Eerdmans, 2006.
———. "Galilee and Judaea in the First Century." In *The Cambridge History of Christianity*, edited by Margaret M. Mitchell and Frances M. Young, 1:37–51. New York: Cambridge University Press, 2006.
———. "Galilee as Laboratory: Experiments for New Testament Historians and Theologians." *NTS* 53 (2007) 147–64.
———. "Galilee, Jesus and the Contribution of Archaeology." *ET* 119 (2008) 573–81.
———. "The Galilean Jesus and a Contemporary Christology." *TS* 70 (2009) 281–97.
Fee, Gordon D. *Paul's Letter to the Philippians*. NICNT. Grand Rapids: Eerdmans, 1995.
Forbes, Christopher. *Prophecy and Inspired Speech in Early Christianity and Its Hellenistic Environment*. WUNT 2, 75. Tübingen: Mohr, 1995.
Fowl, Stephen E. *Philippians*. THNTC. Grand Rapids: Eerdmans, 2005.
Funk, Robert Walter. *Honest to Jesus: Jesus for a New Millennium*. San Francisco: HarperSanFrancisco, 1996.
Garfinkle, Adam M. "On the Origin, Meaning, Use and Abuse of a Phrase." *MES* 27 (1991) 539–50.
Geddert, T. J. "Peace." In *DJG* 604–5.
Gignac, Alain. "Reception of Paul by Non-Christian Philosophers Today." Paper presented to the Romans through History and Cultures Seminar at the 2002 SBL Annual Meeting, Toronto. Online: http://www.vanderbilt.edu/AnS/religious_studies/SBL2002/Philos.htm.

Gitay, Yehoshua. "A Study of Amos's Art of Speech: A Rhetorical Analysis of Amos 3:1–15." *CBQ* 42 (1980) 293–309.

Glasser, Arthur F. *Announcing the Kingdom: The Story of God's Mission in the Bible.* Grand Rapids: Baker Academic, 2003.

Gnilka, J. "Die antipaulinische Mission in Philippi." *BZ* 9 (1965) 258–76.

Goldsworthy, Graeme. *Gospel and Kingdom: A Christian Interpretation of the Old Testament.* Minneapolis: Winston; Homebush West: Lancer, 1981.

Gorenberg, Gershom. "The Danger of Millennial Politics." In *Challenging Christian Zionism: Theology, Politics and the Israel-Palestine Conflict,* edited by Ateek, Dubayis, and Tobin, 192–99. London: Melisende, 2005.

Haija, Rammy M. "The Armageddon Lobby: Dispensationalist Christian Zionism and the Shaping of US Policy towards Israel-Palestine." Online: http://www.informationclearinghouse.info/article15422.htm.

Halper, Jeff. *An Israeli in Palestine: Resisting Dispossession, Redeeming Israel.* Ann Arbor, MI: Pluto, 2008.

Hansen, G. W. *The Letter to the Philippians.* PNTC. Grand Rapids: Eerdmans, 2009.

Hanson, K. C., and Douglas E. Oakman. *Palestine in the Time of Jesus: Social Structures and Social Conflicts.* Minneapolis: Fortress, 1998.

Harvey, Graham. *The True Israel: Uses of the Names Jew, Hebrew and Israel in Ancient Jewish and Early Christian Literature.* AGJU 35. New York: Brill, 1996.

Hayes, John Haralson. *Amos: the Eighth-Century Prophet: His Times and his Preaching.* Nashville: Abingdon, 1988.

Hayes, Katherine. *The Earth Mourns: Prophetic Metaphor and Oral Aesthetic.* Atlanta: SBL, 2002.

Hays, Richard B. *The Faith of Jesus Christ.* 2nd ed. Grand Rapids: Eerdmans, 2002.

Hemer, Colin. *The Book of Acts in the Setting of Hellenistic History.* WUNT 49. Tübingen: Mohr Siebeck, 1989.

Hoekema, Anthony. *The Bible and the Future.* Grand Rapids: Eerdmans, 1979.

Hofius, Otfried. *Katapausis: Die Vorstellung vom Endzeitl. Ruheort im Hebräerbrief,* WUNT 2. Tübingen: Mohr Siebeck, 1970.

Holwerda, David E. *Jesus and Israel: One Covenant or Two.* Grand Rapids: Eerdmans, 1995.

Horbury, William. "Land, Sanctuary and Worship." In *Early Christian Thought in Its Jewish Context,* edited by John G. Barclay and John Sweet, 207–24. Cambridge: Cambridge University Press, 1996.

Horsley, Richard A. *Sociology and the Jesus Movement.* New York: Continuum, 1994.

———. *Galilee: History, Politics, People.* Valley Forge: Trinity Press International, 1995.

———. *Archaeology, History, and Society in Galilee: The Social Context of Jesus and the Rabbis.* Valley Forge: Trinity Press International, 1996.

———. *Jesus in Context: Power, People and Performance.* Minneapolis: Fortress, 2008.

Houlden, J. L. *Paul's Letters from Prison.* Philadelphia: Westminster, 1970.

———. "The Speeches of Acts: II. The Areopagus Address," *TynBul* 40 (1989) 239–59.

Institute for the Study of Christian Zionism. "Challenging Christian Zionism." n.p. Online: www.christianzionism.org.

International Christian Embassy, Jerusalem. "Position: What We believe." n.p. Online: http://www.icej.org/articles/positon.

———. "ICEJ Response To Evangelical Letter To President Bush, 30.08.2007." n.p. Online: http://www.icej.org/article.php?id=4320.

———. "ICEJ Worldwide." n.p. Online: http://www.icej.org/articles/icej_worldwide.

"James Cook: The Voyage of the *Endeavour*." In *The Writing of New Zealand*, edited by Alex Calder, 19–22. Auckland: Reed, 1993.

Jensen, Morten Hørning. *Herod Antipas in Galilee: The Literary and Archaeological Sources on the Reign of Herod Antipas and its Socio-economic Impact on Galilee*. Tübingen: Mohr Siebeck, 2006.

Jewett, R. "Conflicting Movements in the Early Church as Reflected in Philippians." *NovT* 12 (1970) 362–98.

———. "Letter of John Paul II concerning Pilgrimage to the Places Linked to the History of Salvation." n.p. Online: http://www.vatican.va/holy_father/john_paul_ii/letters/documents/hf_jp-ii_let_30061999_pilgrimage_en.html.

Johnson, Dennis E. *The Message of Acts in the History of Redemption*. Phillipsburg: P. & R., 1997.

"Joseph Banks: *Endeavour* Journal." In *The Writing of New Zealand*, edited by Alex Calder, 23–26. Auckland: Reed, 1993.

Judge, E. A. "Paul's Boasting in Relation to Contemporary Professional Practice," *ABR* 16 (1968) 37–50. Now available as ch. 2 in D. Scholer, *Social Distinctives of the Christians in the First Century: Pivotal Essays by E. A. Judge*, 57–72. Peabody, MA: Hendrickson, 2008.

———. "St. Paul as a Radical Critic of Society." *Interchange* 16 (1975) 191–203. Now available as ch. 1 in D. Scholer, *Social Distinctives of the Christians in the First Century: Pivotal Essays by E. A. Judge*, 99–116. Peabody, MA: Hendrickson, 2008.

———. "Cultural Conformity and Innovation in Paul: Some Clues from Contemporary Documents." *TynBul* 35 (1984) 3–24. Now available as ch. 7 in D. Scholer, *Social Distinctives of the Christians in the First Century: Pivotal Essays by E. A. Judge*, 157–74. Peabody, MA: Henrickson, 2008.

Justin Martyr. "Dialogue of Justin, Philosopher and Martyr, with Trypho, a Jew." In *ANF* vol. 1.

Kaiser, Walter C., Jr. "The Promise Theme and the Theology of Rest." *BSac* 130 (1973) 135–50.

Katanacho, Yohanna. "Christ Is the Owner of Haaretz." *CSR* 24 (2005) 425–41.

Kautsky, John H. *The Politics of Aristocratic Empires*. Chapel Hill: University of North Carolina Press, 1966.

Keown, Mark J. *Congregational Evangelism in Philippians: The Centrality of an Appeal for Gospel Proclamation to the Fabric of Philippians*. PBM. Milton Keynes: Paternoster, 2008.

Kim, Lloyd. *Polemic in the Book of Hebrews: Anti-Semitism, Anti-Judaism, Supersessionism?* PTMS. Eugene, OR: Pickwick, 2006.

Klijn, A. F. J. "Paul's Opponents in Philippians iii." *NovT* 7 (1965) 278–84.

Kline, Meredith G. *Kingdom Prologue: Genesis Foundations for a Covenantal Worldview*. Eugene, OR: Wipf & Stock, 2006.

Knighton, Mikael. "The Christian Zionist Hated of the World, Blessed of God." No pages. Online: http://www.zionismontheweb.org/christian_zionism/Christian_Zionist_Hated_of_the_World_Blessed_of_God.htm.

Kohl, Manfred. "The Holocaust and the Evangelical Movement: From German Pietism to Palestinian Christians." Presented at conference "Christ at the Checkpoint: Theology in the Service of Peace and Justice," Bethlehem Bible College, March 2010. Online: http://www.christatthecheckpoint.com/lectures.html.

Bibliography

Köster, Helmut. "The Purpose of the Polemic of a Pauline Fragment." *NTS* 8 (1961–62) 317–32.

Kuttab, Jonathan. "Justice and Mercy: The Missing Ingredients in Christian Zionism." In *Challenging Christian Zionism: Theology, Politics and the Israel-Palestine Conflict*, edited by Ateek, Dubayis, and Tobin, 163–68. London: Melisende, 2005.

Laansma, J. "The Cosmology of Hebrews." In *Cosmology and New Testament Theology*, edited by Jonathan T. Pennington and Sean M. McDonough, 125–43. London: T. & T. Clark, 2008.

———. *"I Will Give You Rest": The Rest Motif in the New Testament with Special Reference to Mt 11 and Heb 3–4*. WUNT 98. Tübingen: Mohr, 1997.

Ladd, George Eldon. "Kingdom of Christ, God, Heaven." In *EDT*, 607–11.

———. *The Presence of the Future*. Grand Rapids: Eerdmans, 1974.

LaHaye, Tim, and Thomas Ice. *Charting the End Times*. Eugene, OR: Harvest House, 2001.

Lausanne Covenant, ¶ 5, "Christian Social Responsibility." n.p. Online: http://www.lausanne.org/covenant.

Lawrence, Jonathan David. *Washing in Water: Trajectories of Ritual Bathing in the Hebrew Bible and Second Temple Literature*. SBLABib 23. Atlanta: SBL; Leiden: Brill, 2006.

Lenski, Gerhard Emmanuel. *Power and Privilege: A Theory of Social Stratification*. New York: McGraw-Hill, 1966.

Lenski, Gerhard Emmanuel, and Jean Lenski, *Human Societies: An Introduction to Macrosociology*. 4th ed. New York: McGraw-Hill, 1982.

Levine, Amy-Jill. "Theory, Apologetic, History: Reviewing Jesus' Jewish Context." *ABR* 55 (2007) 57–78.

Lindsay, Hal, with C. C. Carlson. *The Late Great Planet Earth*. Grand Rapids: Zondervan, 1970.

Littell, Franklin H. *The Crucifixion of the Jews*. New York: Harper & Row, 1975.

Loden, Lisa, Peter Walker, and Michael Wood, editors. *The Bible and the Land: An Encounter*. Musalaha: Jerusalem, 2000.

Longenecker, Richard N. *Galatians*. WBC 41. Dallas: Word, 1990.

Mack, Burton L. *A Myth of Innocence: Mark and Christian Origins*. Philadelphia: Fortress, 1988.

Malherbe, Abraham J. *Paul and the Popular Philosophers*. Minneapolis: Fortress, 1989.

Mandela, Nelson. *Long Walk to Freedom: An Autobiography of Nelson Mandela*. Boston: Little, Brown, 1994.

Marlow, Hilary. "The Other Prophet: The Voice of the Earth in the Book of Amos." In *Exploring Ecological Hermeneutics*, edited by Norman C. Habel and Peter L. Trudinger, 75–83. SBLMS 46. Atlanta: SBL, 2008.

Marshall, Christopher. *Kingdom Come: The Kingdom of God in the Teaching of Jesus*. Rev. ed. Auckland: Impetus, 1993.

Marshall, I. Howard. *The Epistle to the Philippians*. Epworth Commentaries. London: Epworth, 1992.

———. *New Testament Theology: Many Witnesses, One Gospel*. Downers Grove, IL: InterVarsity, 2004.

Martin, D. Michael, *1, 2 Thessalonians*. NAC 33. Logos Library System; Nashville: Broadman & Holman, 1995.

Martin, Ralph P. *Philippians*. WBC 43. Dallas: Word, 2004.

McDowell, Derek. "A Response from Derek McDowell." In *Israel: 5 Views on People, Land and State*, edited by Glyn Carpenter, 71–78. Auckland: Vision Network of New Zealand, 2009.

Mckay, Mary Jayne, "Zion's Christian Soldiers." n.p. Online: http://www.cbsnews.com/stories/2002/10/03/60minutes/main524268.shtml.

Meadowcroft, Tim. Review of *Divine Presence* by W. Brueggemann. *Colloquium* 42 (2010) 102–3.

———. "Some Questions for the Earth Bible." Unpublished paper presented to ANZATS Annual Meeting, Christchurch, July 2000.

Mearns, C. "The Identity of Paul's Opponents at Philippi." *NTS* 33 (1987) 194–204.

Meeks, Wayne A. *The First Urban Christians: The Social World of the Apostle Paul*. New Haven, CT: Yale University Press, 1983.

Meyers, Eric M. "Jesus and His Galilean Context." In *Archaeology and the Galilee: Texts and Contexts in the Graeco-Roman and Byzantine Periods*, edited by Douglas R. Edwards and C. Thomas McCollough, 57–66. SFSHJ 143. Atlanta: Scholars, 1997.

Middleton, Richard J. "A New Heaven and a New Earth: The Case for a Holistic Reading of the Biblical Story of Redemption." *JCTR* 11 (2006) 73–97.

———. *The Liberating Image: The Imago Dei in Genesis 1*. Grand Rapids: Brazos, 2005.

"Monsters." In *DBI* 562–65.

Moo, Douglas J. *The Epistle to the Romans*. NICNT. Grand Rapids: Eerdmans, 1996.

Mosser, Carl. "Rahab Outside the Camp." In *The Epistle to the Hebrews and Christian Theology*, edited by Richard Bauckham, Daniel Driver, Trevor Hart, and Nathan MacDonald, 383–404. Grand Rapids: Eerdmans, 2009.

Moxnes, Halvor. "The Construction of Galilee as a Place for the Historical Jesus," *BTB* 31 (2001) 26–37, 64–77.

Muir, Diana. "A Land without a People for a People without a Land." *Middle East Quarterly* 15/2 (2008) 55–62.

Müller Ulrich B. *Der Brief des Paulus an die Philipper*. THNT 11/1. Leipzig: Evangelische Verlagsanstalt, 1993.

Murray, Iain Hamish. *The Puritan Hope: A Study in Revival and the Interpretation of Prophecy*. London: Banner of Truth Trust, 1971.

Oakman, Douglas E. Review of *Archaeology, History, and Society in Galilee* by Richard Horsley." *CBQ* 60 (1998) 568–69.

O'Brien, P. T. *The Epistle to the Philippians: A Commentary on the Greek Text*. NIGTC. Grand Rapids: Eerdmans, 1991.

———. "Was Paul a Covenantal Nomist?" In *Justification and Variegated Nomism*, edited by D. A. Carson, Peter T. O'Brien, and Mark A Seifrid, 2:249–96. WUNT 2/181. Grand Rapids: Baker Academic, 2004.

Park, Geoff. *Nga Uruora: The Groves of Life. Ecology and History in a New Zealand Landscape*. Wellington: Victoria University Press, 1999.

Paul VI. *Nostra Aetate*: "Declaration on the Relation of the Church to Non-Christian Religions." October 28, 1965. Online: http://www.vatican.va/archive/hist_councils/ii_vatican_council/documents/vat-ii_decl_19651028_nostra-aetate_en.html.

Pawson, David. *When Jesus Returns*. London: Hodder and Stoughton, 1995.

Peskett, Howard, and Vinoth Ramachandra. *The Message of Mission: The Glory of Christ in All Time and Space*. BST. Downers Grove, IL: InterVarsity, 2003.

Plantinga, Cornelius. *Engaging God's World: A Christian Vision of Faith, Learning, and Living*. Grand Rapids: Eerdmans, 2002.

———. *Not the Way It's Supposed to Be: A Breviary of Sin*. Grand Rapids: Eerdmans, 1995.
Preston, Don K. *Israel: 1948 Countdown to Nowhere*. Ardmore: D. K. Preston, 2002.
Prince, Derek. *Promised Land: God's Word on the Nation of Israel*. Christchurch: Derek Prince Ministries, 2006.
Proclamation of the Third International Christian Zionist Congress. Jerusalem, February 25–29, 1996. n.p. Online: http://christianactionforisrael.org/congress.html.
Rapinchuk, Mark. "The Galilee and Jesus in Recent Research," *CBR* 2 (2004) 197–222.
Rees, Matt. *Cain's Field: Faith, Fratricide, and Fear in the Middle East*. New York: Free Press, 2004.
Reed, Jonathan L. Review *Palestine in the Time of Jesus: Social Structures and Social Conflicts* by K. C. Hanson and Douglas E. Oakman. *RBL*, February 15, 1999. No Pages. Online: http://www.bookreviews.org/pdf/71_385.pdf.
———. *Archaeology and the Galilean Jesus: A Re-Examination of the Evidence*. Harrisburg, PA: Trinity, 2000.
———. "Archaeological Contributions to the Study of Jesus and the Gospels." In *The Historical Jesus in Context*, edited by Amy-Jill Levine, Dale C. Allison Jr., and John Dominic Crossan, 40–54. Princeton: Princeton University Press, 2006.
Renan, Ernest. *The Life of Jesus*. London: Kegan Paul, Trench, Trübner, 1893.
Reumann, John. *Philippians: A New Translation with Introduction and Commentary*. AB 33B. New Haven, CT: Yale University Press, 2008.
Richardson, Peter. *Israel in the Apostolic Church*. SNTSMS 10. Cambridge: Cambridge University Press, 1969.
Ricoeur, Paul. *Essays on Biblical Interpretation*. Edited by Lewis S. Mudge. Philadelphia: Fortress, 1980.
Ridderbos, Herman N. *The Gospel according to John: A Theological Commentary*. Translated by John Vriend. Grand Rapids: Eerdmans, 1997.
Riddlebarger, Kim. *A Case for Amillennialism: Understanding the End Times*. Grand Rapids: Baker, 2003.
Riggans, Walter. *Israel and Zionism*. London: Hansell, 1988.
Roberts, Vaughan. *God's Big Picture: Tracing the Storyline of the Bible*. Nottingham: InterVarsity, 2002.
Robertson, O. Palmer. *The Israel of God: Yesterday, Today and Tomorrow*. Phillipsburg, NJ: P. & R., 2000.
———. "A New-Covenant Perspective on the Land." In *The Land of Promise: Biblical, Theological, and Contemporary Perspectives*, edited by Peter W. L. Walker and Philip Johnston, 121–41. Downers Grove, IL: InterVarsity, 2000.
Sanders, E. P. *Paul, the Law, and the Jewish People*. Philadelphia: Fortress, 1983.
Sawicki, Marianne. *Crossing Galilee: Architecture of Contact in the Occupied Land of Jesus*. Harrisburg, PA: Trinity, 2000.
Schmithals, Walter. *Paul and the Gnostics*. Translated by John E. Seely. Nashville: Abingdon, 1972.
Schenk, Wolfgang. *Die Philipperbriefe des Paulus: Kommentar*. Stuttgart: W. Kohlhammer, 1984.
Schröter, Jens. "Jesus of Galilee: The Role of Location in Understanding Jesus of Galilee." In *Jesus Research: An International Perspective*, edited by James H. Charlesworth and Petr Pokorný, 36–55. Princeton-Prague Symposia Series on the Historical 1. Grand Rapids: Eerdmans, 2009.

Schuler, Mark T. "Recent Archaeology of Galilee and the Interpretation of Texts from the Galilean Ministry of Jesus." *CTQ* 71 (2007) 99–117.

Scott, James M. "'And Then All Israel Will Be Saved' (Rom 11:26)." In *Restoration: Old Testament, Jewish, and Christian Perspectives*, edited by James M. Scott, 489–527. JSJSup 72. Leiden: Brill, 2001.

Sheldrake, Philip. *Spaces for the Sacred: Place, Memory, and Identity*. Baltimore: John Hopkins University Press, 2001.

Silva, Moisés. *Philippians*. 2nd ed. BECNT. Grand Rapids: Baker Academic, 2005.

Sizer, Stephen. *Christian Zionism: Road Map to Armageddon?* Leicester: InterVarsity, 2004.

———. *Zion's Christian Soldiers?: The Bible, Israel and the Church*. Nottingham: InterVarsity, 2007.

Smith, James A. *Marks of an Apostle: Deconstruction, Philippians, and Problematizing Pauline Theology*. Semeia 53. Atlanta: SBL, 2005.

Snodgrass, Klyne. "The Use of the Old Testament in the New." In *New Testament Criticism & Interpretation*, edited by David Alan Black and David S. Dockery, 409–34. Grand Rapids: Zondervan, 1991.

Snyman, S. D. "The Land as a 'Leitmotiv' in the Book of Amos." *Verbum et Ecclesia* 26 (2005) 527–42.

Stegemann, Wolfgang, Bruce J. Malina, and Gerd Theissen, editors. *The Social Setting of Jesus and the Gospels*. Minneapolis: Fortress, 2002.

Stevens, R. Paul. *The Other Six Days: Vocation, Work, and Ministry in Biblical Perspective*. Grand Rapids: Eerdmans, 1999.

Stott, John. "The Place of Israel." In *Zion's Christian Soldiers: The Bible, Israel and the Church*, by Stephen Sizer, 164–72. Nottingham: InterVarsity, 2007.

Strathmann, H. "πόλις, πολίτης, πολιτεύομαι, πολιτεία, πολίτευμα." In *TDNT* 6:516–35.

Strom, Mark. *Reframing Paul: Conversations in Grace and Community*. Downers Grove, IL: InterVarsity, 2001.

———. *The Symphony of Scripture: Making Sense of the Bible's Themes*. Downers Grove, IL: InterVarsity, 1990.

Swanson, J. *Dictionary of Biblical Languages with Semantic Domains: Greek (New Testament)*. 2nd ed. Oak Harbor, WA: Logos Research Systems, 2001.

Tate, Randolph W. *Biblical Interpretation: An Integrated Approach*. Peabody, MA: Hendrickson, 1991.

"Te Horeta Te Taniwha: An Account of Cook's Visit." In *The Writing of New Zealand: Inventions and Identities*, edited by Alex Calder, 26–30. Auckland: Reed, 1993.

"Te Rangi Hiroa: The Discovery of New Zealand." In *The Writing of New Zealand: Inventions and Identities*, edited by Alex Calder, 15–18. Auckland: Reed, 1993.

Theissen, Gerd. *Sociology of Early Palestinian Christianity*. Translated by John Bowden. Philadelphia: Fortress, 1978.

———. *Social Reality and the Early Christians: Theology, Ethics, and the World of the New Testament*. Translated by Margaret Kohn. Edinburgh: T. & T. Clark, 1993.

Thurston, Bonnie Bowman, and Judith M. Ryan. *Philippians & Philemon*. SP 10. Collegeville, MN: Liturgical, 2005.

Turner, Mary Donovan. "Daughter Zion: Giving Birth to Redemption." In *Pregnant Passion: Gender, Sex, and Violence in the Bible*, edited by Cheryl Kirk-Duggan, 193–204. Leiden: Brill, 2003.

Vale, Ruth. "Literary Sources in Archaeological Description: The Case of Galilee, Galilees, and Galileans." *JSJ* 18 (1987) 209–26.
Van Buren, Paul Matthews. *A Theology of the Jewish-Christian Reality*. Part 1: *Discerning the Way*. New York: Seabury, 1987.
Waard, Jan de. "The Chiastic Structure of Amos V 1–17." *VT* 27 (1977) 170–77.
Waard, Jan de, and William A. Smalley. *A Translator's Handbook on the book of Amos*. Help for Translators. Stuttgart: United Bible Societies, 1979.
Wagner, Donald. "A Heavenly Match: Bush and the Christian Zionists." n.p. Online: www.informationclearinghouse.info/article4960.htm.
———. "Beyond Armageddon." n.p. Online: http://www.christianzionism.org/Article/Wagner04.asp.
———. "From Blackstone to Bush: Christian Zionism in the United States (1890 – 2004)." In *Challenging Christian Zionism: Theology, Politics and the Israel-Palestine Conflict*, edited by Ateek, Dubayis, and Tobin, 32–44. London: Melisende, 2005.
Wakefield, Edward Jerningham, and John Ward. *The British Colonization of New Zealand: Being an Account of the Principles, Objects, and Plans of the New Zealand Association*. London: J. W. Parker, 1837.
Walker, Peter W. L. *Jesus and the Holy City: New Testament Perspectives on Jerusalem*. Grand Rapids: Eerdmans, 1996.
———. "The Land in the Apostles' Writings." In *The Land of Promise: Biblical, Theological, and Contemporary Perspectives*, edited by Peter W. L. Walker and Philip Johnston, 81–99. Downers Grove, IL: InterVarsity, 2000.
———. "The Land and Jesus Himself." In *The Land of Promise: Biblical, Theological, and Contemporary Perspectives*, edited by Peter. W. L. Walker and Philip Johnston, 100–120. Downers Grove, IL: InterVarsity, 2000.
Wallace, Daniel B. *Greek Grammar beyond the Basics: An Exegetical Syntax of the Greek New Testament*. Garland: Galaxie Software, 1999.
Walls, Andrew *The Cross-Cultural Process in Christian History: Studies in the Transmission and Appropriation of Faith*. Maryknoll, NY: Orbis, 2002.
Walsh, Brian J., and Sylvia C. Keesmaat. *Colossians Remixed: Subverting the Empire*. Downers Grove, IL: InterVarsity, 2004.
Waltke, Bruce. "The Kingdom of God in Biblical Theology." In *Looking into the Future: Evangelical Studies in Eschatology*, edited by David W. Baker, 15–27. ETS Studies. Grand Rapids: Baker, 2001.
Walton, John H., and Victor H. Matthews. *The InterVarsity Bible Background Commentary: Genesis-Deuteronomy*. Downers Grove, IL: InterVarsity, 1997.
Walton, John H. *Genesis*. NIVAC. Grand Rapids: Zondervan, 2001.
Walvoord, John F. *Israel in Prophecy*. Grand Rapids: Zondervan, 1962.
Waner, Mira. "Music Culture in Roman-Byzantine Sepphoris." In *Religion, Ethnicity and Identity in Ancient Galilee: A Region in Transition*, edited by Jürgen Zangenberg, Harold W. Attridge, and Dale B. Martin, 425–47. WUNT 210. Tübingen: Mohr, 2007.
Wenham, Gordon J. *Genesis 16–50*. WBC 1. Dallas: Word, 1994.
Wilkinson, Paul Richard. *For Zion's Sake: Christian Zionism and the Role of John Nelson Darby*. SEHT. Milton Keynes: Paternoster, 2007.
Wilson, Dwight Julian. *Armageddon Now! The Premillenarian Response to Russia and Israel Since 1917*. Grand Rapids: Baker, 1977.

Winter, Bruce W. *Seek the Welfare of the City: Christians as Benefactors and Citizens.* First-Century Christians in the Graeco-Roman World 1. Grand Rapids: Eerdmans; Carlisle: Paternoster, 1994.

———. *After Paul Left Corinth: The Influence of Secular Ethics and Social Change.* Grand Rapids: Eerdmans, 2001.

Wolters, Albert M. *Creation Regained: Biblical Basics for a Reformational Worldview.* 2nd ed. Grand Rapids: Eerdmans, 2005.

Wright, Christopher J. H. *God's People in God's Land: Family, Land, and Property in the Old Testament.* Grand Rapids: Eerdmans; 1990.

———. "A Christian Approach to Old Testament Prophecy Concerning Israel." In *Jerusalem: Past and Present in the Purposes of God,* edited by Peter W. L. Walker, 1–19. Grand Rapids: Baker; Carlisle: Paternoster, 1994.

———. *Knowing Jesus through the Old Testament.* Downers Grove, IL: InterVarsity, 1992.

———. *Salvation Belongs to Our God: Celebrating the Bible's Central Story.* Downers Grove, IL: IVP Academic, 2007.

Wright N. T. *Jesus and the Victory of God.* Christian Origins and the Question of God 2. Minneapolis: Fortress, 1996.

———. "New Exodus, New Inheritance: The Narrative Substructure of Romans 3–8." In *Romans and the People of God: Essays in Honor of Gordon D. Fee on the Occasion of his 65th Birthday,* edited by S. K. Soderlund and N. T. Wright, 26–35. Grand Rapids: Eerdmans, 1999.

———. *Paul: In Fresh Perspective.* London: SPCK; Minneapolis: Fortress, 2005.

———. *Simply Christian: Why Christianity Makes Sense.* San Francisco: HarperSanFrancisco, 2006.

———. *Surprised by Hope: Rethinking Heaven, the Resurrection, and the Mission of the Church.* New York: HarperOne, 2008.

———. *The New Testament and the People of God.* Christian Origins and the Question of God 1. London: SPCK; Minneapolis: Fortress, 1992.

———. *Acts for Everyone.* Part 1: *Chapters 1–12.* London: SPCK; Louisville: Westminster John Knox, 2008.

Yaakov, Ariel. "An Unexpected Alliance: Christian Zionism and Its Historical Significance." *Modern Judaism* 26 (2006) 74–100.

Yule, Rob. "Christians and Israel." In *Israel: 5 Views on People, Land and State,* edited by Glyn Carpenter, 55–68. Auckland: Vision Network of New Zealand, 2009.

Zangenberg, Jürgen. "A Region in Transition: Introducing Religion, Ethnicity, and Identity in Ancient Galilee." In *Religion, Ethnicity and Identity in Ancient Galilee: A Region in Transition,* edited by Jürgen Zangenberg, Harold W. Attridge, and Dale B. Martin, 1–10. WUNT 10. Tübingen: Mohr, 2007.

Index of Ancient Sources

OLD TESTAMENT

Genesis

1	46, 61, 65
1—2	67, 135, 138
1—11	64, 65
1:1	46
1:10	46
1:20	138
1:24	138
1:26–28	60
1:27–28	64
2	63, 64
2:2	54
2:5	46
2:15	60, 64
2:18	145
2:19	144
2:20	145
3—11	67
12	9, 67
12:1–3	17, 49, 66, 152
12:3	20, 46, 107
12:7	108
15:1–19	49
17:1–8	49, 66
17:7–8	3
17:8	67, 110
17:10–12	33
17:13	66
18:2	46
26	81
28	136, 139, 140
28:10–18	134, 135, 137, 145
28:11	139, 141
28:12	141
28:13	137, 140, 141
28:13–14	50, 65
28:13–17	81
28:14	137
28:17	137
28:19	144
30:37–43	142
30:41	142
47:13	46
47:20–23	46
49:15	53

Exodus

12:14	66
15:13–17	47
17:1–7	52
19:3–6	17
19:4–6	151
19:6	152
20:12	50, 66
23:9	113
23:10–11	46
29:9	66
29:28	66
31:16	66
35:2	53

Leviticus

18:26–28	66
19:34	113
20:22–26	66
23:22	11

Index of Ancient Sources

Leviticus (cont.)

24:22	11
25:23	2, 113
25:35	113

Numbers

10:23	53
14:1–35	52
15:15–16	11
20:1–3	52
26	80
26:53	2, 80
26:55	80
26:56	80
31:36	80
36:2	2, 46

Deuteronomy

1:16	113
4:21	2, 46
4:25–27	66
4:38	2
5:16	50, 66
9:26	60
10:9	80
10:18–19	11
12:12	80
14:27	80
14:29	80
15:4	2
25:19	47

Joshua

6:17–21	110
6:23	57
11:23	2
12:7	80
13:7	80
14:4	80
14:5	80
15:13	80
17	83
17:2	80
17:5	83
17:14	83
18:2–10	80
19	83
19:9	80, 83
19:29	83
19:51	80
22:8	80
22:25	80
22:27	80
23:14	47

Judges

18:1	46

1 Samuel

13:19	46

2 Samuel

7:13	4
7:16	4
14:17	53
22:50	152

1 Kings

8:56	47, 53
21:1–16	2

2 Kings

5:17	46
25	61

2 Chronicles

6:41	47

Ezra

4:3	108

Nehemiah

2:20	108
9:36–37	47

Psalms

18:49	152

Index of Ancient Sources

Psalms (cont.)

21:29	60
22:28	60
27:13	46
29:10	60
47	77
67	77
74	4
79	4
80:8	71
80:14	71
95	52, 53, 54
95:1–7a	52
95:7b–11	52
95:11	53
105:11	2
110:2	50
117:10	152
135:12	2
136:21	2
145:11–13	60

Isaiah

2:2–4	20
5:3–7	71
8:23	89
9:6	64
11:10	152
19:17	47
27:19	113
32:43	152
49:6	47
52:7	64
58:14	2
59:20	50, 156
59:20–21	16
61:5–6	109
66:1	49, 60

Jeremiah

2:7	46
2:21	71
3:19	2
12:10	71
22:13–17	129
31:31–34	3, 149
35:18–19	4
45:3	53

Ezekiel

16:49–50	129
20:42	47
36–39	9
45:1	2
47:21–23	112
47:22–23	11
48:29	2

Hosea

2:25	151
6:2	71
10:1	71

Joel

4:4	89

Amos

1	76, 80
1—2	80
1—4	84
1:1	79
1:2	75, 79
1:4	76
1:7	76
1:10	76
1:12	76
1:13	76
1:14	76
2	80
2:2	76
2:5	76
2:6–8	85
2:6–16	79
2:7–8	85
2:9–10	85
2:10	80
3:1–2	80, 85
3:3	80

Amos (cont.)

3:6	76
3:9	76
3:9–10	85
3:9–11	76
3:10	76
3:11	76
4	84
4:1	85
4:6–8	76, 80
4:6–11	80
4:7	76, 80
4:9	75, 80, 82
4:10	80
4:11	80
4:12	80
4:12–13	80
4:13	80
5:1–17	81, 84
5:2	81
5:3	76
5:4–6	81
5:5–6	81
5:7	81, 85
5:8–9	81
5:9	76
5:10	85
5:11	75, 82, 85
5:12–13	85
5:14–15	85
5:16–17	82
5:17	75, 76
5:18–23	85
5:24	85, 114
5:27	85
6:2	76
6:3	85
6:8	76
6:8–14	85
7	82
7:2	75, 82
7:4	76, 80, 82
7:10	83
7:10–11	82
7:10–17	82
7:11	82, 83
7:12	46
7:17	76, 80, 83, 85
8	83, 84
8:1–2	84
8:3	84
8:4	83
8:4–6	84, 85
8:7–14	85
8:8	83, 84
8:9	83
8:11	83
8:11–13	84
8:12	85
9	83
9:1–4	83, 84
9:2–3	85
9:4	85
9:5	84
9:5–6	84, 85
9:7	85
9:8–9	84
9:9	84
9:11–12	151
9:11–15	79, 84
9:14	75, 76
9:15	84

Micah

6:8	11, 114

Habakkuk

2:14	70

~

NEW TESTAMENT

Matthew

1:17	17
2—5	6
2:15	73
2:20–21	48

Matthew (cont.)

3:17	73
4:15	48
4:15–17	17
5:5	8, 66
5:17	73
6:10	66
11:28	73
13:47	59
19:16–25	62
19:24	62
19:28	62
20:1–16	71
21:28	71
21:32	71
21:33–41	71
24:22	9
24:30	41
25:46	63
26:63–64	41

Mark

1:1–3	17
1:15	59
3:6	88
4:26	59
9:45	63
9:47	63
10:17	63
10:23	62
10:24	63
10:30	63
12:1–12	71
12:13	88
13:20	9, 157
13:26	41
14:62	41

Luke

1:1	58
1:32–33	4
1:55	49
1:67–79	17, 48
1:73	49
2:25	48, 70
2:38	48, 70
4:21	17
4:25	48
9:29–30	8
13:35	6
18:24	62
18:30	62
19:41–44	6
20:9–19	71
21:20–24	6
21:24	9, 157
21:27	41
23:28–31	6
24:21	48, 70

John

1:14	5, 73
1:29	73
2:19–21	73
2:21	5
3:16	65, 70
3:22	48
4:7–14	73
4:20–23	72
5:9	68
6—8	8
6:32–35	73
8:12	73
9:5	73
10:11	73
15	73
15:1	71, 73
15:1–5	73
15:5	71
21	68
21:14	68

Acts

1	6
1:3	7
1:6	48, 70
1:7	70
1:8	4, 16, 48, 50, 70

Acts (cont.)

1:11	41
2—3	4
2:22–36	73
2:29–31	69
2:33	69
3:1	8
3:12	48
3:19–21	65
3:21	70
3:22	73
3:25	48
3:26	49
7:3–4	49
7:17	50
7:47	49
7:49	53
7:58—8:4	33
9:4–5	33
11:19	33
13	49, 51
13:19	49
14—15	33
15:1	31
15:14	151
16:11–40	38
16:21	38
17	22
17:23	21
17:23–28	19
21:26	8
22:3	33
22:4	33
22:7–8	33
23:6	33
26:5	33
26:11	33
28:15	42

Romans

2:25–29	32
3—8	17
3:2	20
3:29–30	8
4	17, 32, 50
4:13	4, 44, 50, 66, 67
5	20, 72
5—8	72
6	72
7	72
7:12	33
8	72
8:16–17	2
8:19	41
8:19–23	42, 65
8:20–23	17, 23
8:21	63, 65
8:23	41
9	17, 50
9:6	156, 157
9:6–7	154, 155, 156
9—11	16, 148, 154, 155
9:11	50
9:23	151
9:25–26	151
9:33	16
11	155
11:1	xi, 147, 155
11:1–2	155, 156
11:5–7	156
11:13–14	156
11:14	156
11:15	156
11:25–26	156, 157
11:25–27	155
11:25	9, 156
11:26	16, 50, 155, 156, 157
12:2	14
15:9–12	152
15:25	17
16:25	25

1 Corinthians

1:17	41
1:20	14
1:22–23	18
1:23	23, 38
1:27	14

1 Corinthians (cont.)

1:31	32
3:16	32
3:16–17	5
6:19	5, 32
10	17
10:1–4	8
11:1	27
15	20
15:3–8	18
15:9	33
15:23	41
15:24	18
15:27–28	43
15:42–57	42
15:45–49	21
15:45	73
15:52	41
16:3	17

2 Corinthians

1:18–20	127
1:20a	69
3	17
3:3	32
4:6	14
10:5	14
10:17	32

Galatians

1—2	23
1:13	33
1:14	8, 17, 33
1:18	17
1:23	33
2:14–16	19
2:21	39
3	17, 32
3—4	50
3:7	152
3:8	67
3:15–18	127, 154
3:16	73, 180
3:18	50
3:26	72
3:26–29	2
3:28	21, 111
3:29	67, 72, 73
4	16
4:25–26	40
4:25	21
5:3	19
5:4	33
5:5	41
6:15	20
6:16	150

Ephesians

1:8b–10	111
1:9	25
1:9–10	65
1:9–11	17
1:10	20
2	114
2:11–12	151
2:11–22	18, 67
2:11–23	2
2:13–14	70
2:14	8, 21
2:14–15	111
2:14–22	21
2:15	151
2:15–16	68
2:19	151
2:19–20	111
2:19–22	32, 112
2:21–22	5
3:3–9	25
3:5–6	112
3:6	18
3:9	111
6:1–3	50
6:2–3	66

Philippians

1:5–7	36
1:6	35
1:7	36

Philippians (cont.)

1:11	39
1:12–26	38
1:14–18	36, 38
1:19–26	36
1:27	40
1:27—2:4	35
1:28–30	38, 43
1:30	38
2	32
2:5–11	28, 36
2:6–8	34, 36
2:6–11	34
2:9–11	32, 43
2:11	39
2:11–16	35
2:13	35
2:16–18	36
2:17–18	36
2:19–30	36
3	39, 43
3:1–2	43
3:2	28, 30, 36, 37, 40
3:2–9	8
3:2–10	39
3:2–11	29, 30
3:3	23, 28, 29, 32
3:3a	32
3:3b	32
3:3c	32
3:3d	33
3:3–11	31
3:3–12	31
3:4–6	17, 29, 33, 36
3:4–8	36
3:5–6	36
3:6	8
3:7–11	29, 34
3:8–11	29
3:8	21
3:9	31, 32
3:10–11	29, 34
3:12–14	35, 36, 37, 39
3:12–17	29, 35
3:14	36
3:15–17	29, 36, 37
3:17	37
3:18	28, 37
3:18–19	29, 36, 37, 39
3:18–21	29
3:19	39
3:20a	39, 40
3:20b	39, 41
3:20–21	29, 36, 39
3:21	42
3:21a	39, 41
3:21b	39, 42
4:2–3	36
4:10–14	36
4:20	39

Colossians

1:15–20	17, 23
1:19–20	65
1:26–27	25
2:3	14
4:11	18

1 Thessalonians

2:1	38
4:16	41
4:17	42

2 Thessalonians

1:7–10	41
2:8	41

1 Timothy

1:13	33

2 Timothy

1:14	32
2:18	38

Hebrews

1:1–2	73
1:3	55, 70

Index of Ancient Sources

Hebrews (cont.)

1:13	55
2:9–10	55
3	52, 53
3—4	4, 51, 52, 53, 55
3:1	57
3:1–6	8, 52, 73
3:7	52
3:7–11	52
3:11	53, 54
3:12–19	53
3:12—4:11	52
3:13	52
3:15	52
3:18	53, 54
4	53, 54
4:1	53, 54
4:1–11	73
4:3	53, 54
4:4	53, 54
4:5	53, 54
4:7	52
4:8	53, 54, 56
4:9	53
4:10	53, 54
4:10–11	54
4:11	53, 54
4:14	73
4:14–16	55
6:19	55
7:1	56
8:1	70
8:1–2	55
8:7–13	4
9:28	41
10:2	51
10:10–22	5
10:12	55, 73
10:12–13	70
10:19–20	55
10:19–25	55
10:25	52
10:32–39	51
11	56, 57
11:8–10	73
11:8–16	68
11:8–19	56
11:9	45, 51, 56, 68
11:10	56
11:16	56
11:19	x
11:31	57
11:39–40	57
12:1–4	51
12:2	55, 56, 70
12:22–24	53, 55
13:13–14	55, 56, 57
13:14	45, 56, 68, 73
13:17	52

1 Peter

1:1–2	152
1:3–4	2
1:14	152
1:18	152
2:4–8	5
2:9–10	2, 8, 152
4:3	152

2 Peter

3:10–13	65

Revelation

4:1–11	55
5:10	65
15:3	8
19:11–21	41
20:1–6	49
20:9	49
21—22	64, 73
21:2	65
21:3	63, 64

~

APOCRYPHA

1 Maccabees

5:15	89

PSEUDEPIGRAPHA

1 Enoch
14:8–34　　　　　　　　55

DEAD SEA SCROLLS

4Q394 (4QMMT)
3–7 II 16–18　　　　　55
8 IV 10–12　　　　　　55

4Q405 (4QShirShabb^f)
20 II 21–22 8　　　　　55